THE PUSH FOR A CHILD PHILOSOPHY
WHAT CHILDREN *REALLY* NEED YOU TO KNOW

DR MAXINE THÉRÈSE

childosophy™

Copyright © 2017 by Maxine Thérèse

First Published in 2017 reprint 2018, 2024.

All rights reserved. No part of this publication may be reproduced, distributed, or transmitted in any form or by any means, including photocopying, recording, or other electronic or mechanical methods, without the prior written permission of the publisher, except in the case of brief quotations embodied in critical reviews and certain other noncommercial uses permitted by copyright law. For permission requests, write to Dr. Maxine Thérèse at the address below.

P.O. Box 1168, Geelong, VIC 3220, AUSTRALIA or contact Dr. Maxine Thérèse at www.childosophy.com

This book is catalogued as follows: Name: Thérèse, Maxine, author. Title: The Push for a Child Philosophy: What Children Really Need You to Know/ Maxine Thérèse Description: Australia Identifiers ISBN 9780994641311 (pbk) - ISBN 9780994641335 (e-book) Subjects: Parenting: Educational Psychology: Developmental – Child Psychology: Education: Philosophy: Consciousness.

The case studies used in this book are based on the experience of real people, whose names and identities have been changed to protect their privacy. Any resemblance to actual persons is entirely coincidental.

Cover Art: Melanie Bedford - Cover design: Pixel –Studio

Cover photo of Maxine Thérèse: Baby Buddha Photography

To my parents for birthing me,

To my sons Dillon and Austin, for birthing my soul,

And to St. Thérèse,
for holding my hand every step of the way.

TABLE OF CONTENTS

Who Is This Book For? 1
How To Read This Book 11
Let's Begin 15
PART I: THE PUSH FOR UNITY 31
   Chapter One: Seeking New Interpretations 33
   Chapter Two: The Child As A Soul 59
   Chapter Three: The Child Embodies the World 85
   Chapter Four: Mapping The Soul 117
PART II: THE FOUNDATIONAL NEEDS 135
   1. Children Need To Be Safe And Secure: Soothe Me .. 137
      Case 1: Sally 138
   2. Children Need To Feel: Free Me 171
      Case 2: Tommy 172
   3. Children Need To Act: Allow Me 207
      Case 3: Jeremy 208
   4. Children Need To Love: Love Me 239
      Case 4: Ella 240
   5. Children Need To Speak: Hear Me 265
      Case 5: James 266
   6. Children Need To See: See Me 291
      Case 6: William 292
   7. Children Need To Know: Know Me 323
      Case 7: Mimi 324

PART III: SUPPORTING THE SOUL 351
    Chapter Five: Being In The Question 353

Conclusion 375

Acknowledgements 397

Glossary 401

Appendix 1: A to Z of Children's Ailments 405

Appendix 2: Foundational Needs at a Glance 413

Index 417

Notes 431

Who Is This Book For?

Life doesn't make any sense without interdependence. We need each other, and the sooner we learn that, the better for us all.

~Erik Erickson[1]

Bringing forth a new generation is definitely recognised as one of the most important tasks one can undertake. Many adults are preoccupied with doing this task perfectly. There is a myth that adults must impart their knowledge onto the child and the adult has to somehow hold a superior position to the child. This myth however is no longer supporting parents or children to thrive. Because of this view, we have collectively been stuck in a loop where adults teach and tell children, and children grow up to be adults who teach and tell children. This way of relating is really just transmission of knowledge as opposed to *transformative* growth. It appears that we have forgotten that we are actually here to teach each other and grow together toward unity – we are interdependent; we need each other to be whole.

There is a deep motivation in all human beings to live a life that matters, which actually grounds the individual in a state of wellbeing. This motivational *push* arises in the very beginnings of life and yet our children have not been recognised as being active in their own self-development. There is so much happening for our children that even a generation ago we would not have considered possible. Reflect for a moment on the number of children that do not fit within the developmental frameworks and are then labeled with developmental deviations. Because we have not been able to recognise what is happening for the child outside of developmental staged frameworks many children just do not get the support they need. If you feel unsatisfied with, or limited by, the models and concepts of child development you've previously encountered – this book will illuminate fresh understandings.

When I became a mother, 30 years ago, I felt like I needed a handbook or at least some type of map to be equipped and ready for my role as a mother. Since then, I have worked with many parents and families who feel the same. I have seen countless parents become consumed with supporting their children to be the best they can be, without realising that they are often just projecting their unhealed past onto the child, even with the very best intentions. The interesting thing is, that when we become parents or caregivers of children, we find ourselves in a position of having to meet our children's needs whilst we are in effect, often, still seeking affirmation of our own needs. This book is for you if you are seeking to understand the meaning of why our children are responding to life as they are and also if there are some aspects of your own childhood still misunderstood. Given that all of humanity is involved with the care of children, this book has a broad readership. What follows is a description of the book's particular audiences.

Parents and Families

The parenting journey generally begins with awe and exploration, and can quickly turn to concern and discomfort, especially if children do not meet certain parameters according to standardised norms. As parents record the ways the child meets itself and the world and measure their growth, they can overlook the fact that they do so largely against standards that are just an image of what should be occurring; these 'images' are not a true measure of the child personally, and are based upon limited models of the child. The unique differences that are a hallmark of every individual are soon overlooked or resolved into sameness as we aim for our children to be, do, and act more in line with other children. The appreciation that every child is a unique expression and therefore will never really fit within a mould, is counter to the many milestone and developmental approaches that reassure adults, albeit falsely, that a child is on the path to a certain destination.

In this book you will see that how we have been led to believe children grow is only part of a much bigger picture. Children do not just grow in a linear way up a ladder of sorts, but rather in a holistic manner in each and every moment. If the child can maintain a balance of self, moment-to-moment, the linear growth takes care of itself. Seen in this way, the child is always seesawing to a degree, as it attempts to regulate itself and be whole through all of life's experiences. If there is imbalance in self the child's natural transitions may be harder for them. If there is residue in the way of unhealed aspects from generation(s) before, these further impact the child. Through the science of epigenetics as you will come to see, we have amazing insight that supports the notion that unmet needs that arise in our children are not only from unconscious parental patterns but move within the generational line and the family system as a whole.

If our children struggle with balance, the solution is not always about giving them more to make up for what we perceive we never had; it is an opportunity to reconsider loops of patterning and relating from our own past. Paradoxically, these patterns are often hard to see, let alone exit, without our children bringing attention to them. The impact of those things unmet in our lives as parents becomes magnified very purposefully through our children, so we may review them and heal them. Grandparents therefore also play a very pivotal role in the wisdom of childcare, often in ways that go far beyond offering advice or looking after children whilst parents work. Many grandparents have conscious memories of a time long ago, and because of this, can offer much insight into the patterns they see emerging in the child's behaviour.

Educators

Educators are aware of the importance of their profession in the overall wellbeing of children. Many teachers appreciate that the purpose of education is more than just learning math, science, and passing examinations, and are constantly on the lookout for improved ways to support the children in their care. Teachers are exceedingly aware that they are transmitting information to malleable beings that are ingesting so much more than just formal lessons. Many teachers are dedicated beyond their call in seeking up-to-date research and information that might assist them in implementing new strategies to support children in enhanced ways. However, teachers are often frustrated with gaps between the philosophies of children—the pedagogies and the practical methods that are available to assist children in their daily lives. Philosophies of education are often positioned within, or come from, the broader childhood developmental philosophies. Some great educators have promoted the focus on the whole child, and yet these seemed to be located within select schools and there remains no educational theory that suggests what the unified child is. If you are an educator you will find an evidence-based philosophy of the whole child in these pages that will hopefully empower you with new ways of seeing and working with children.

Practitioners

Practitioners and therapists of children have become an indispensable part of modern society. This demand has arisen in order to assist children to cope in a changing world. Due to time constraints and other restrictions that have developed as habitual patterns within families and schools, parents and teachers can relate to children in a programed way. Because of this, children's emotional expression can get relegated to something that is separate from the everyday, rather than incorporated into daily life. Practitioners and therapists however, generally work with children in a retrospective way, which is always after a problem has presented. Something may have occurred for the child without any awareness from other adults in the child's life, and a problem has become apparent or unavoidable, so help is sought. It is the cause of the *problem* that the therapist is trying to determine. The therapist is trained to see the child's life more objectively than the parent, and therefore is positioned to be impartial. This impartiality, whilst necessary, is only really an advantage if the therapist is attuned to the child's whole experience and has a model to understand the child's inherent unity. Maps that assist the practitioner to understand the child from a holistic perspective have been limited. If you are a therapist of children you will find a true transpersonal and integral approach to the child in these pages. This approach allows you to meet the depth of the child, and safeguards them from bypassing certain aspects of the whole self, as they grow.

Researchers

Researchers and scholars are challenged by the large undertaking they face in studying how to best meet the needs of children to sustain wellbeing. This is due in part to the significant impact that we know this stage of life has on the broader human development. On top of this, the study of children, their needs and wellbeing, requires a cross-disciplinary and cross-cultural inquiry. The merging of broad fields of thought is often difficult, and thus philosophies of childhood are still often studied within separate fields of expertise, meaning insight and research into children's wellbeing remains largely divided. This is problematic because these endeavours underpin policy and other measures in place for children, which depict only part of the child. Most scholarly research into the child also comes from a foundational difficulty, viewing the child as disconnected in body and mind, and further largely disregards the concept of spirituality and the vital role it plays in regard to the child's integrative and unified wellbeing. The child's needs arise as a result of an intricate dance between the child's biological and spiritual needs. The spiritual life of the child has more recently been a topic of interest within the realm of childhood studies and more detail concerning the spiritual aspects of the child's life are found as we move through the pages of this book.

If you are a researcher and scholar interested in the emerging theories of the whole child you will find the theory of the child as a soul, as well as the *Foundational Needs Model* (FNM) presented here, allows you to situate anew the complex interplay of the body-mind-spirit as it presents in the child.[2] The child's body (their sensory, biological and cellular processes), their mind, (mental, neurological, cognitive, and brain approaches) and their spirit (actions in the form of the child's behaviours and responses) are all accounted for within the one model. Maintaining this unity of self in childhood transpires to the most amazing outcomes as we further explore the many and varied dimensions of what it means to be human.

We are Born Philosophers

Children are natural philosophers; in fact, childhood is the very beginning of philosophy. The questions of children are a pursuit of Good, Truth and Beauty and to see them as anything less, is misinterpreting the brilliance of the child. We can encourage children to pursue an interest in those things they are drawn to know more about because there is much information in such inquiry, information that will guide the child toward its destiny. And as adults we must remember to pursue what we are drawn toward for ourselves, especially if we are in a caring role around children. Adults can support children by continuing to be in the question for themselves and maintain their own curiosity in life. By doing this, adults help children to maintain unity. When a child is able to feel, think, and act in a unified way they are aligned and experience growth that is best for them. When we can allow the child to unfold according to its own pattern of development, and also do what we need to unfold ourselves, we are observers to the unfolding of humanity and what children really need is revealed.

When I pose the question to adults, "What does the life of the child look like when we can allow children to truly *know thyself* and become the authority over their lives, even in the earliest of years?" I often get an immediate response, ranging from shock and dismay, to one of wonder and curiosity. Perhaps how one even begins to consider this question is very telling. If we can let the children lead the way, we are getting closer to the principle on which philosophy is founded; that is, the dictum, *know thyself*, which means that in order to live a good life, we need to come to know ourselves. What might the child really need from us if we as adult caregivers were coming from our own highest potential, utilising the energies in our body and life in the most optimal way.

The phrase *know thyself* pertains to children as well as adults knowing themselves. In essence, a calm centered energy and self-mastery emanating from an adult will calm and still even the most troubled child. As caregivers then, we might see that there is no need to continue to hold a narrative about our child's responses to life -- which are often just a story of what is happening based upon our own past, or limited models -- and is not always the truth. Instead of justifying that the effort required to meet all of the child's needs is too much for us, we can look to why we feel this way in the first place. In our need to control our children we focus on training away the child's behaviours, symptoms, and issues, intent on instilling proper conduct, and thus can remain stuck in a loop. I know many parents who feel that no sooner is one thing sorted out; something else that the child needs takes its place. In all honestly, if we can relax and look to ourselves as a first point, we can see that trying to fix a child is a lot of work, and in my experience, not the most optimal use of energy. We can instead look at what we might cultivate in ourselves.

Consider for a moment your own childhood; perhaps there were things that you felt or things you were curious to understand, things that the grown-ups could not help you resolve. Now, imagine instead, that you had been encouraged to self-explore as if you were actually assumed to hold your own wisdom, and the adults around you were interested in this and encouraged this in you as well. In attempting to explore the considerations above, one might reflect and realise that they did not get this type of regard as a child. However, at any point in life, one can begin to explore questions such as, How might I begin to determine how I manage and control myself? You can also consider - how do I myself discern right from wrong? How do I do the right thing when no one is watching? How do I discover the best ways to learn? How do I decide what I am to be at my best expression as an adult?

If adults can transcend the belief that children can only be raised well and flourish if adults alone teach them how to do this, we can then open to activating our potential for ourselves without projecting our own past onto our children. If we can bring more awareness to the notion that we can grow with children – it enhances the conversations that adults have with children as well as the conversations that our children have with themselves. The statement that children are our teachers comes to have a whole new meaning.

How To Read This Book

I am here. I brought my whole self to you. I am your mother.

~ Maya Angelou[1]

Parents often feel frustrated that their children don't come with a set of instructions. They search for solutions to problems that arise as their children grow and implement new strategies and tactics, even if they don't *feel* quite right. There is no shortage of parenting theories, philosophies and expert opinions available to fill this need for external instruction. What makes this book different is that it asks you to trust your relationship to your child as you grow in self-belief and self-awareness. Without developing a sense of self-competency, that you are indeed the best person to support your child as it grows, it is impossible to develop trust in a child's unfolding. Essentially, the greatest gift you can give a child is to help them to learn to trust and know themselves and it is also one of the most difficult to do. This book allows you to deepen your relationships to yourselves as caregivers, so you can develop trust in your role with children. It also allows you to enhance your relationship with children as they grow, which are the keys to understanding what they *really* need.

Whether you are a parent, grandparent, teacher, practitioner, or researcher; if you feel called to strengthen your own self-awareness and to deepen your role, this book is your invitation to a whole new way of relating with the children entrusted to you. When my children were little, no one told me that they were helping me grow in ways that were different to anything I could teach them. By knowing ourselves as the needs of our children arise, we are better positioned to care for children. This book supports adults and children to grow together. This book does not only ask to be grasped intellectually; it asks to be integrated at a soul level. As such, this book may challenge and even trigger you. When you reach a passage that feels beyond your understanding, trust that there will come a time when it will resonate deeply. For this is a book born to be re-visited and re-membered.

The book is divided into three parts. You have permission to read this book out of order, if you wish. Whilst each part builds upon the next, in reality, we each learn in our own way and sometimes in a non-linear manner so allow your curiosity guide you. Part One, *The Push for Unity*, offers the philosophical and scientific support for the notion of the child as a soul. I offer research that shows how the child as it grows, purposefully brings forth the personal and collective past, so that we all (adult and child) may review any imbalance or fragmentation in order to secure whole and unified growth. The second part of the book examines each of the seven *Foundational Needs* within my FNM showing the complex interplay of the body-mind-spirit composite. After each individual *Foundational Need* is considered in light of key themes and a case study, you will find tips to encourage the cultivation of these needs. Finally, Part Three, *Supporting the Soul*, offers a way of being, or an approach to relating with children, that I call, 'Being in the Question.' This approach outlines an affirmative relational skill for adults to use in their interaction with children. Supporting children to explore the questions they have is vital to their wellbeing, and keeps them connected, balanced and well. Effectively, when adults know more about their own unmet needs in a purposeful way, and how they surface in relationship with children, they deepen their own self-awareness.

WAYS TO DEEPEN YOUR UNDERSTANDING

Journal

As you read this book, you may like to keep a journal. Use this to record the fears, memories and musings as they arise. In accepting that nothing is a more triggering subject than how we ourselves were raised and how we are raising our children, we are ready to explore; track what triggers you. You may find yourself with more questions: ones that don't offer immediate answers. By keeping a journal you are inviting the answers you seek. Be patient and open and allow the feeling to surface.

Become a reflective observer

This book invites you to become a reflective observer of the child/children and of oneself. We may feel *pushed* to take action and think we know what to do for our children before we have fully understood what is really going on. By slowing down and staying curious we often find that the answers we seek spontaneously arise.

Discuss

You may wish to invite a friend, partner or colleague to read this book alongside you. Sharing our insights and struggles through a rich, curious dialogue can open new doorways of understanding. You may even like to dialogue within a small group who are interested in children's needs. Perhaps you might like to open the dialogue with your parents around the ideas in the book. In my experience, there is much growth to be had discussing the needs that have not been collectively met as we grow, an encounter which can soften the most challenging relationships. Such active endeavours and conscious dialogue offer a new way of integrating the whole message of the book.

Let's Begin

"The study of the child may have an infinitely wider influence, extending to all human questions. In the mind of the child we may find the key to progress."

~Maria Montessori[2]

There is a much deeper purpose beneath our children's behaviours and actions than we can currently grasp. If we examine the child from a soul perspective, I believe that we see the actions and the motivations of children reveal much more than we could ever imagine possible. Appreciating more fully why children do what they do will certainly have consequences for our human progress. How children should act in the world however, has largely been dictated by adults, rather than from what is necessary for the child, according to the child's own soul. Philosophies of the child, as well as childhood growth and development models have historically interpreted this vital stage of life and children themselves, from a very limited and fragmented perspective. Because of this, the support children have received has been very limited and fragmented as well. In fact, there has been no theory in Western psychological, philosophical, psychiatric, or medical disciplines that conveys the idea of the child as an already existing composite whole. Additionally, the current models of childhood growth and development bypass the inherent wisdom of the child altogether. Not only are you about to learn a theory that confirms the child is indeed whole, you will also discover a *model* --and a *map*-- that helps you to support the child's unity as they grow.

The Push for a Child Philosophy is a call to adults to expand their horizon in regard to understanding what children really need. By offering a workable theory of the child as a soul – unified in body-mind-spirit, this book allows adult caregivers to begin to address the whole child's needs in a way not possible before. This book brings forth evidence that shows how children begin life feeling, thinking and acting as a unified whole and the impulse to crawl, stand and walk actually derives from this naturally integrated process. Over time and over the course of life, there are many situations, events and circumstances that cause a child to fragment from experiencing life in a unified way.

We have not really considered it a serious proposition that children themselves know what *they need* as they grow and in fact they are communicating this in the best way they can, through their actions and behaviours. If there is a lack of unity in the child's feelings and thoughts due to unmet needs there will be an imbalanced action. If there is a lack of unity due to unmet needs arising in parents, family, or other environments, the child purposefully reflects this imbalance as well. The child's feelings and thoughts, which are so often disregarded by adults, are the energetic drivers of every action the child takes in the world. A child's resistance to going to school or into care, for example, or a bizarre set of behaviours, even a troubling symptom at a certain age, or perhaps a fascination toward certain things, are indicating something important for adults about children. These are not simply problems to be fixed; or deficiencies to be overcome; they are an invitation into a deeper inquiry.

Because we have not collectively recognised that children are indicating vital unmet needs through their actions, behaviours, symptoms and obsessions we have overlooked important information. The issues and challenges for children, those things that arise as a matter of growth, are not complications, but rather a natural response to the child's separated self, and thus offer opportunities to distinguish what needs of the child may be unmet. The adult expectation of how children ought to feel and think (based on how we have been taught to feel and think in the past can now be reconsidered) and instead of projecting our feelings and thoughts on children we can gain more respect for the child as a self-directed being. Then, if a child has difficulty with something or someone, or when they experience a challenge in life, we will be less inclined to judge them, or judge ourselves, and more eager to look to see what it means for the child according to them. We may also be keener to pause and see if our own unmet needs from the past might be showing up. Growth models that expect our children to develop and be ready when they are told to be ready are defunct because they have ignored the inherent wholeness of the child.

Unity and Wholeness

When I use the terms unity and wholeness, I am in essence referring to a relationship between feelings, thoughts and actions. If I had known when I became a mother that my lack of unity (incongruence of feelings and thoughts) would hinder my children and if I had known that the very things that would challenge me as a mother were not my children at all, but my own unmet needs, I might have been more interested in consciously working on these imbalances. I did not know that my children would constantly mirror back to me all of my unrealised potentials, extending out and back in both time and space to a collective past. Those things unrealised or in opposition within me, that had not been cultivated as I was growing, those things, which lay as deficient or even excessive responses within my own energy (thoughts, emotions, beliefs and other stressors), were actually awaiting enlightenment through my children. And because of this largely unknown dimension to caring for children, my children have had to endure certain things that I would never consciously choose to repeat.

Over time, whilst engaging in various roles with children, it became evident to me that it is natural for children to carry the family, social and cultural patterns of energy forward. Indeed my own children have had to review any lack of unity that came before them in order to integrate and maintain their own unity. I have come to see how this is the case for all children. In my desire to look toward better ways of living and being for my own children and for myself, I was led to explore many fields of study. As you will come to see in the pages to follow, this journey actually began in my own childhood and has been an integral part of me since my earliest years. Since I was a young girl, I have been trying to uncover the meaning of my feelings and thoughts specifically about two things: firstly, the child and children, and secondly, the soul. My curiosity about 'the soul' and 'children' always held a kind of conflict for me. These themes for me were embodied as a real opposition, which I experienced between those things I felt as important, the indicators via the language of my body (my feelings) and the interpretations that I made of these feelings (my thoughts as well as what others told me to think, the beliefs and attitudes of my dominant culture). This gap between what I felt and what I thought, eventually always led me to experiences that gave me answers to my questions. I often wondered why my intense desire to unify my feelings and thoughts was such a *push*. Now I realise that I was in a process of becoming whole again.

It seems to me also, that to a degree, we all experience a prompt toward a unified way of being, to be whole. I have always questioned if there might be a better way to assist children to keep their feelings and thoughts connected as they grow and more importantly perhaps for children to learn to do this for themselves? Perhaps you too have experienced a prompt in the form of a feeling that there might be an alternative approach to what others pronounce is best for children. Or it may come as a more obvious prompt, such as a strong emotion that arises and lingers after you have witnessed an injustice take place with a child, in a classroom, playground, or shopping centre. Perhaps you have become aware of a child knowing things they have not been taught, or knowing about something that happened before they were born, but you have not been able to communicate this knowing to others. Maybe you are drawn to reading vast amounts of literature on any topic that might broaden your own perspective and beliefs about what is best for children. Maybe you are a curious teacher or a practitioner working with children and are frustrated with the gaps between the theory and the practical approaches available for children. Or perhaps you are exhausted from the daily demands of a challenging child and want to learn how to create a more harmonious relationship. These prompts are all indicators that even though you may not have all of the answers you need right now, there is a deep *push* demanding that there must be another way, and more importantly, that this other way is possible—somewhere, somehow.

This book therefore, urges the *collective push* for a child philosophy, for all who care for children and in doing so;

the *push* ultimately requires that we become more attuned to the oblique *push of the soul*. The word push itself is used variously throughout the book and is referred to in three specific ways. The first meaning of the push is in reference to the *child push* toward the adult. The second is the adult *push* toward the child. The third is the *soul push*, which is the push toward unity and our unfolding human destiny.

The first push, the *child push*, is significantly inspired by words from my own childhood. When I was a child, I often heard the phrase, "Don't push me," or, "You are pushing me." When I was truly overstepping the mark and challenging family pattering, then I would hear the taunt "Go on, push me." These expressions and assertions signified that if I were to push the boundaries or the rules of the house too far, there would be consequences. I grew up knowing only too well the consequences -- and I often held back from acting on or expressing all of the things that I felt and thought were important to me, as well as things that troubled me -- because of the impending consequences. I know that I am not alone; many people grow up experiencing the same. This first push then, the *child push* toward the adult, is often perceived to be a personal crusade against the adult. When it is, the child, smaller and more vulnerable than the adult, is dominated and controlled because of its *push*.

Children *push* adults, however, because they come from a different time, and they also have a very different future. As we progress through the pages you will see how the *child push* is a wonderful opportunity for adult caregivers to review their own unrealised potential. After all, the unmet needs that present in the child are a mirror for the unmet needs in the child's environment. The *child push* as an evolutionary act just like crawling and walking then should be natural, and yet it is often dealt with negatively, which can be harmful to the child. Whilst children push to remain whole in how they feel, think and act in the world, there are simultaneously many external forces in familial, social, and cultural environments that can hinder their growth and cause fragmentation.

The second push, the *adult push*, conveys the substantial push that children receive from adults who believe that it is their responsibility to motivate and direct children according to what they think is best. This *push* is based largely upon the fact that the adults themselves often never had the opportunity to achieve certain things in their childhoods (or things misunderstood from their childhoods), are seeking both their own expression and their own meaning through the child. The dynamics underlying such parental motivation are discussed in more detail as the book progresses. When acting in this way, adults often defend and justify the notion that they know what is best for children, and that children ought to be thankful for all of the opportunities available to them. From the child's point of view, the *adult push* is often a negative force and actually creates an imbalance in the child. Some adults take this push to the extreme and hijack the child's inner life, hovering over him or her, interrogating every feeling and thought and projecting their own conditioning upon the child.

Research into extreme parenting approaches, such as the so-called Helicopter or Tiger parenting styles, reveal that the *adult push* creates issues of relational control and submission of children.[3] These approaches are aligned with the philosophical idea that 'might is right' and take advantage of human vulnerability and dependence on family to meet even the most basic needs of food and shelter. They also imply that the child is not at all capable without the *adult push*. Because of the threat of loss of basic needs from adults who are mightier, some children will resist conflict and surrender to the dominant push. Thus, many children learn very early to adapt, to fit in, which actually makes them more controllable and pliable to the instructions of others, but more fragmented in themselves. Some children push harder against the structural *adult push*, which is evident in the adult frameworks and other embedded doctrines and structures that place adults in a powerful and often dominant position over the child.

The *adult push*, in its most affirmative expression, can however be a valuable contribution to helping the child embody its unique potential. An adult that urges the child at a soul level, is perhaps most obvious in what we term a mentor. The recognition of one's soul is a powerful touchstone that can comfort a child, often in ways that are immeasurable. However sometimes, adults (parents mostly) go to the opposite end of the spectrum with children, and focus too much on their 'specialness.' This appears more often today in the endeavour to encourage positive approaches in the ways we respond to children, and in doing so rejecting any negative expressions in the hope of being happy. This way of relating can be a challenge for a child who will not know how to be at peace with troubling feelings, thoughts and emotions and may grow up in a type of void of feelings because they are encouraged with words such as "Don't be sad, think happy thoughts" or alternatively they grow with an elevated sense of self, where they are told that "Whatever you choose to do will be alright, you cannot fail." These statements and attitudes place a lot of expectation on children who still need a degree of guidance, nurturance and support from adults to process feelings and emotions and to feel they matter. It seems to me that a parent will always come to hold some imagined idea about their child's future, which is to a degree necessary, because such an imagining elevates interest in the child's potential. To decide what that potential specifically might be, however, is missing the point -- because that is just seeing the child as the fulfillment of the parent's own needs.

The third, and the most significant push therefore is the *soul push*. The *soul push* is the ultimate push for a unified way of being, because from this soul unity one's potentials will be expressed. This push for unity arises within each of us. Often the child's *soul push* is not recognised and mistaken for bad behaviour. I know for me, that I have always (and often against my better judgment), pushed the boundaries in all aspects of life, sometimes without knowing why. This characteristic has created discomfort for me, as well as for all those whom I have pushed. Even so, over time I have come to realise this pressure from children on adults to evolve is very real and very purposeful. It is in my clinical practice over the years, where I have seen that it is natural for children to push to grow beyond the boundaries of their upbringing. This *soul push* brings forth all sorts of information to help them realise potentials that have been denied, repressed, and conditioned away. I have also learnt that as adults, if we have suppressed or bypassed our own *soul push*, our self-potential, we risk unconsciously projecting this onto our children.

A Model of Wholeness

As I could find no theory that conveys the idea of the child as a soul - as an already existing composite whole, much of my research was interested in developing one, so that we may support the child's inherent unity as they grow. By having a model that accounts for the child's complete experience as a unified soul, incorporating body-mind-spirit, we begin to appreciate how the child's physical, emotional, mental, and spiritual needs actually interact and inform each other even at the cellular level. When we can see the child as a soul (and for children to see themselves as souls) we can begin to interpret the discourse that occurs between the various aspects of the *whole* child in a way that has not been available before, and as a result, we are informed about the vital role adults play in the life of the child, like never before. The complex interplay between the various energetic aspects of the child has been difficult to truly map, however, in my work with children I began to identify how the unmet need at the origin of the child's behaviour, issue or symptom, circled around particular themes. I then saw a correlation between these unmet needs and the seven main Chakras found within the *Yoga Sutras*[4] and *Upanishads*. The Chakras offered a way of accounting for the energetic patterns of influence I had discerned, both within the child and also outside the child (as the unseen energetics of thoughts, beliefs, emotions and stressors that are within the child's environment.) My research and findings allowed me to begin to chart the child's growth holistically, rather than hierarchically. Over many years this research developed into the FNM. Below, you can see how I have assigned the seven *Foundational Needs* as they closely align with the seven principal Chakras and the themes of each need.

The Chakras as they correspond with the Foundational Need

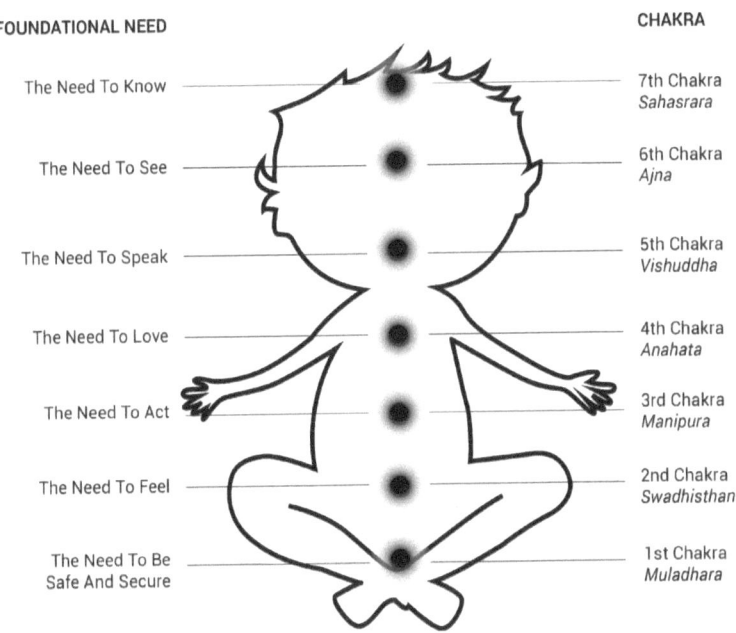

Figure 1. The Foundational Need as it corresponds with each Chakra[5]

- **The first need is the *Need to Be Safe and Secure*.** The need the child is, in essence, proclaiming is: ***Soothe Me.*** This first Chakra's key theme encompasses the variety of needs around safety and security, preservation, and prosperity.

- **The second need is the *Need to Feel*.** The child is, in essence, proclaiming ***Free Me.*** This second Chakra's key theme encompasses the needs around pleasure, the flow of emotions, and bodily sensations.

- **The third need of the child is the *Need to Act*.** The need the child is, in essence, proclaiming is

Allow Me. This third Chakra's key theme encompasses the needs around expressing our individual will and motivation, self-esteem and personal power.

- **The fourth need is the *Need to Love*.** The child is, in essence, proclaiming ***Love Me.*** This fourth Chakra's key theme encompasses the needs for relating, unconditional love, and connection and compassion.

- **The fifth need is the *Need to Speak*.** The child is, in essence, proclaiming ***Hear Me.*** This fifth Chakra's key theme encompasses the needs of expression, voice and creative communication.

- **The sixth need is the *Need to See*.** The need the child is, in essence, proclaiming, is ***See Me.*** This sixth Chakra's key theme encompasses the needs around vision, imagination, symbolic sight and intention.

- **The seventh need is the *Need to Know.*** The need the child is, in essence, proclaiming is ***Know Me.*** This seventh Chakra's key theme encompasses the needs for unity, highest power, universal knowledge and connection.[6]

With the FNM, we can begin to look more impartially at those things that occur in the daily lives of children and help children notice when they have become disconnected from their unified state of being, from their soul. As you will come to see throughout, by way of many examples as well as the research presented, any disparity between one's feelings and thoughts leads to imbalance and ill health. For instance: when a child has to hide or deny aspects of themselves and how they feel, or believe they have to think about things in ways that please others, it causes incongruence between their feelings and thoughts, and this affects their body and energy system, resulting in the health problems and behavioural issues that are most common in childhood today.

The FNM allows for an account of a physical location in the child's anatomy, the corresponding thought patterns and psychological aspects, as well as the often-inhibited potentials as they manifest through the child's behaviours and issues. In this way the FNM offers a distinctive way to translate the complex integrative dialogue occurring between the child's body (sensory, biological and cellular processes), their mind (mental, neurological, cognitive and brain approaches) and their spirit (actions in the form of the child's behaviours and responses.) These parts of the self, work as one and are all connected through the human nervous system, which operates holistically, not hierarchically, as a place to get to.

Seeing children's seven *Foundational Needs* as energy patterns that are always present, which become activated when nurtured and lay dormant when neglected, allows us to easily identify the unmet needs that drive certain behaviours and expressions in children. If there is congruence in the child's feelings and thoughts in regard to one particular theme, for instance the *Need to be Safe and Secure*, in circumstances where the child is soothed when frightened, the child's actions will reflect balanced wellbeing. Likewise, when there is incongruence in the feelings and thoughts about the *Need to be Safe and Secure* the child's actions will reflect imbalance through certain types of behaviours, symptoms, and other indicators. Some common expressions of this unmet need are anxiety, and resistance to change. The impact on the child of the complex unseen energies within family, society and culture, offers an expanded interpretation of why children do what they do and why certain things are presenting in our children.

So we can know in a practical way, that when a child is challenged or struggling with life, there will be an unmet need at the origin creating an imbalance. Equally, we can know that even when a child has a particular physical symptom such as a rash or allergy we can look to the unmet need for clues of imbalance, which are creating physical imbalance. The varied expressions of any physical, emotional, mental or psychological imbalances in our children present either as a deficiency or excess. That is, the energy from a *Foundational Need* left unmet, will present as a deficient or excessive response, which really just means that energy will be directed in particular ways based on the meaning of the unmet need for the child.

If we know that a child is feeling, thinking, or acting in a way that may not be optimal for them, the energy in the Chakras is affected. In fact, everything the child feels and thinks has an effect on the body and their life. Interpreting the meaning beneath the child's expressions, behaviours, symptoms and fascinations, requires that we comprehend that children respond purposefully to unmet needs, and that the child's actions convey vital information about the feelings and thoughts driving their behaviours.

There is much more detail of how the unmet needs present as particular energies in the second part of the book, where I position the child's *Foundational Needs* on a seesaw of balance. Cultivating children's *Foundational Needs* from the beginnings -- at each age -- is ultimately offering a touchstone for more affirmative ways of being in the world. It also sets and establishes in the earliest of interactions the foundations for lifelong wellbeing. By continually supporting children to welcome their own *soul push*, to stay unified, connected and balanced as they transition through life, we are beginning to flow with life instead of against it.

PART I
THE PUSH FOR UNITY

Chapter One
Seeking New Interpretations

There can be no keener revelation of a society's soul than the way in which it treats its children.

~ Nelson Mandela[1]

Philosophies of childhood ought to support adults to interpret children's needs and provide possible ways of meeting such needs. However, since the origins of child development theories, the child has been poorly regarded and many needs of the child have gone unmet. The dominant perspective of *the child* is still today, a developmental one. The developmental perspectives of human growth largely position the child as incomplete and in stages of becoming. The models and theories that help adults to understand children all have as the main feature a 'lifespan perspective' which views human growth occurring in developmental stages and states of becoming -- where the child is simply not ready for some things. Viewing the child from adult based frameworks and lifespan perspectives alone is still an *adult push*. This presumption of adults to know what the child really needs in order to become an adult, does not always account for what the child needs in the present moment. Additionally, when we see a child for the adult they are to become, this always comes with a projected past that is entangled with the adult caregivers own childhood and the models they grew with.

The way any society treats its children is determined by the philosophies of childhood a society ascribes to and because the invisible or energetic aspects of children's lives have not been easy to understand, they have never been included in the broader philosophies of childhood. This oversight has created a lot of additional confusion for those who nurture, care for, educate, and heal children because there is so much more to children than our theories can explain. So much has been missed in our adult centered interpretations of the child from the current models, and as a result, the interpretations children make about themselves. Vital information about the child is missed or bypassed because we have not had a way of discerning how the child perceives and interprets information between the various aspects of the whole as it is growing and why it does so in the manner that it does. A new interpretation of what children really need consequently is well overdue.

There are two very culturally entrenched and well-established ideas about the child in Western societies, present since the beginnings of philosophical and psychological thinking about what children need. One such idea is that it is up to adults to decide for the child what children need and what is best, because it has *not* been recognised that children themselves may know what they need. The second, is that children must wait until adulthood to experience higher order needs, often referred to as peak experiences and spiritual capabilities. Because these limiting assumptions of children are still entrenched in our approaches to children, this first chapter examines how we have understood the child in the past with a view to exploring these two main ideas. This allows us to begin to broaden the interpretations we make of the child's experience to include many of the aspects of the human growth that have been discarded or overlooked.

It has not been considered a serious proposition that children themselves offer vital information about what they need by way of how they feel and think about themselves and life. Nor has it been considered in our current frameworks that the child purposefully brings forth the personal and collective past, so we all (adult and child) may review any imbalance or fragmentation in order to secure whole and unified growth. As this chapter progresses you will see that the past ways of conceptualising and treating children are much harsher than the present. However, we still have a way to go in regard to the full recognition of children and what they truly need. This expansion will come when we consider the human self as whole from the beginnings and thus reconsider the significance of the child-adult relationship in the evolution of humanity.

What is the Child?

The embedded *adult push* is evident historically as we have placed the child's value on what they will become, rather than by virtue of their existence. Childhood has largely been regarded as the optimal time to seize the future adult and make a mark. This is a principle, which has enjoyed various applications and interpretations over time and is most evident in the Jesuit maxim, "Give me a child until he is seven and I will give you the man." The awareness of early childhood as a time in which future (adult) beliefs and attitudes might be formed and embedded was recognised by the Jesuits, who proposed that by the time a child had reached seven, his character would largely be set. Consequently, the Jesuits invested considerable time and effort in ensuring that Roman Catholic teachings were instilled into the child. This is indicative of the function and purpose of childhood; where 'training' is shaped and designed in the formative years to correspond with how well the child will fit within the larger structures that form their world. There is more detail of the significance of the earliest years in chapter four where I discuss the idea of the *adult push* to teach children versus the *child push* ignited naturally as the sensory system of the child educates itself.

Adults historically have seen it as their role to shape children to become model citizens who can distinguish right from wrong, who will grow into social and political agents, who have access to particular knowledge and resources, aiming toward a good life, which has been seen to be a noble undertaking. This is why, over time, many people have made suggestions about what is best for children. Stages of child development have been rigorously formulated with the intention of understanding how to cultivate and best relate to children, as well as what to expect from them as they grow. Whilst it can be verified that the child is a biologically vulnerable being that requires support from caregivers until it can independently care for itself, and some children require more specific care than others, at the same time the child is mastering many complex foundational skills within their biology that will serve as a template for their later development and wellbeing. If we are not aware of what children really need as they grow, when they exhibit certain behaviours or challenges -- those things that are indicating what is happening in their complete system as a whole – then we are missing much in our support for them.

The *adult push* has collectively been very strong, and because of this it has been difficult for many adults to allow the full freedom of the child. As adults we have to be watchful to ensure that we do not reduce the child's expression by continuing to use limited interpretations, those that suggest children do not possess certain types of knowing, or certain types of needs because they are still in a state of becoming. The lineage of *Needs Theory* as exemplified in Maslow's hierarchy of needs, and the consequent needs discourses compel us to believe that lower order needs have to be met before higher order needs can even be considered. You will come to see this is flawed thinking as a research study outlined in the *Need to Act* demonstrates that many higher order needs are more important to a person, even if many of the most basic needs are unfulfilled. The failure to acknowledge that children have complex foundational needs at all times and across all aspects of growth, has impacted the supports children receive. Those material wants, satisfiers, and objectives, are only a part of the child's needs, which encompass those unseen and energetic in nature, which often get ignored. Needs discourses therefore hold the same biases of the hierarchical and developmental type growth models that perceive the child as lacking compared to adults. Such beliefs concerning children, as well as the ways of relating with children, originate from the philosophical notions about the child.

The following points highlight the current philosophical definitions and conceptualisations of the child.

1. Child 1 is the child of one or more parents (child is any age and may be an adult, that is, I will always be my parents' child.)

2. Child 2 is the person at an age where adult rights and responsibilities have not been bestowed, generally aged 0-18 years.

3. Child 3 is 'the novice' – incapable, uncivilised, 'not yet learnt', 'not yet ready' – and all people are this from time to time.[2]

These three distinctions of the child all refer to the child in relation to the adult, either as parent, teacher or policymaker. Also, the child is referred to in the eyes of the law as being dependent, needy, not able to take responsibility, unreasonable, incapable or uncivilized based upon the idea that adult ways of interpreting reality are superior to that of children.

As you can also see the child is considered less than, incapable and deficient, as they are perpetually framed to be in a state of becoming an adult -- and the *adult push* predominates this very relationship. The many demands explicitly and implicitly placed upon children to perform, fit in, achieve, and excel based on defunct growth models means that many children are constantly given the message that they need to be more than they are at any given moment, and that the present moment experiences and the things they feel are not important in this becoming. The results of such convictions could be said to be evident in children's angst, and a rise in anxiety levels in children. The fact that adult rights and responsibilities and certain needs are not bestowed upon children, has given adults a superior position in the child-adult relationship.

Well-meaning attempts by adults to civilise children and help them become accepted into society, often instead ends up repressing children's exuberance and vitality, the sharpness of their senses, and their curiosity about their bodies and their lives. We have therefore largely taken it to task that any aspect of child development that does not fit within current frameworks must be fixed so they do fit. Whilst as already mentioned, I do recognise that the nurturance of children requires that adult caregivers interpret the needs of the child, paying particular attention in the early years. At the same time, the child is skilfully aware of what they need, although they are not always able to verbalise this. The indications of children in the form of quirks, questions, frustrations, and behavioural challenges are all pointers for the adult about the child's innate knowledge and wisdom.

Often the child's innate knowledge cannot be expressed verbally, is not allowed to be expressed at all, or cannot find another way to be expressed and thus will come through the child's behaviours. Irrespective of how the child communicates it, we must be attuned to all the child's expressions, as they are vital indications about what they need. Knowing the *child push* is a vital signal of need means that adults are required to know more about children's body knowledge and establish a way of connecting and attuning to this wisdom, without intellectualising the interpretations they make about the child's behaviours. There is more detail on how adults can connect with children's body wisdom in upcoming chapters. Children are rather extraordinary; astonishingly in studies of embodied cognition, researchers have concluded that no Artificial Intelligence can match the three year old in terms of genius. The child is an embodied complete system and because of this, it truly does know what it needs. Yet adults still deem what the most appropriate growth is for the child and perceive any suggestion otherwise from children as distractions that move the child away from what they (adults) want the child to achieve.

This book therefore advocates and advances the further philosophical definition of the child:

1. Child 4 is a soul: whole, unified and composite body-mind-spirit, (connected to a source of energy supporting its best growth) and an active participator in its own destiny.

The definition of the child here does not reject all of the previous definitions, such as the idea that children have parents, and in this sense we will always be somebody's child – nor does it dismiss the idea that the child grows across a time and age continuum. It does, however, cast-off the idea that children are not complete and do not have the potential for wholeness at each of the otherwise noted stages and across the time continuum. It is my contention that the *child push,* to seek to understand itself more deeply, happens independent of age in a unified way that supports its best growth. It is also my contention that the adult-child power dynamic, or the *adult push,* has left children with many necessary human needs neglected.

The notion that childhood is a time of putting information and knowledge into the child as opposed to allowing the child to unfold according to its own pattern of growth and development, as a soul, has been restrictive for our children. Further to this, orthodox developmental theories inadvertently and constantly diminish children's emotional, social, spiritual and mental growth. Because of this, many of the supports provided for children, actually fall short of meeting their needs as they arise, that is, those things that the child indicates they need as they are growing and transitioning through each age. The tendency of the *adult push* as you will come to see more specifically in the next chapter has been to want to instil particular values or principles in children and this is strongly ingrained. The *child push,* therefore, challenges the past in so many ways.

A Soul Seeking Itself

When I was a child, the models to help me understand my human experience, and the world I lived in, were limited. This, however, did not inhibit the innate connection I felt toward people, natural environments, plants and animals, nor did it prevent the feelings and energies that came through me when I was in certain places and in particular situations. What these frameworks did restrict was the way in which I was able to interpret many of my experiences, as well as the important messages that they offered me. I was born in Australia in the late 1960s, a time noted historically for rapid and far-reaching social change. Whilst many of these changes were global in character, I grew up in a somewhat sheltered environment; the family was the nucleus of my childhood and could be said to be the main influence on my development. The social changes that were occurring at a structural level, challenging dominant paradigms at the time of my childhood (especially in regard to women), did not transpire to real changes at the family level. I grew up in a lower middle-class Catholic family, in a small coastal town. I was the second youngest of seven children. The female role and identity was strongly rooted in a patriarchal model.

From an early age I held a deep feeling that I wanted to look after many children. I would play with dolls, animals, and plants, and care for them as if they were my children. I was often overcome with a sense and strong feeling that *this is what I am here to do*. I expressed one day that I wanted to be a doctor and to take care of children. I don't even remember why I used the word *doctor*, but I suppose it was the closest word to express the type of care I wanted to give. I was informed that, "Girls don't become doctors—they become nurses and mothers look after children—but *not* doctors."

To be fair, when I was a child the only type of doctor known to me was the general practitioner type, a medical doctor, and in Australia in the 1970s this was definitely a male dominated field. I still recall feeling shocked by the response I received, because at this young age I still held the belief that I could do whatever I wanted to do.

At this point, a conflict between what I was feeling, and what I was told to think about my feelings, was established. Of course, this conflict is common to many; when the beliefs and stories of one's outer world, do not mirror one's inner world. In retrospect, I realise I repressed a deep part of myself at this age, and at the time I had no way of understanding that this is what had occurred. A tension between what I felt and how I interpreted those feelings was founded, and I reconciled this tension with the idea of growing up to become a mother, which became the dominant idea that satisfied the perplexity of my inner feelings. After all, this reasoning corresponded with the beliefs of my home environment and most of the social world I was part of.

At around the time of my announcement of what I felt to be my life purpose, my beliefs about life were sharply impacted by the death of my eldest sister. When I was 8, my sister was in a motorcycle accident. She had been a pillion passenger on her boyfriend's motorbike, and a drunk driver had failed to stop at a stop sign. Both my sister and her boyfriend were severely injured, and my sister died a few days later whilst in a coma. She was 19 years old and had just completed her nursing degree. My sister's death was difficult for the whole family. When she died, family life changed dramatically. Although there were many of us children, I learnt at a early age that no one and no thing could fill the gap that was left by someone when they're gone. This type of loss requires we adapt to a whole new way of being. There was so much sorrow and heartbreak for a very long time. My parents were so sad, my mother in particular, and I couldn't even begin to imagine what it was like to lose a child. It was hard enough to lose a big sister. The sleeping arrangements in our family, due to its size, meant my sister and I had shared a double bed. In the evenings I missed her physical presence very much, but I would often still feel her close to me. I wondered about where she had gone. I always felt my sister simply existed somewhere else - maybe as something else - but she still continued to exist somewhere. The pain and trauma I felt, as a result of my sister's tragic and sudden death, was somewhat relieved by my childhood pondering about the soul.

The idea of the soul was spoken about a lot in my family, and we held the shared belief that my sister's soul was the eternal aspect of her that survived physical death and had gone to heaven. I took comfort in being told she was now a nurse in heaven. I also wondered what heaven was like; I think any child faced with the loss of a loved one wonders the same thing, especially if heaven is part of their cultural or religious beliefs. I wondered if I would have to wait until I got to heaven, wherever that might be, to know my own soul? The answers I received to my questions about the soul from others never really satisfied the thirst I had for understanding it. I would often wonder why so many people had trouble explaining the soul. Many people told me that the soul could not be described. Or I was given responses that signaled to me that such questions were not for children to concern themselves with, and yet the soul was a great concern for me. Somehow, I knew that the idea of the soul was not just a story that helped me cope with loss, or allowed me to soften the blow of facing the reality that my sister was gone.

Intuitively, as a child I felt that the soul existed; not in a rational way, but in a way that seemed to be such an obvious, yet invisible, thing. How does one even talk about such things, especially when what is invisible can be reduced to childhood fantasy? I have always, in some way, been seeking a new interpretation of these childhood experiences and the meaning they held for me. A yearning to be in touch with the aspect of my human life that I was told would continue to exist after death. Over time, due to a lack of ability to solve the complexity of the problem, I repressed feelings I had about the soul, yet the questions never left me. Like all repression, and perhaps philosophical inquiry itself, hunches resurfaced when the time and space could support my expansion and inquiry. The way I thought and felt about the themes of caring for children and the soul changed shape as I grew, and at certain pivotal moments, it was clear to me that they were not going to go away; at least not until I had found the answer to the meaning they held for me.

The Search for Meaning

I can recall the frustration, as well as the optimism, I felt as a child in regard to any clues I received from the adults in my life about the soul, and its meaning to my life. Children take great delight in asking questions and playing in the realm of possibilities of what something might mean, and particularly what it might mean to them. For me to cease asking questions about things that mattered to me was like asking me to stop wondering about my possible existence, and even though I had no idea why at that point, these questions about the soul truly mattered to me. I did not know then but evidently, the tendency to imagine a greater version of our human existence has been ever-present since the earliest philosophies and mystical traditions. These qualities of greatness are tied to our human search for meaning. Searching for answers to the questions that we have about our place in the world and the meaning of our existence seems to guide our lives. Victor Frankel in his book, *A Man's Search for Meaning* (1963), tells us that we all have a will or drive to seek meaning regardless of the circumstances.[3] The drive and will for meaning is present even from the beginnings. Yet this freedom is not often granted to us as children.

As we transition through our early life, we are often not met in the way we need to be met. That is, many of our feelings are often not recognised or validated and we are often told what to feel and what to think. If we question too much, then our questions may bring up unease in adults, and thus for adults to respond or consider our questions it requires they must be comfortable with unease. When children are directed to be a particular way, or told to ask only certain types of questions, they are forced further away from their curiosity and their innate wholeness. As we navigate our lives, we are simultaneously managing the push of our own innate will to meaning versus the push that comes from others, external demands and factors (*adult push* on children within familial, social, and cultural environments). The search for meaning is a tension of sorts between what truly gives one's life meaning and what meaning someone else wants to attach to one's life; the tangible tension between the *child push* and the *adult push*.

The thoughts and beliefs we come to hold about our feelings then are largely influenced by the external world of parents first, followed by others. There comes a point in which we all begin to interpret life and come to conclusions about our experiences based predominately upon what other people think, rather than relying on our own innate processes. When the child's body responses and feelings are regulated and restricted, what the child thinks also becomes measured. As we grow it seems inevitable then that we develop defences, complexes, behaviours, and even physical illnesses, which are symptomatic responses to the underlying core factor: the felt knowing that we possess is being challenged as we struggle to keep our unified connection in body-mind-spirit. This period of movement away from existing as a self-operating whole, to a way of being in which one experiences life as a fragmentation of thoughts and feelings has been referred to differently depending on the school of thought. Sociologists, for example, refer to this movement from a feeling of unity to one of separation of self as the generalised other, object relations theorists call this the *false self*, and psychoanalytic and transpersonal theorists call it the ego. It appears a ubiquitous occurrence, nevertheless, that we experience a division between feelings and thoughts as we grow and that we are in essence seeking to maintain unity.

Of course, as I will discuss in detail in chapter three, the symptoms and behaviours that present in the form of defences, complexes, and physical illnesses are not the reality of who we are - they are not our *true self* - and yet our personality holds strongly to these ways of relating. After all, they have often been established in childhood in order to survive. The various transitions we all must make as we move forward in life can cause fragmentation and thus necessitate reintegration. One will often remain fragmented until it is safe to heal. Perhaps then we can see that the search for meaning is somewhat difficult, and yet thankfully, as we expand from the immediate environment where we grew up, our perspective generally broadens, and in this experience, we have a chance to revisit the past and heal from it.

Experiences that caused us to fragment aspects of what really mattered to us in order to be loved and receive recognition from others now become available for review. It seems that in a way, as life moves forward, we continually revisit the past in an attempt to rewrite any limited interpretations. Over time, over the course of a life, we go back somewhat spontaneously to resituate or retell what is already present, but has been largely misunderstood. This resituating and reinterpretation allows the previously misunderstood to be seen from a new perspective. It appears that we go back to see what information these past experiences, especially traumatic or troublesome ones, might hold if we can just see the meaning in them.

Regardless of whether we are aware of it or not, as adults, we mostly continue to search for recognition and validation of the feelings, thoughts, emotions, and intuitions that we experienced as children. Thus, we are searching for meaning in the hope of finding the larger meaning to the 'story of us', our true selves reflected by the outer world. As adults then, we are largely living a life searching to have the unmet needs of our own childhood fulfilled. Even if we become parents, we may not realise we are searching to have our unmet needs met through our children's lives so we may return to a wholeness and unity.

Whilst many adults attempt to reclaim a misunderstood past of their own, they are not able to be present to the child's needs in the way that children require. Many adults cannot open to the child's perspective because they are too wounded. This neglect sees the unmet needs simply, but often painfully left unresolved. And if left too long the wounds unresolved are repeated by the next generation. If we as adults do not seek new ways of meeting our own needs, whilst we care for children, then our children, naturally, albeit mostly unconsciously, become a surrogate for our own search for meaning based upon our unmet needs. Unless we truly know what, the child's needs are, and even if we are *aware* in our parenting, we can still subtly project our own unhealed past upon our children.

Growing Up with our Children

When our children's behaviours mirror our unhealed past, we may not see this and then we blame the child's behaviour on the child. Many adults do not realise the child is not against them, nor are they exhibiting certain behaviours in an attempt to get us upset. Rather they are working with us. As adults, we are called to grow with children, not against them. I often say as our children grow up; we adults are continually being asked to grow down. We are spontaneously called to revisit each and every age alongside the literal aging of our children. Every experience or issue that presents in the child offers an opportunity for transformation, for him/her and for us as his/her caregiver. The resituating or retelling of what is already present, and yet largely misunderstood, can be seen anew with our children. This happens spontaneously without any force as the unhealed or projected imbalance becomes evident in the child and yet if unrecognised the *adult push* continues to inhibit this natural emergence. Growing with children requites a certain way of relating with children that has not been easy for adults to achieve when holding the idea that adults know more than children. Part three details this relational process called 'Being in the Question' which guides adults in a sequence to support improved relationships with children.

The fact is: parents can only relate to their children from the level of emotional stability they hold in themselves. In his book *The History of Childhood* Lloyd deMause examined the way adults have related with children overtime and states, "The history of childhood is a nightmare from which we have only recently begun to awaken." [4] DeMause proposed a 'psychogenic theory of history,' and in doing so proclaims that childhood has been a painful progression for parent, adult caregiver and child. The parent in the past, according to deMause, lacked the "emotional maturity to see the child as a person separate from himself." Even with all the difficulties present historically, he suggests the parent arguably always had the best intentions. "All of this is not to say that the parents didn't love their children in the past, for they did."[5] It was not the feeling that was at fault, but rather the expression. The way parents have related with children over time has been seen on a range. Children throughout history, deMause tells us, have been treated on a spectrum that places children being perceived as dispensable, or treated with increasing dominance, toward the other end, which has only historically been more recently from an empathetic interaction called the 'helping mode.'[6] Within this broader spectrum of relating deMause theorised that adults relate with children in three obvious ways, first; a projective reaction, where the adult uses the child as an instrument for the projection of his/her own unconscious; second, the reversal reaction, where the roles of adult and child become reversed, and the child is used as a surrogate or replacement for an adult figure that was important in his/her own childhood; third, the empathic reaction, where the adult empathises with the child, and is able to meet on the level of a child's need. This allows the adult to correctly identify the child's need without imposing adult projections to satisfy it.

The most evolved approach according to deMause is helping mode and is used by the empathic parent who can be emotionally available for the child. We see this type of approach adopted when the parent is attuned to the child's needs and view the child as an individual that is separate from them with their own dreams, abilities, and aspirations. The projective and reversal reactions are just that, reactions and largely unconscious. Adults reacting in this way are often left at a loss as to why the child is behaving as they are. They cannot see their role in the child's behaviours or symptoms. Parents who complain about their children having certain characteristics or exhibiting behaviours they do not like seem unaware that the child is repeating and imitating unresolved issues in its environment. There is more detail of this dynamic as the book moves forward. Most of these unresolved issues, however, are energetic and therefore unseen, or unspoken, and have complex emotional dynamics resonating within the familial, social, or cultural environments. In effect, we cannot notice the child's wound if our own longstanding unhealed wound is taking all of our energy and requiring constant attention. The tiger parenting and helicopter parenting approaches seem a perfect example of an adult's unprocessed emotional life becoming projected onto the child. From deMause's work we can see that past ways of conceptualising and treating children are harsher than the present, yet, there is also the thought amongst many that the present way of treating and relating to children is far from the end of the progressive history of the child.[7]

Today as we are growing in emotional awareness, we see deMause's helping mode evident in 'conscious parenting' and other 'aware parenting' approaches, which place the improved empathic reaction of the adult to meet the child's needs from the child's level. The success of these conscious approaches is only possible to the degree that the unseen energetics (thoughts, emotions, beliefs, and other stressors) is acknowledged within the models in place to support children. If the adults in the child's life can understand their own energetic patterns, account for genetic stressors, and know how these often-unseen patterns present as issues in the child's life, it increases the support they offer the child. Part two and three provide tips and suggestions that help adults to begin to see these often-unrecognised dynamics from an objective position. When we can see the reason and necessity for these energetic drivers, such as beliefs and emotions, and the measurable biological expression of such, we become better at responding to our own as well as our children's needs. In essence, we become better at responding to needs instead of reacting to them. DeMause's empathetic reaction, however, will remain just a concept, if the parent knows the child ought to be related to with empathy, but is exhausted by this approach due to other demands, constraints, and unrealised potential. If this is the case, there will be continuing unmet needs within the child's life, and for the parents too; in fact, it affects the whole family system.

DeMause also tells us that when the adult becomes a parent, they spontaneously regress to the age of a child.[8] The importance of this process comes to mean that when we attend to the needs of our children as adults, we really do have a *double push*. We must overcome our own unmet needs, and then we must be watchful to allow the children in our lives to have their needs met. Thankfully, this push arises as a shared push, as the review of our own unmet needs is triggered spontaneously when the child is beginning to express its own needs. Enabled to reconsider our own past as the child is growing, we are given an opportunity for great growth because we actually share far more than we realise. If we can relate to this purposeful dynamic consciously, the child will not have to process our past experiences as well as its own current ones, before it can unify and move toward its potential. This analysis certainly accounts for the reason why many adults struggle with objectively directing their attention toward the child's needs, as they are not fully aware of the degree to which they have not had their own needs met in their own childhood, and are reenacting them as adults when the child proclaims that their needs be met. If we are not aware of this, as I certainly was not in my early parenting, then we loop patterns from specific ages and phases of our growth, through the lives of our children.

The child's unmet needs therefore are a gift that help us identify our limitations and unmet needs too. In essence, by looking to our own unrealised potential before we look to improve our children, we witness a wonderful phenomenon. The child does not need much at all; in fact, they offer us more than we realise. Our children are mirroring all of our unmet needs purposefully; in fact, they are also assisting the evolution of human consciousness. This spontaneous regression is not just due to an individual unconscious reaction, but a collective one, which pervades cultures and humanity as a whole. The small child actually reflects back family patterning so eloquently that sometimes even the parent themselves cannot see this gift. We often *do not* recognise the child's patterns as our own, because they have taken a different shape in the child, thus they can appear strange to us. Part two gives detail and much research to digest so you can to begin to recognise your own unmet needs (individually and collectively) as they present in the child within the various roles you play as you parent, teach and support children.

Taking responsibility for your own past limitations means that you may relate with your children without needing to project your own unhealed past upon them. This is only possible when we identify the ways that we can subtly project the unhealed past. If we take, for example, a mother who is emotionally available for her children, this may trigger unhealed wounds in her (adult) partner that stem from his lack of support from his mother in his childhood. The reaction of the father might be to act like a child to get the same attention. He may also resent the mother, or the child, or both, because of the unconscious, unhealed response to his own parent (mother). We can simply reverse the roles and see how just as easily this example applies to a mother (adult) who acts like a child seeking the same attention her child might get from the father. Part two also gives more detail about the varying responses that arise from specific unmet needs within families, and demonstrates how they manifest in a variety of ways, which can be at times both excessive and deficient.

When we dismiss the various expressions of our children as merely bad behavior, for example, we shut down any exploration of the associated themes of why the child is responding the way they are. We then, albeit unconsciously, teach them dysfunctional ways of dealing with their concerns. Because by blaming the child we are not taking responsibility for the ways in which the child is a mirror for its environment and we are projecting our own past onto the child. No one is perfect, and yet we often expect perfection from our children.

If you witness something that you do not like in your child, you can pause for a moment and see, feel, and attune with your child as a first point, you may just find your child is sending you a message about something that you can first change in yourself. In order to support children to bring forth their potential in accord with what is best for them, we have to be able to hold the space for children's emotional expression rather than projecting the way we feel or think onto them.

It can seem difficult to accept the reality that we may not always know how to meet the needs of our children and so we are also in need of some assistance. The value of being vulnerable and open to admitting that we are not perfect is immense.

This is a point Carl Jung recognised:

> *The more "impressive" the parents are, and the less they accept their own problems (mostly using the excuse of "sparing the children"), the longer the children will have to suffer from the unlived life of their parents and the more they will be forced into fulfilling all the things the parents have repressed and kept unconscious. It is not a question of the parents having to be "perfect" in order to have no deleterious effects on their children.*

> *If they really were perfect, it would be a positive catastrophe, for the children would then have no alternative but moral inferiority, unless of course they chose to fight the parents with their own weapons, that is, copy them. But this trick only postpones the final reckoning till the third generation.*[9]

If we as adults can explore what meaning our own lives might contain for us, that is, focus on our own *soul push*, we can look to the *child push* as a way to explore our possible potential.

None of our approaches to children's needs or wellbeing have seriously considered or incorporated into their theories the degree to which we, as adults, become a child again in the company of children, or the degree to which we embody the same patterns of energy, and the reasons why this is so. In effect then, it is found here that the needs arise in the child as an opportunity to reunite fragmentation from the past so we may all exist as a harmonious whole. As children mirror our unmet needs, we get another chance to unify what we have not. By having a map of those patterns of energy as we do with the FNM, we become more aware of the needs we all share that get purposefully activated in our care of children. The point is that as adults, we can often get caught up in unconsciously trying to meet our own needs or looking outside to find the cause of the issue in our children, that we do not realise that we are projecting our unhealed past on the child. If we can know this, then we can look to the child as our reflection, and thus they purposefully bring forth valuable information for us as parents and caregivers.

As our children transition through life, through the *child push*, they offer many reflections to adults that are not always easy for the adult to see, hear or tolerate. Perhaps it is easy to see that in the past it was much less onerous to engage the *adult push*; to put information, ideas, and beliefs into the child, rather than allowing what is within the child to come forth. Collectively, however, we have in a way just been postponing the inevitable transformation of consciousness and fighting and resisting the *child push* rather than deciding to work with it. As parents, we are all at times often so concerned about why our children are behaving in certain ways, that we can forget to examine our part in the child's life. Carl Jung tells us: "If there is anything that we wish to change in the child, we should first examine it and see whether it is not something that could better be changed in ourselves." Rather than restricting the child's expression, or projecting and pointing the finger, we can now open to a type of wonder in regard to the child's actions.

Know Thyself

A deep level of self-awareness is required on the part of the adult; as adults, we must *know thyself* and truly come to know the meaning of our own feelings, thoughts, and actions. My clinical work is founded on the assumption that when a child is feeling, thinking, and acting in a manner that supports optimal growth for them, their body responds by holding strong. When the child's feelings, thoughts, and actions are not optimal for them, the body will not hold strong. When adults have a deeper understanding of the energetic interactions of the child and how certain things affect our ability to hold strong in life, it allows adults to identify the possible unmet need that might be driving any imbalance. With self-awareness we can begin to recognise that many unseen aspects of the child's life, such as their feelings and thoughts, actually become manifest in their behaviours.

When we are balanced and whole in ourselves, we can begin to wonder what the child's imbalance might be revealing. We can ask a question such as 'What might my child be experiencing to be responding to life in a particular way?' In the past, there have been concerns that allowing children to feel and think for themselves is too dangerous, or that they will not even know what they need. This thinking has been present since Socrates, who was sentenced to death for corrupting the youth of Athens by encouraging them to think for themselves, because he believed children actually contained their own wisdom. A midwife of the soul was a term attributed to Socrates; as his philosophical enquiry supported others to birth their souls, as a guiding force in their lives. Socrates stated, "The many admirable truths they bring to birth have been discovered by themselves from within." [10] Socrates knew that he could only draw forth what was already within a person, and that in doing so; people could discover their own wisdom. Socrates, however, advocated the greatest position to meet another from, in order to help them bring forth their own wisdom – was to *know thyself*. More recently, many thinkers have recognised that allowing children to feel and think for themselves has many benefits. If we as children were encouraged to know ourselves, then we would never doubt that our children ought to be encouraged in this way too.

Knowing ourselves means that we need to trust our feelings and the body wisdom which helps us to understand the ways we have moved away from our innate self-knowledge and wholeness. When we can support children to understand why they act the way they do, based on a larger story of their unmet needs, we are allowing them to know themselves and activate their own capacities. Children need to be given a degree of freedom to find the meaning of why they do what they do, no matter how odd it may seem to anyone else. This ought to be based upon what the child's body is indicating, not what we believe, but rather what the child is experiencing.

Assisting children to know themselves for the truth of who they are entails that we as adults do too. The cycle of wounded adult—wounded child can then stop; but we must all start now. If we as adults do not begin to seek different interpretations of what the child might be offering us in way of awareness about our needs, the unmet needs will reoccur and persist through their behaviours and responses to life. Common themes and patterns will continue to resurface or remain present for all of humanity until healed. If we contemplate the idea that we are all part of the one evolving humanity, seeking unity, then we must do what we can do to return to unity now as adults. If we leave it up to the next generation to answer the questions we have not, in essence to do our *soul push* for us, then they will simply inherit our fragmentation and carry it as their own.

Chapter Two
The Child As A Soul

It is impossible to see the angel unless you first have a notion of it.

~ James Hillman, The Soul's Code[11].

Imagine if you grew up knowing you are a soul with a divine purpose that is unique to you? Ever since I was a little girl, I have been drawn to images and symbols that convey a message about one's greatest potential images that represent being the best one could be. I believe every soul has an individual image that is uniquely theirs and each soul seeks unity of self, so it may grasp its unique destiny, and then as a natural consequence, reflect that image out into the world. I have therefore looked to the outer world, to some external image to find a reflected form of my own deep inner feelings. It was in reading stories about the lives of the Christian saints that opened me to representations of a broader possibility of my human experience than the one I had in my everyday life. One saint was particularly interesting to me as a child—a saint who is also my namesake, St. Thérèse. I did not know it then, but I was to come to learn later that St. Thérèse actually wrote an autobiography of her life that she called, *A Story of a Soul*.[12] According to St. Thérèse, God initiates relationship, makes all things possible, and nourishes us. I also felt, as St. Thérèse did - that each one of us is imbibed with divinity - and yet, I did wonder if this belief was just a childhood wish or illusion based upon my own familial, religious, and cultural conditioning.

As my own journey to find meaning regarding the soul progressed from an aspect of my personal life, to my research and my professional life, it became apparent to me that many thinkers before me had questioned the same. In my own childhood the only representation of the soul was within religion. Yet, as I expanded out into the world, this idea that our human life has an ideal image kept coming forward as a common theme and I came to see it was a similar idea in many cultures. It seems to me, that it is acceptable to speak of the soul in a religious framework such as discussing the lives of the saints, and in what are referred to as mystical or even new age environments. Elsewhere however, the soul is often reduced to a supernatural phenomenon, or a metaphysical idea, that has no place in the dialogue of the rational academy or serious philosophies of the child.

I could, however, feel a push within me to bring the notion of the soul forward, as a real idea, in the serious philosophies of childhood. In the same way that I have always been looking for the best images in my own experiences, those things that resonated with me, I believe that every human life is infinitely deeper and much more dynamic than we can see. I also feel that our human experience is connected to and informed by something that extends beyond any personal motivation. The *soul push* actually comes through the child in a unique way that is necessary for both the child's individual growth, as well as for the survival of the species. This is not a survival of the fittest mentality, but rather an evolution of consciousness, which Sri Aurobindo tells us, will result in human beings actualising their full potentials as divine vessels.[13]

The particular focus of this chapter then, is to take a look beyond our Western inheritance of the soul and to make the leap in our thinking to apply the notion of the soul as the unified whole child; a composite of body-mind-spirit. Positioning the child as a unified soul as a key concept allows us to begin to encourage children to know their soul wisdom; to effectively *know thyself*, and to bring this wisdom forth in the here and now. In the vein of this chapter's opening quote by James Hillman, I believe that it is impossible to see the *child as a soul* unless you first have a notion of it.

Following My Push

Those early intuitions I had as a child concerning the soul as you are coming to see have been something I have needed to reconcile. The invisible meaning regarding the questions about the soul and caring for children were revisited most persuasively when I became a mother. When my first son was born I felt like I had been reborn too. I remember reading the following quote by Shree Rajneesh (also known as Osho) and it resonated so deeply with me; "The moment a child is born, the mother is also born. She never existed before. The woman existed, but the mother, never. A mother is something absolutely new."[14] The transition for me from woman to mother allowed for a conscious review of my previous ways of being, as well as an opportunity to integrate the new and to be reborn. The seeds of this conversion came as I made a commitment to my unborn child that I would try to be the best mother I could be. I even had a clear image in mind of what that would look like.

However, even with good intentions, the commitment to be a better version of myself seemed faint, particularly when I was actually giving birth. When the midwife advised that I was at a stage of labour where I ought to push, I nodded in response, but my focus was fully intent on just breathing. "Next time the contraction comes," she said, "you have to push." In between my breaths, I murmured, "I can't." She responded, "You will *have to push* if you want your baby to be born." I didn't feel ready yet and so my initiation into motherhood began in that moment with those words. I was encouraged to push so my baby could be born. And trying to hold back from this push, we are told, leads to much pain for both mother and child, not just in labour, but also in life. New evidence suggests however that this age old preference on the *adult push*, in labour might be best left to the *child push*, in allowing the baby to emerge when it's ready - which actually avoids a mother's physical injury. [15] Perhaps a mother's (and a cultural) resistance to allowing the *child push* in this symbolic and real way is meaningful for the type of relationship she holds with the child as it grows. In birthing my first child and the above-mentioned point with the midwife, I had the strangest feeling come over me that I had given birth before. I let that feeling go, as there was much else to focus on; the birth process literally is nature's way of readying the mother to pay attention to every push her child will expect her to make.

What I was not fully aware of and did not know then, were the ways that my children would push from that day on. Of course, not every birth can be the result of a literal push, for either baby or mother and not every mother has physically birthed the child they mother. These facts do not reduce ones role as a mother, and every mother is required to push herself in a particular way for her particular child. Within my own *soul push*, which has been present since I can remember, is the embedded desire to understand and advocate for broader concepts of children and childhood, and to account for the meaning of the soul in this relationship. It was my first birthing experience that allowed me to see the degree to which these themes are always connected, interdependent, and form a large part of who I am.

In asking the question to align with being the best for my children, I opened to the opportunity to explore and revisit all of the possible potentials that lay within me as a mother, woman, and human being. Of course, it meant that I had some work to do, and that I always will, because as my children grow and move through the many transitions in life there will always be new reflections. And then, if and when my children are ready to welcome new life of their own, whatever I have not processed will be left to them. In order to assist my children and my children's children to be their greatest self and to achieve their best outcomes in body-mind-spirit (feeling, thinking, acting—emotionally, mentally, psychologically, and physically), I have to at least attempt to do this for myself. And, so my entire journey as a mother has become absorbed by this ideal.

~~~

When my own children began school, I became a caregiver to children with severe medical challenges, as well as an integration aide in the Australian education system. During this time, I began to witness many gaps, both in the professional understanding of the child's experiences, what we broadly term their health and wellbeing, and in the ways that adults and institutions assist children to flourish. I noticed that many of the structures, namely the conceptual frameworks embedded within the educational system and educational policy that were in place to supposedly support the child, actually created more imbalances and inhibitions to childhood wellbeing than they resolved. In 2002 I returned to study psychology, motivated by this 'lack of fit' that I saw for our children. I found that it was difficult to locate the child in the academy; the child's voice was not heard or acknowledged. I also felt somewhat despondent when I encountered the various clinical and quantitative methodologies that characterised contemporary psychology. Here, a positivist statistical approach to human experience across the lifespan, as well as the objectification of those things that give meaning to human lives, were embedded features of the discipline, especially at my own university.

I found that my search for meaning in my inquiry into childhood wellbeing lay more within the field of philosophy. Given these realisations, I took a double major in psychology and philosophy, particularly because philosophy engaged with the nature of reality and the human experience in ways that were meaningful to me personally, and helped in my quest to understand children's wellbeing and child development. The child, however, was not really a strong area of inquiry in this discipline either. Just as women's rights in Australia would have been unthought-of as a serious area of study in the 1960s, here I was in the first decade of the year 2000 and the child was still mostly unseen and unheard in the Australian academy.[16] The parallel between the feminist movement and emerging directions for children has not gone unnoticed. The degrees to which women have paved the way for a new understanding of children is largely due to the fact that women and children share many of the same concerns, and literally grow up in the same space.[17] As this book progresses, you will see other parallels drawn between the liberation of women, and how women have paved the way for the freedom of children, as well as just how much our children push us to grow.

When it comes to understanding children's growth, within the academy, we are still collectively stuck looking for what children are supposed to do according to defunct models. Classifications, developmental models, and methods that frame childhood growth, diagnose any imbalance in the self as a disorder or pathology, rather than an opportunity to discover the blockage to the innate wellbeing of the child, or the unmet need(s) beneath the surface of the behaviour, symptom, or illness. Furthermore, these models often fail to recognise the important impacts on the child's life, such as emotional tension and stress, which are not always easy to discern because they are energetic and thus invisible in nature. Nor do they recognise that the source or origin of these stressors may not be within the child at all. I often remark that our psychologies are interested in *how* we do things as human beings and our philosophies are interested in *why* we are motivated to do things. With our children, it seems we have been trying to measure the *how* without any parameters that measure the *why*.

My desire to find a better image and way forward for the little ones led me to consider any means and methods that might help me better interpret the meaning of some of the things that I was seeing in children. I was drawn to learn techniques that gave me information of another type. Studying kinesiology and other energy approaches heightened my intuition and I was somewhat reassured as to the importance of the language of the body and the energetic and metaphysical messages contained within. These modes gave me confidence in the notion that if you or I feel something then it is important to understand what this feeling means. The feelings we feel are the directors of our life as they are felt for a specific reason, the reason known often only to our soul. There is much wisdom contained within the soul and the child's feeling nature allows us to tap into this wisdom. When a child expresses something that we as adults are not sure of, or something that seems like a grand idea that has no basis or rational logic, we need to listen to him or her anyway.

It was around this same period that I began to assist others with their children's concerns in a therapeutic way. By having a mode of reading the child's body wisdom as it presented in various forms in the child, I came to offer insight in regard to other possible solutions for a resistant or non-responsive child by reading energies with kinesiology. Seeing many shifts take place in my own children as well as with other people's children, was reassurance to me that there was some deep meaning being made in children, when what they *feel* actually gets recognised as vitally important. Feeling the feelings fully and working with them allows the opening of many interpretations of what our children are experiencing, and why they are doing what they do, that even many adults have not considered. As my own curiosity about the soul deepened when I became a mother, and further intensified through research and my clinical practice, I came to sense that the concept of the soul might actually be better understood as a living, breathing reality. At least it deserved attention as something we needed to know more about in aiming to bring forth the best in our lives, and interpreting why we do what we do—and such a task ought to begin with children.

Talking about the soul, and references to the soul, as well as any further exploration into notions of God or even uttering the word God within philosophical circles always seemed to land me in a spot of bother. This did not stop me from exploring these concepts. Concepts of the soul and God throughout history and across culture generally seem to be referred to together. Most people would agree that it is hard to refer to one without the other, or agree that they form part of the same idea. These two concepts are certainly interconnected in 'two worlds' theories, which support the idea that there are two distinct realities to our lived experience, one at the level of the un-manifest or the formless and a second at the level of form termed material reality.[18] Two worlds' theories are found within ancient Eastern mysticism and philosophy, and also within the early philosophical thought of Plato and perennial philosophies. These all include as a basis a belief in the transitory interconnected nature of all things and the illusion of separation of thought and existence. I define God as a field of energy that is invested in our highest growth according to our unique destiny.

The drive for me to explore the energetic interaction between the aspects of body-mind-spirit, as a soul, and the relationship between these aspects, as well as one's feelings, thoughts, and actions were a far cry from definitions of the soul that I grew up with, where the concept of the soul is tied to the afterlife. In these worldviews one is not really encouraged to reveal or even posit our soul's wisdom, and bring it forth in our here and now life - unless it is a purpose tied to an improved afterlife. I was never told, nor did I have the capacity or tools to understand, that every action I took was an expression of my soul. Presented below are the main assumptions that underpin my theory of the soul and a diagram of the soul.

A Soul Theory

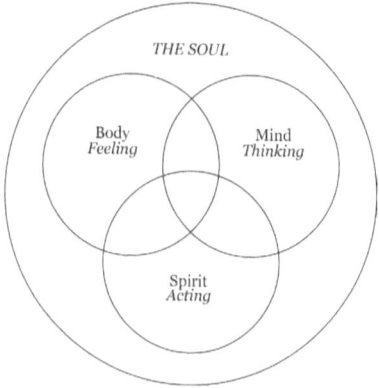

1. Children are energetically integrative in body-mind-spirit. This energetic integration is ever present, at each moment of growth even at the conception of human growth. (Whole self as a soul.)

2. The quality of the connection of the body-mind-spirit is variable. That is, it is an energetic vibration of the soul that can be effected by, and also affects, external forces (people, places, and events), as well as internal forces (feelings, thoughts, beliefs, emotions, and behaviours). The effect of the quality of connection can be both positive (enhancing equilibrium and wellbeing) and negative (challenging equilibrium and wellbeing). The variability or strength of the soul therefore will depend on a range of forces.

3. If we can maintain the integrity or unity of the soul at all times and in each moment (beginning in childhood and continuing on into adulthood), our experiences will be informed by the full range of resources available to us through our body-mind-spirit.

These assumptions of the soul posit the idea more firmly, that in every moment when I feel, think, or act in any way, it impacts and affects all of the varying aspects of me (body-mind-spirit), extending out in time and space. We can think of it in this way: the soul is body-mind-spirit in each moment, and has always been—then, now, and after. If there is an imbalanced action, we can look to the origin of this imbalance, which will be an environment that has not supported the feelings and thoughts in unity (on an individual level or a collective one), either in the past or the present. The beliefs and emotions, as well as behaviours that we have experienced within our own lives as well as those of our family, society and culture, can all inhibit the soul's unity. The degree to which I remain integrated or unified as a soul, and the degree to which I become fragmented and separate, is dependent upon how I feel, think, and act.

I Feel, I Think, and I Act are a tripartite process occurring in the self as further correlated to the child's body-mind-spirit. These parts of the self work as one and are all connected through the human nervous system, which as you will come to see as the book moves forward operate holistically within a greater field of energy supporting its best growth. Children's needs are not just things to cultivate to endow children with character or instil certain virtues; they arise as a result of an intricate dance between the child's biological and spiritual lives. Children store and hold memory, beliefs, emotion, and other energetic information within their bodies and these invisible energies arise in response to the environment. Because the feelings, thoughts, and actions of the whole child is a central concept in our understanding of the child as a soul, I express again that the child's unified self works in the following way—I feel, I think, and then I act.

~~~

The Soul Process

I Feel – Children absorb the energies from their environment (inside and outside), and as they *perceive* this energy, it is first through their body and their nervous system. The child feels all energies.

I Think – At almost the same time as the child feels (give or take a few milliseconds) they also determine what to do with this information. The child *interprets* -- thinks about -- the meaning of the energies it feels based on their own body wisdom. This interpretation is made from an astute operating system (the child's energy body) that has no set location, where past, present, and future merge. The interpretation and thinking about feelings therefore is not just based on the current environment, but on all environments from the past, the present, and the future.

I Act – The child then acts or distributes the information obtained from the *perceived* feeling and the *interpreted* thinking in a way that is best for the child; in a way that will lead them to unity as a whole soul. It is from a unification of self that one's potential may be realised.

Before we go into mapping the soul needs more directly, it is important to visit the early thinking about the soul, so you may come to see how these questions about knowing the self as a soul, have always been present in one form or another.

Early Philosophies of the Soul

The idea that a potential greatness is intrinsic to our human experience, that perhaps that there may be something beyond the physical has roots within the founding Western philosophical traditions. This is where the philosophical discourses of the soul came to prominence and where the idea of the three parts (tripartite notion) of the soul originates. Within these early discourses we find the origins of most thought about what comprises a good life, the meaning of life, as well as ideas about human motivation and wellbeing. How one might know and educate the soul was a point of great significance for both Plato and Aristotle, and yet there were differences of thinking between them. Plato's notion of the soul is presented here first, before moving on to Aristotle's notion. There is, of course, a significant body of work from both these early philosophers, and the inclusions here are to demonstrate the origins of how we have come to think about and apply theory of the soul.

Plato's concept of the soul led to an actual categorisation of the soul. In order to convey his ideas about the divine design and unity of the soul, Plato offered an allegory called *The Chariot*. The story of *The Chariot* paints a picture of the role of the different parts of the soul. Plato classified the soul into three parts—the *Rational Soul* that was the driver of the chariot, the *Appetitive Soul* a black horse, and the *Spirited Soul* a white horse. The charioteer driving the chariot must maintain harmony; that is, must stop the two horses from going in different directions.[19] If the driver can keep the horses working together, the whole soul will proceed upward towards enlightenment. Further, and more practically perhaps, Plato contends that any action that a person takes in the world is a reflection of the state of the whole soul. Plato creates a powerful image of how the aspects of the soul need to be kept together as a means of reaching its greatest potential. I think we all know too, that it is a very real task to keep all of the aspects of ourselves together.

To find the soul described, categorised in this way, as you might imagine was very exciting to me. I became absorbed with much of these early philosophies as they resonated with what I felt to be true, and they made a great deal of sense in regard to my own questions about the soul, and particularly what I was observing in children. I came for the purposes of my own research to position Plato's conceptions of the *Appetitive Soul* in parallel to our feelings (body), and the *Rational Soul* in parallel to our thoughts (mind), and finally, the *Spirited Soul* in parallel to our actions (spirit).[20] The idea that the feelings, thoughts, and actions of the child need to remain in harmony in order for the child to maintain a balance within the self, and to reach their potential, you can see is resonant with Plato's early thinking.

Aristotle, a student of Plato, also divided the soul into three key categories that are similar to Plato's parts of the soul. The harmony of the whole soul, however, was not the focus for Aristotle—he was interested in the part of the soul where human functioning resided. Aristotle held strong that the *telos* (final cause) of the human being resided in the rational part of the soul.[21] This is important in regards to both the notion of the child, as well as the notion of the soul, because Aristotle placed predominance on the fact that humans possess reason, and other living creatures do not. For Aristotle, the human good had nothing to do with God or connecting with the divine unity consciousness. Instead, the goal we should aim for in life is *eudaimonia,* which is variously translated as doing well, living well, happiness or wellbeing. Aristotle said the human purpose is "an active life of the element that has a rational principle."[22] We might all agree that a good life equates to happiness and wellbeing, but what that looks like will vary between people. For Aristotle, the human good is the action of the rational part of the soul and, performed well, is in accordance with virtue. Aristotle listed numerous virtues that a person could cultivate, and children could have instilled in them, eventuating into a happy rational adult.

Cultivating the Soul

In early Greece, the education of the child and the soul were seen to be interrelated principal concepts. Plato discusses the child as a soul in *The Republic*. Plato saw the human being as a soul, and childhood was the beginning of the human life. For Plato, a child's harmony of the whole soul was obtained by surrounding the child with the right objects. Plato said the purpose of education is to "turn the eye, which the soul already possesses, to the light." [23] Plato's metaphor conveys that the purpose of education is not about teaching knowledge to the soul, or putting information into the child, but to bring out the best things that are latent in the soul, and to do this by directing it to the right objects. Objects reflective of the Forms of Good, Truth, and Beauty, allow the child to naturally bring forth or activate in itself capacities to reach their highest potential in accord with their own soul. In essence, Plato believed that if a child is raised knowing that they are a soul that is good and connected to the highest idea about themselves and life, they would draw on this ideal to guide them. Little children in early Greece were told stories through myths about the gods as a guide to bring forth their Good. Plato believed the purpose of the human life was to become the best one could be, based upon a bigger picture idea of our human existence; one that included a divine aspect. The child therefore is a harmonious whole soul who need only be surrounded by the ideals of Good, Truth, and Beauty for it to exist as that. Plato observed that just as a plant grows in accordance to the soil and atmosphere it is surrounded by, so it is with the soul.[24]

For Aristotle, the education of the child involved instilling certain habits or customs of behaviour according to his virtues. Aristotle implies that we are not naturally virtuous, but we can become so by being taught. "The child must be trained to act well by getting into the habit of doing it."[25] This habit of acting well then becomes the child's behaviour, which becomes part of its nature; second nature, for Aristotle. The function of the child, according to Aristotle, is to become an adult. "It is that only by being trained, by some external authority, to behave well that they will acquire the habit of behaving virtuously."[26] When Aristotle says that the child is "doing just acts", he says the child is not Just already; he is merely mimicking being Just. Only after acquiring just habits, will the child go on to learn to understand what he is doing, and why it is virtuous.

The legacy of Aristotle's thinking is evident in the *adult push*, with the largely repeated belief that societies must educate the young, irrespective of the young person's wishes. Another is that childhood must be transcended and left behind. Philosopher Gareth Matthews has highlighted that "dominant conception of the child remains, that a human child is an immature human, which by nature, has the potential to develop into a mature adult but that the child must be taught how to become this mature adult by other mature adults."[27] Actually, many of the current assumptions about how we should deal with children tend to have been derived from Aristotle -

recalling for a moment those definitions of the child presented in chapter one. It is recognised that while accounts of childhood, or conceptualisations of children, have not remained fixed since Aristotle well over 2000 years ago and are by no means universal, they still have recognisable origins in the Aristotelian tradition. Aristotle's thinking essentially not only dominated the forward progress of philosophy, but science as well. In fact, the idea of genetic determinism is present in Aristotle's thinking about the inheritance of acquired character traits.

For Aristotle, only the mature (adult) human being could attain *eudaimonia*—happiness, or wellbeing. Aristotle's aim for the soul's good life was to become a virtuous mature human. The issue remains that we still largely believe it is up to adults to instil habits in children, and yet many mature adults are still looking back to their own childhood, unconsciously seeking to have their needs met. Of course, there is one main sticking point when it comes to both Plato's and Aristotle's early philosophies of the soul - that they both, to varying degrees, positioned the rational aspect of our being as the driver of the whole soul - especially in Aristotle's perspective. Because Aristotle did not see the spiritual and physical, or material, world as connected to our humanness in the same way as Plato did, there is no room in Aristotelian thinking for a metaphysic, a force such as God to be ascribed as a driver to the soul. To re-cap, the main difference between these two thinkers was that Aristotle saw the human being pulled by the rational part of the soul into a virtuous happy adulthood, and Plato saw the human being pushed toward a unity of the soul as self-realisation or enlightenment to be aligned with part of a greater ideal of *God*. I argue that the child becomes the adult not because of rational, reasoning logic, but because of a teleological force (final cause inherent in the soul's divine design) to become unified.

It was Plato's insistence on the interrelatedness of the soul with another more perfect divine reality that tells us something else very important about Plato's bigger picture concept of the soul and its role in the human experience. According to Plato, the soul is self-moving and is united to the human being when it is forming and remains united until it dies, at which point the soul leaves the human body. Almost in a contradictory way, whilst positing the human soul (consisting of the tripartite body-mind-spirit), Plato also tells us that the soul is at the same time the immortal, eternal aspect of human existence and that a characteristic of who we are, is in fact tied to the eternal and immortal. He states, "All soul is immortal; for what is always in motion is immortal."[28] This particular feature of Plato's definition of the soul seemed to be more in line with the belief that I grew up with in the Catholic religious tradition; an encouraged belief helping me to be satisfied that my sister had gone to heaven.

And so, here again we may face confusion about the idea of the soul. Plato, one of the greatest recorded thinkers of all time, argues on the one hand that the soul has a very human experience of keeping the tripartite aspects of the self together, aspects I have come to name the body-mind-spirit, our feelings, thoughts, and actions in harmony in order to reach the highest of human potentials. Yet, on the other hand, Plato also tells us that the soul is self-moving and self-generating, and furthermore that something that is self-moving cannot be destroyed nor created. As such, there is an eternal aspect to the soul that leaves the body and regenerates. According to Plato, death is described as *the separation of the soul from the body,* but is not the end of the soul. There is a further element to Plato's soul theory, an element that was not part of the catholic faith in which I was raised; Plato held that there was a movement of souls from one living thing to another, and movement, or reincarnation and rebirth of soul, into new bodies.[29]

~~~

As you take a moment to reflect on some of the points raised about the various approaches to the soul within Plato and Aristotle's thinking, as well as those regarding the child, you may be feeling that there are still some important questions to explore, or that still need to be answered. Such as:

How are we categorically to understand the soul as the composite body-mind-spirit?

To examine this more clearly, Plato claims that the soul is a non-physical aspect of our human life, which is in essence immortal. It is united to the human being when it is forming, and remains united until it dies, at which point it continues to exist. Aristotle holds contrary; that the human soul is *not* capable of existence or activity apart from the body, and is *not* immortal. To be fair to Aristotle, Plato's thought about the soul existing separate from the body are a metaphysic and rather otherworldly -- therefore difficult to reconcile in rationalist thought as an important notion pertaining to our human experience. It is very logical for you to wonder that if I am suggesting the soul equals the composite body-mind-spirit as it appears now, and if the body is mortal and can die, how then does this contradiction of the soul being a non-physical aspect of our self even resolve itself?

Cyclic Existence?

As with my own childhood wonder about the soul, you may also question how we can truly know the whole soul in the here and now, as an active *push* guiding our human experience, if the concept of the soul remains tied to the afterlife? This paradox has already been resolved in a very important way by Plato himself, where he speaks of a journey of the soul in another story, *The Myth of Err*. This myth is found in the last section of *The Republic* where Plato introduces the idea of reincarnation by discussing a man named Err, who is a dead soldier who comes to life and recounts his experiences in the afterlife, including an account of reincarnation, as well as a description of the celestial spheres of the astral plane.[30] The doctrine of reincarnation, however, is not just limited to Plato's myths and, is also found as a central tenet of the religions of Hinduism, Jainism, Buddhism, and Sikhism.[31] It is also a common belief of other tribal societies, in places such as Siberia, West Africa, North America, and Australia.[32] Tibetan Buddhist doctrine, for example, holds a view of the cyclic nature of life and that there is an existence between the 'two worlds' (merger of material and spiritual). These doctrines also take it as a feature of our human experience that we are born with many abilities and human capacities as well as memory that have been carried over from past incarnations.

In the West, Ian Stevenson became internationally known for his research into reincarnation, positing the idea that emotions, memories, and even physical injuries in the form of birthmarks, can be transferred from one life to another. Stevenson traveled extensively over a period of 40 years investigating 3,000 cases of children around the world who claimed to remember past lives.[33] Stevenson's position was that certain phobias and unusual abilities and illnesses could not be explained by heredity or the environment, and that 'personality transfer' provided a third type of explanation, though he was never able to suggest what kind of physical process might be involved. Stevenson's major work was the 2,268 page, two-volume, *Reincarnation, and Biology: A Contribution to the Etiology of Birthmarks and Birth Defects* (1997) which reported 200 cases of birthmarks that he believed corresponded with a wound on the deceased person whose life the child purported to recall.

In an article, 'The Phenomenon of Claimed Memories of Previous Lives: Possible Interpretations and Importance', Stevenson says:

> *"Several disorders or abnormalities observed in medicine and psychology are not explicable (or not fully explicable) by genetics and environmental influences, either alone or together. These include phobias and philias observed in early infancy, unusual play in childhood, homosexuality, gender identity disorder, a child's idea of having parents other than its own, differences in temperament manifested soon after birth, unusual birthmarks and their correspondence with wounds on a deceased person, unusual birth defects, and differences (physical and behavioral) between monozygotic twins."*[34]

Of course, we need a whole new perspective to approach a belief in reincarnation or transmigration of the soul, when it comes to understanding our children—but do we really, because we actually witness this belief every day when we consider the life of the Dalai Lama.

According to Tibetan Buddhist doctrine, the Dalai Lama is the rebirth of a long line of Lamas. Tibetan doctrine views the evolving consciousness, or stream of consciousness, that is within the human being upon death, as one of the contributing causes for the arising of a new aggregation. The consciousness in the new person, according to this belief, is neither identical nor entirely different from that in the deceased, but the two 'existences' form a continuum, or stream. The Dalai Lama is believed to be the rebirth of a long line of *Tulkus* who are considered to be manifestations of the bodhisattva of compassion, *Avalokitevara*. The current Dalai Lama is thought of as the latest reincarnation of a series (the fourteenth) of spiritual leaders who have chosen to be reborn in order to enlighten others.[35]

In a book titled, *Dalai Lama, My Son: A Mothers Story* by Diki Tsering, the Dalai Lama's mother, gives a moving account of her experiences as the mother of His Holiness.[36]

> *"Lhamo Dhondup was different from my other children right from the start. He was a somber child who liked to stay indoors by himself. He was always packing his clothes and his belongings. When I would ask what he was doing, he would reply that he was packing to go to Lhasa and that he would take all of us with him. When we went to visit friends or relatives, he never drank tea from any cup but mine. He never let anyone except me touch his blankets and he never placed them anywhere but next to mine. Our friends told us that for some unaccountable reason they were afraid of him, tender in years as he was. This was all when he was over a year old and could hardly talk."* [37]

Tsering continued that, "One day he told us that he had come from heaven." In her memoir, she recounts that a month before his birth she had a dream of two green snow lions flying around a brilliant blue dragon. All three beings smiled at her and greeted her in traditional Tibetan style. She thought her son might become a high Lama, but she says, "Never in my wildest dreams did I think he would be the Dalai Lama."[38]

Of course, the Dalai Lama's mother had been raised in a culture that accepted reincarnation as part of their cultural belief system, so she had a cultural model in which to see a deeper motivating push beneath the manifest experiences of her child, and even in her role as his mother. The Buddhist culture, with its broad cosmology, two-world theory as well as a cyclic view of existence, has produced one of the greatest spiritual teachers of all time. It could be said that the Dalai Lama is a conscious, creative participator in the knowing and wisdom that he is a soul. With conscious participation between the soul of the Dalai Lama and God (divine consciousness), we see a tangible bringing into form of the values of the highest human potentials.

To consider an integrative whole soul might be in a relationship with a consciousness that encompasses all time and space, one that is invested in its best growth motivating an evolution of consciousness has been difficult to reconcile. However, in the interest of the child, I have always been curious to at least consider what we might be missing in our interpretations of why children do what they do, when we continue to base our interpretations on limited stories?

The medical texts of ancient India, *The Chakara Samhiti*, suggest that even what we term nature-nurture are integrative, and suggest that even the child's genetic characteristics extend beyond the family genetic inheritance. They are said to comprise:

1. The father's characteristics
2. The mother's characteristics
3. The mother's environment whilst pregnant (diet, conditions, etc).
4. The past of the child as a continuum or the consciousness of the soul.[39]

Eastern non-dual philosophies therefore have an account for the soul that is an eternal and governing principle of the individual. The goal of human life is the merging of one's individual self with God as this the highest potential man could emulate and embody. The Eastern philosophies, with their broad worldview and account for the soul, such as the example of the Dalai Lama, differ slightly too from both Plato and Aristotle's concepts of the soul. It is interesting to consider, however, what our children's capacities might reveal if we perceived them as little Buddhas with a continuum of consciousness that is pushing for its evolution in this lifetime.

~~~

Many cultures have models of the child as a soul that place the child as central to directing its own way forward and welcome the *child push* as it is in accord to the child's destiny. In some Buddhist traditions children are considered to know more about their destined path than adults because the child is deemed to have capacities that are often not recognised in the West. In fact, both Tibetan and Indian traditional medicine practices offer great insight into the way that the human life is understood from an energy perspective.[40] These traditions also offer a view counter to the dualistic and separate notions of self and world often prescribed in the West. Ancient Indian texts describe the human body as well as the therapeutic measures one may take to heal, and are a vast resource for anyone interested in the body-mind-spirit relationship.

From the very beginnings of life energy moves and operates within the human body frame and is a direct relationship with the energies outside itself in effect giving and receiving energy.[41] This wisdom comes from the basic stance that assumes an inter-connectedness of all things; the whole self then is seen to be in a direct relationship with the outer world and all of nature. Further, this whole self is considered to have innate qualities that transcend those of purely genetic inheritance. The child's character or disposition in these cultures is seen to be part of a much bigger story.

Chapter Three
The Child Embodies the World

> *What kind of God would push only from outside,*
> *letting the cosmos circle round his finger?*
> *He likes to drive the world from inside,*
> *harbours the world in Himself.*
>
> - Johann Wolfgang von Goethe (1749-1832).

When we consider why our children do what they do and consider questions about children's behaviours and motivations in the West, we still predominately vacillate between nature and nurture determinants. When it comes to the common understanding, there are two sides to why children behave as they do. One is nature; that is, based upon one's genetic determinants or heredity. These traits or behavioural dispositions are viewed as being adjustable according to the type of environment a child is in. The other therefore is nurture; that is, the environmental influences of familial, social, and cultural worlds, and how these shape the child.[1] What we are now coming to know and as this chapter reinforces, is the fact that the child's environment is much deeper and wider than we previously imagined. Children's past experiences are operating on a continuum of consciousness and containing memory from a past. The idea of this past originating in a past incarnation, which is influencing the child's behaviour in the here and now, has been hard to reconcile within a rationalist paradigm. And yet we see this same idea already present within the Eastern knowledge systems, Plato's philosophies, and my observations and experiences of children with whom I have worked.

The actual motivation behind why children do what they do, will sometimes almost be alien to the child. Consider asking a child why they acted in a certain way, and you may have noticed they often look at you in disbelief. They acted in a way that seemed appropriate for them; it is up to adults to interpret these actions in the most positive light. Because we have a tendency to interpret children's experiences from the models that are available to us, we may not look outside those models when looking for answers. In this way, we may not consider some possible explanations of why the child is responding as they are.

Outdated models impact even those who are interested in understanding more deeply what drives the child to act in certain ways. A case in point is Anna Freud, who prompted Robert Coles, a student of hers, to see if he had missed anything about what children were expressing, how they found meaning, and how they interpreted life, in his previous works. She was adamant that current models (particularly her father's –Sigmund Freud) had no frame for many of the child's experiences. As a result of this prompt, Coles went back over his research to see what he may have missed and subsequently wrote a book called *The Spiritual Life of Children*.[2]

The fact is, like Coles, when we explore openly what is happening with children, we come to see that the reason for a challenge or a particular issue faced by some children, actually originates in something that happened when 'I lived in another time' or 'Before I was born'. We now know, from what has been presented earlier that children may indeed have access to an ever-present and all-encompassing consciousness. The reality of the continuum of memory – as the Buddhist doctrine holds – is also found in quantum theory and now most recently in the emerging field of epigenetics. Both these sciences are yielding amazing insight assisting us to interpret how the past variously appears in the child's body and subsequently their behaviours in the world. Before I delve too deeply into the inner cellular world of the epigenetic process operating within the child, and how the child actually perceives (feels), interprets (thinks) and acts in the world based on the past, it is important to look at the idea that the child is not at all separate from the outer world. And in fact, the child is pushing the world forward as it embodies the past, present and future within its actual being.

Quantum physicists claim that we are part of, and not separate from, a larger energetic field. The founders of quantum mechanics actually believed that quantum theory meshed well with the aforementioned 'two worlds' or metaphysical theories indicated in the last chapter. Quantum theorists see the energetic field as analogous in this way with Eastern and Western mysticism and perennial philosophies, which all include as a basis a belief in the transitory, interconnected nature of all things and the illusion of separation of thought and existence. In the book *The Tao of Physics*, Fritjof Capra (1975) discussed the idea with Werner Heisenberg (a prominent quantum scientist in 1972) that there was an interconnected and unified reality beyond the manifest material world we experience. He mentioned in the following interview excerpt:

> *I had several discussions with Heisenberg and I visited him several times in Munich and showed him the whole manuscript chapter by chapter. He was very interested and very open, and he told me something that I think is not known publicly because he never published it. He said that he was well aware of these parallels. While he was working on quantum theory he went to India to lecture and was a guest of Tagore. He talked a lot with Tagore about Indian philosophy. Heisenberg told me that these*

talks had helped him a lot with his work in physics because they showed him that all these new ideas in quantum physics were in fact not all that crazy. He realised there was, in fact, a whole culture that subscribed to very similar ideas. Heisenberg said that this was a great help for him. Niels Bohr had a similar experience when he went to China.[3]

In quantum theory, consciousness is transcendent to all phenomena and is not bound purely by neurological activity in the body's nervous system. Furthermore, consciousness is transcendent to both time and space. Quantum theory helps us understand the interconnectedness of human beings with a greater field of energy. This energetic field has been recognised by many others in the last few decades.[4] David Bohm, in his book *Wholeness and the Implicate Order* (1980), says that quantum theory and relativity (classic physics) contradict one another, and that this contradiction implied that there existed a more fundamental level in the physical.[5]

Danish physicist and Nobel Prize winner, Niels Bohr (1885-1962), before him explored the notion that "classical physics is intrinsically incapable of explaining the holistic aspects of consciousness." This more fundamental level to return to Bohm represents an undivided wholeness and an implicate order, from which arises the explicate order of the universe as we experience it. Bohm's implicate order applies both to matter and consciousness, and he suggests that it could explain the relationship between them. Mind and matter (body) are here seen as projections into our explicate order from the underlying reality of the implicate order.

In trying to describe the nature of consciousness, Bohm discusses the experience of listening to music. He says that the feeling of movement and change that make up our experience of music derives from both the immediate past and the present both being held in the brain together, with the notes from the past seen as transformations rather than memories. The notes that were implicated in the immediate past are seen as becoming explicated in the present. Bohm views this as consciousness emerging from the implicate order. There is a communication occurring that has a transformative property in that the unknown (from the past as energetics - from a field of consciousness) or out of the ordinary aspects of consciousness, seem to be shaping the child much more than we realise. We can say that quantum physics offers support for the idea that the child is both shaping and being shaped by the external world of which it is a part and this world has no set time or space location.

Embodying The Past

The nature-driven (genetic) explanations of human development and behaviour and even the notion of consciousness more broadly have been challenged by epigenetics. Epigenetics studies the changes in gene expression caused by means other than changes in the DNA sequence. Research in epigenetics demonstrates that the child's environment changes the biological and genetic structure of the child. Further, we now know through quantum theory that what we have called the environment actually extends beyond the seen to the unseen influences of the feelings, beliefs, and emotions that exist in the child's family, social, and cultural relationships. The energetic field, or those non-physical energies, to evoke Bohm, are merging with the physical and existing as an undivided wholeness and/or the implicate order, from which arises the explicate order of the universe as we experience it.

Epigenetics allows us a way to unite the child's actions in the world within a quantum understanding. In a practical way epigenetics shows us how children's responses to self and life are to a large degree patterned and programmed epigenetically at a cellular level. The child absorbs or picks up memory of the past in the cells of the DNA by a process called implicit memory, which does not require conscious thought. I will elaborate on this in more detail soon. Epigenetics declares the child's environment is embedded into the child's subconscious mostly by the time they are around six years of age. This occurs due to the genes carrying certain memory. The child's environment (the ways we nurture and the unseen intentions as well as the influences) therefore has now become the predominant arena to consider when looking to our children's actions in the world.

The importance of this discovery is the idea that what we have believed to be the environment afforded to preceding models is actually much broader and deeper than we have known or apprehended. There is much more discussion in part two about the real effects that the environments of the past have on children and many examples are presented.

Epigenetics clearly contests existing biological reductionist theories of inheritance and evolution, and argues that the genes that we have presumed for so long to be fixed can be altered. Phillip Hunter explains, "Many geneticists now think that the behaviour of our genes can be altered by experience, and even that these changes can be passed on to future generations." [6] Cell biologist Bruce Lipton has made significant discoveries about the behaviour of cells, and his work was pioneering in the field of epigenetics. Reviewing the work of Dr. Thomas Verny, as well as many others involved in prenatal and perinatal psychology, Lipton claims the research has established *beyond any doubt* that parents exert overwhelming influence on the mental and physical attributes of their children *in utero*, and not just after children are born; the mother's perception of the environment while carrying the child *in utero* is considered to be decisive in shaping the child's constitution at a cellular level.[7] Even one's grandparents' experiences are said to leave a mark on the child's genes. There are many studies' highlighted to support this process in the next part which charts the FNM.

Lipton tells us that for parents with children who have very different personalities compared to their biological siblings, the nature theory (of genetic determinism) can be appealing to them. Lipton explains especially considering children grow up in the same environment (nurture). But epigeneticists verify that it is not primarily the genetic structure, but importantly one's environmental influences, including the parent's beliefs, thoughts, and emotions, that significantly shape the way that genes are expressed. Stressors in the environment literally determine the biological mechanisms.

Parents, in this way, are prototype genetic engineers, according to Lipton, who states that parents do not just pass their own genes onto their children and then take a "back seat in the children's lives" whereby they "need only refrain from abusing their children, feed and clothe them and then wait to see where their programmed genes lead them."[8] They have already and unconsciously transferred all of their previous experiences onto the child. The fetal and infant nervous systems have vast sensory and learning capacities. Epigeneticists concluded that newborn babies possess the type of memory mentioned earlier called *implicit memory*.

Implicit memory is a category, or partly a function of, memory in which the past or previous experiences are said to make the performance of a task easier. Implicit memory operates without any conscious awareness of the previous experiences of others. The individual's epigenome pattern, thought to be set during early fetal development and largely established in this phase, has recently been discovered to change in response to the environment throughout the whole lifespan even though the fetal stage is still seen as a critical period.

For parents, this offers a lot of new questions to consider, and if you are a parent and have more than one child, you may consider for a moment the different type of energy that was present in you and your life while one child was *in utero* compared with another. How was your emotional, physical, spiritual, and mental state? Were you in 'a good space', so to speak? Upon reflection of such enquiry, you will most probably notice an imitation or characteristic in your children that mirrors the state of consciousness you were in while the child was being welcomed into the world. Again, there is much more information regarding this type of patterning as we move through the second part of the book exploring each of the needs.

The point to highlight is that children are not blank slates; any emotional patterning and habits we have in ourselves as parents will be embodied by the next generation. The child acts as a total mirror for the past. This manifestation of the past in the child beautifully illustrated with epigenetics is also answered in part by quantum physics as well. This idea of habits of the past becoming a present reality is also affirmed by Rupert Sheldrake in his biological theory called *Morphic Resonance*. On top of this past becoming present, Sheldrake says the child also contributes to the collective memory, affecting other members of the species in the future. The human morphic fields, which are part of this larger field, according to Sheldrake, are the fields that establish and unify the activity of the nervous system which are inherited through morphic resonance. The theory of morphic resonance posits that all living organisms have a prototypical energetic field that supports growth and evolution. Sheldrake sees this resonance as transferring a type of collective, instinctual memory:

> *"Each individual both draws upon and contributes to the collective memory of the species. This means that new patterns of behaviour can spread more rapidly than would otherwise be possible. For example, if rats of a particular breed learn a new trick in Harvard, then rats of that breed should be able to learn the same trick faster all over the world, say in Edinburgh and Melbourne."*

The child's body, having a cellular memory, therefore holds and contains the trauma of the past. The trauma may not be in one's conscious memory but, as noted earlier, the body holds and stores a vast amount of memory, emotion and habits. The idea that trauma is carried over from the parent or grandparent from cellular memory shaping the child's behaviour, has offered much support for the insights I had in clinic, those real life examples of what is being carried forward with our children.

Epigenetic research contends that often trauma does not originate with the child, and yet the child is acting it out. [10] It is no wonder then that our children are so confused about the things that they feel and think. Sometimes they are not even their own feelings and thoughts but come from their parents and grandparents leading back often to a very distant past. The consequences of knowing with more accuracy the reasons why children respond the way they do and what their unmet needs are, will have a direct and positive impact on the child and its own self-understanding, and then the loop of trauma can stop.

It seems natural then that the child activates a certain response from its environment until the message is heard and acknowledged; and the longer it takes, the more momentum it will build. Unfortunately, we have a tendency to blame the messenger. The next part on the FNM, in the *Need to Feel*, the emotional expression of the child is addressed and the process of the child as the messenger of the past in much more detail. The discussion on trauma is also continued in more detail in part two, in the *Need to Be Safe and Secure*.

Child as Genius

The insistence on putting virtues into a child as many positive approaches still advocate versus bringing forth the child's inherent capacities has meant that the *adult push* which has seemed intent on fixing or moulding children since Aristotle's day, does not allow a child to evolve according to their own pattern of unfolding. The child is a unified being who perceives the rich environment and interprets the information it finds and acts accordingly. Children operate from a multimodal sensory system and embodiment research looking at childhood and what is broadly termed the child's intelligence reveal that as an extension of the innate epigenetic and instinctual morphic mechanism, teaching a child anything may not be nearly as effective as modeling it. From Western science, we know that when children's cognitive capacities have been considered in light of designing artificial intelligence (AI); theorists recognise the body itself is critical to intelligence in both how it is affected by, and also how it affects, the physical world. Linda Smith and Michael Gasser concluded that due to the fact that the child is embodied (that the physical and emotional self expresses a human interpretation of the complex external environment) means that no AI could compete with a three-year-old in terms of intelligence. Smith and Gasser stress that this is because humans have bodies that are, "multiple overlapping and time-locked sensory systems that enable the developing system *(child)* to educate itself— without defined external tasks or teachers—just by perceiving and acting in the world."[11]

Eva Simms, in her research, looked to the theme of gestural presence in children -- the idea that children are moving their body in way that gesture what they need and how they find meaning, and clarified the unifying perception of infants. Simms suggests that gestural presence offers a basis for reinterpreting the discoveries of developmental research, and in particular, those adult-centric or deficient models of psychological and cognitive development.[12] To demonstrate the unity of the child and the gestures indicating the way the child is working as whole, Simms looked at pacifier studies, which were conducted by Meltzoff and Borton (1979). These studies showed the degree to which infants actually perceive across different sensory modalities, without the need for prior learned correlations. In the study, three-week-old infants were blindfolded and given one of two different pacifiers to suck on; one pacifier had a round-shaped nipple, and one had nubs on the surface. "The babies were allowed to touch the nipple of the pacifier with their tongue and mouth and suck on it for a while; then the pacifier was removed and placed next to the other one and the blindfold was taken off. After a quick visual comparison, infants looked more at the nipple they had just sucked." The results were interpreted to indicate that, "infants store abstract information about objects in their world that facilitates recognition of objects across changes in size and modality of perception." [13] The children were able to recognise something they had only felt. Another way to express this is, that the body-mind-spirit, the child's feelings, thoughts, and actions exist as a unified whole processing information in an integrated way.

Our human potential definitely begins in childhood and yet very little is known about the neural mechanisms of human flourishing from western science. The aim of cultivating energy in the body accounting for the whole of the child is found in Eastern yogic practices and Chakra theory, which offers a biological basis of human flourishing. The next chapter highlights this energetic potential as the Chakras are positioned as the FNM, the most unified model of childhood growth.

The idea that something critical is happening in the early years of human growth has been recognised by many. Maria Montessori maintained that the absorption of and adaption to beliefs, values, as well as familial, social, and cultural patterns of relating to self and others has occurred by the time the child is around six years of age. The science of epigenetics claims the child embeds its environment subconsciously by the time they are around six. Neuroscience tells us that this is happening a little earlier and that the child has formed vital pathways in the brain from its environment by around the age of three or four.

Historically, we see there has been importance placed on teaching a child by the age seven, because these early years have been recognised as a crucial time for the child. Because the critical early life of the human being has been the time to instill certain values and teachings into the child, it has resulted in an *adult push*. However, we have missed vital clues and have misinterpreted the child's needs and their growth and development by holding the idea that we have to shape and direct the child in a certain way, rather than allowing the *child's push* to emerge. The maxim of St. Ignatius of Loyola mentioned earlier, "Give me the child till the age of seven, and I will show you the man"[14] was popularised in the social experiment that was documented and aired on the BBC in England, and then around the world beginning in the 1960s, called 7Up. This series was inspired by the Jesuit quote and it follows the lives of children from age seven years through to adulthood. The most recent installment in 2013 saw the children of seven, now 56 years of age. The documentary has received broad analysis over many years to comprehend if in fact the child does become the man, and the series offers a unique look into the lifespan experiences of a group of people every seven years with this view in mind.[15] The focus on instilling as much as one can into the child in this time has distracted us from the fact that it is actually a critical time precisely because it is an optimal time to notice through the child, the things that they are actually assimilating - those things we do not like or want to see - those unhealed or fragmented phenomena within a family, society and culture.

What if we celebrated this critical period as a profound opportunity to transform the unhealed patterns from the past?

We are all tempted to want to accelerate the child's potential when we glimpse a seed of it, it is more helpful, however, when such a genius comes to light that we offer an environment to the child that might support the child's uniqueness rather than suggest we know the right path for the child. The great thinker St. Augustine (300 CE) recognised that the child was not a *tabula rasa*, or blank slate, onto which the teachings given to the child became inscribed, but that the child was indeed a remarkable creature who grabs at the world and pulls large parts of it into himself.[16] Much of St. Augustine's writings on the child came as result of observations and dialogue with his own son, Godsend.

These insights are captured beautifully in the work *Confessions*. In fact, Gary Wills, the author of *Saint Augustine's Childhood*, illustrates how many of St. Augustine's observations are now confirmed by neuroscience. The discoveries in epigenetics as well as quantum theory have expanded in a profound way what we have conceived as the child's environment. The previously set boundaries of a social and cultural nature as well as a time condition, no longer applies. We now know the child's environment is those seen and unseen dimensions as well as the past and the future. This extends out to every field of influence, which had for a very long time been beyond any current understanding of *why* children do what they do. Contemplate this: if we are aware the child comes into the world with the memory of all that has gone before contained within its cells, and then makes a choice, conscious or otherwise if this patterning will serve or not, then we as adults can see that we have never been more responsible for revolutionising the way we see this period of human growth and childhood itself. If we as adult caregivers can consciously consider our personal and unconscious repetitive cycles and patterns, and see them as fields of influence on our children, we might be more serious in our attempts to transform ourselves. We might also be more interested to know our family, social and cultural histories and be open to the child's expression of what they are feeling as well as what the challenges they face mean for them. We might be more interested to listen to the child and we might also take more responsibility for the way we mirror what we hold as valuable, spoken or unspoken and realise that these dimensions of our own lives are shaping the human potential in our children.

Expressing the Soul

By being unified in body-mind-spirit, one has the opportunity to impact the world through a soul expression. In order to allow our children to express their soul, we are then faced with the stark realisation that we do indeed have a *double push*. On the one hand as adults, we have a responsibility to undo our own limited and restrictive patterns and conditioning, whilst we also have to support our children to transcend theirs. As adults then, it might be best to first look to our unhealed past before we project any further fragmentation onto our children. This however has not been easy to do because collectively, as you are beginning to see, there has been a lack of understanding of the child as well as what children really need. Each generation therefore has carried the burden of what has been left unresolved and unknown. The problem of fragmentation circulates because as we grow, we are told, and come to believe that the self and the world are separate. However, in contrast we feel differently. We don't actually feel (perceive) separate from the world at the most fundamental level.

One touchstone to demonstrate this point arises as a memory when I witnessed a child of age five in a guided group meditation become rather confused after the meditation and so asked the teacher what had been meant by saying inner and outer. The teacher whilst in the meditation had directed the students with the words "focus on your inner and let this become one with the outer." The child with no experience of concepts of inner and outer until it had been suggested, had confusion about this idea. She had never before considered that there was such a seperation. The expansive feeling of being connected to *all* in this way is known as a non-dual state of consciousness, a state of consciousness in which there are no binary oppositions and one's experience is of a unifying nature, that is, with no separation between self and other, self and world, or self and God. Children actual experience a constant non-dual awareness.

Lynne McTaggert states that the "EEG studies of the brains of children under the age of five show that children permanently function in an alpha mode—the state of altered consciousness in adults—rather than beta mode of ordinary mature consciousness."[17] Electroencephalography (EEG) is a method to record electrical activity in the brain. This research supports the notion that children transit between the two realities, or those aspects of the human and divine consciousness more easily than most adults. These conceptual realities can now unite in the emerging energetic model. Research measuring children's brain functioning shows that the non-dual or alpha states of altered consciousness are actively engaged, not just sometimes, but a lot of the time. This type of brain activity goes underground or becomes inactive as we grow. Then non-dual states can be regained with conscious effort later in life, which ironically is the aim of most spiritual practice. There are blocks established in accessing this state of consciousness, and then the previously unified and natural processes in the child as well as their potential capacities become obstructed. As mentioned, this is variously understood as the development of the ego, the appearance of the *False Self*, or the emergence of the generalised other. These various concepts all describe the one idea: that is, they mark a separation or fragmentation from a unified state of existence. An occurrence that can be portrayed as how I felt before - and how I am told to think about my feelings now.

Perhaps we need to pause and truly feel the implications of the *adult push* with regard to the early life of the child. What we now know is that the early life of the child (perhaps up to the first seven years) is a phase in which the child is more receptive and open; as demonstrated with the EEG studies, the child exists in a non-dual state of consciousness, so they are absorbent and pliable, and have not fragmented from their natural unity to the degree that many adults have (as was the child in mediation). At the same time, we can see how the inherited collective memory from the past members of the species (parents and grandparents most particularly, but this can extend out to cultures and nations, too) already sits in a type of transformative suspension within the child. Children adapt to their parents' beliefs and past unconsciously too, as well as to one another and to the greater evolution of the species.

Recalling the details of the process of the unified soul as I Feel – I Think – I Act, in which the child firstly feels all energies in and around them. The child then interprets the meaning of these energies it feels based on their own body wisdom. The child's body has a vast store of information allowing for the interpretation to extend beyond the seen and current environment, to all environments from the past, the present, and the future. The child then acts or distributes the information obtained from the perceived feeling and the interpreted thinking in a way that is best for the child. Sometimes as we are coming to see, what the child deems best based upon his or her unique soul, is not what adults deem is best. This is why it is vitally important for caregivers to allow children to trust their own feelings and to use their own resources as much as possible in order to stay unified in feelings and thoughts.

A Childosophy

The genius of the child's body wisdom is most apparent in my work as a Childosophy practitioner, in which I use a strength technique (kinesiology muscle test) that supports a tangible response from the body. The technique allows child or adult to determine and understand the body's response to any concept or emotional state.[18] Child-centred approaches that address the body and ways of reading the child's body language (such as Childosophy) obtain body information as biofeedback, and offer a brilliant support to both adults and children. The method of a muscle test is one way of receiving feedback from the body in much the same way as intuition. In fact, I assert these muscle responses or testing techniques operate as an extension of our natural intuitive function and are truly only necessary until we have re-established our own unity of feelings and thoughts within ourselves. When we have a unity of self and can feel and think in harmony, we have equilibrium, and from such equilibrium one's intuition is fine-tuned. We might evoke here the skill an intuitive practitioner uses, a person more commonly referred to as an energy worker, who feels the variance in a person's physical presentation energetically; they are watchful and present to the affects and movement of the body, as well as verbal language and the breath, under certain situations.

Children are very intelligently indicating to the adults around them through their behaviours, issues arising, and challenges, exactly what they need. The child's innate body wisdom is expressed in physical, emotional, and behavioural expressions and comprises a language that expresses the underlying need of the child. The virtue of a body-based language to interpret the child's needs (which children predominantly use) gives a register of the status of the child's current experience in ways that are meaningful for the child. Children exploring the meaning of their body responses often find a very deep value in being able to dialogue with their body. Children challenge the adult's tendency to think through problems and encourage them to adopt a more body-based interpretation. This body-based approach toward interpreting children's needs is less distorted or biased than other approaches because a body-based interpretation of the child's experiences is multimodal, and does not depend on rational assumption alone.

William Braud highlights that the body is a good place to look for clues to validity, especially in the oft-quoted expression, 'The body does not lie.' Regarding body indicators, Braud notes that:

> *"Even (or especially) in children and in animals, bodily movements and selections can reveal somatic deficiencies—for example, of vitamins and minerals—and can provide unconscious access to substances that can correct deficiencies. This is the well-known wisdom of the body. We speak of having "gut*

feelings", of something "touching the heart", and of feeling something "in the pit of our stomach". Situations prompt feelings of chills and shivers up and down the spine or "make our hairs stand on end". It is possible that certain bodily reactions could provide indications of the truth or validity of statements or conclusions in research, and other reactions could signal something is amiss. But can we always trust such bodily indicators? Can the body lie? Some maintain that the body itself never lies, but that should we go astray, it is because we intellectually distort or misinterpret the body's wisdom"[19]

Physical symptoms, and even and in particular, the bodily reactions in children, can reflect the child's current experience in ways that are less distorted or biased because the intellect is not engaged in interpreting the issue or problem.[20] As with many alternative approaches to our lived experiences, the muscles in our body, as well as silences, body movements, facial expressions, and even tone of voice are all valid modes of human expression, that are missed when we consider one means (e.g. verbal language) alone to be the best indicator or interpreter of human experience. This awareness has been heightened for me in my clinical practice, where a narrative or story tied to the origins of certain issues for children becomes apparent through a designed body guided process, but one does not have to be a kinesiologist to measure the energetic imbalances within the child's body and life or to see the child's genius in this regard.[21] By having knowledge of the child's *Foundational Needs* as they are presented here, the caregiver's sensitivity is generally increased, and thus an appropriate responsiveness can be given to the child's signals of need.

As adults become more aware of the correlations and associations of the themes of the Needs as they correspond with the energies of the Chakras, they learn how the child's complex needs are depicted at the most subtle level, and how specific themes can also be located within the physical body. This will be demonstrated within the second part when I cover the seven *Foundational Needs* where we see issues of the child further corresponding with the child's anatomy and body-systems central to these needs. From a holistic approach you will come to see how physical symptoms, mental imbalances and social problems all circulate around these needs. In short, the emotional, mental, spiritual, and physical aspects of each child comprise a whole system that ought to be considered in discerning the *cause* of any imbalance, illness, or presenting symptoms in children. From this awareness, we are better positioned to assist children to cultivate body awareness for themselves. Ultimately, such knowledge leads to enhanced self-understanding.

Children are influenced (influences we term both positive and negative) from their social and broader environments and express this through their body. A storehouse of energy is available to the child through its human body, this energy is not finite, nor is it restricted to certain periods. In order to connect with children's wisdom and know how to work with the child's body's energy, we have to come to believe that the body's wisdom is not lesser than any other aspect of what we broadly term intelligence. As we look to observe intelligence in children, we must incorporate children's embodied intelligence into the equation. People who know a three-year old might agree with AI studies that their adult rational intelligence is no match for this embodied intelligence and innate brilliance.

Children develop agency and belief in self when we allow them to trust their feelings and body sensations as a guide.

Adults therefore must begin to pay attention to the child's sensory life. How one might activate such attunement with a child, when we have not known how to attune within ourselves is described in part three *Being in the Question*. When we come to know that what the child feels is pivotal to staying whole and balanced, which requires a degree of body awareness, we can encourage them to utilise all the energies available to them. We all begin life integrated and every infant comes into the world as a sensuous being according to Violet Oaklander.

> *"She sucks to live, must be held to thrive, looks at everything, touches everything, tastes everything as she develops. Her body is in constant motion and as she grows she does not restrict her body movements. She crawls, walks, climbs, runs exuberantly and zestfully. She expresses emotions congruently; you know when he or she is sad, or frightened, or happy or angry. Her intellect thrives; she learns language, explores, asks questions. Her organism, made up of senses, the body, the intellect and the ability to express emotions is functioning in a beautiful, integrated way as she grows"*

However, Oaklander also tells us that over time and over the course of growth, "the senses become anesthetised, the body is restricted, the emotions are blocked, and the intellect is diminished."[22] Oaklander, to use my words, is indeed highlighting that overtime due to trauma the integrative body-mind-spirit becomes fragmented. This fragmentation happens when the child encounters traumatic experiences like abandonment, illness, and violence. Further, "there are a variety of developmental stages and social factors in the child's life that also cause him to restrict, block and inhibit himself."[23] The notion of what constitutes trauma in a child is discussed in part two, but suffice to say here, the same chemical and subsequent reaction to stress occurs in a child who is disregarded emotionally, as in a child who has been physically harmed or experienced violence. With epigenetics we also know that the child does not have to experience a trauma first hand, but will respond to trauma as its own, if trauma exists in its environment. Effectively, and as a very sensible response then, as Oaklander suggests, the child cuts himself off from his self instinctively when facing trauma as a protective act. These behaviours, in the service of protecting himself, can, and often do, follow him through life.[24]

Transitional Growth

When children move through life they are not really aiming to get anywhere; they are actually continually striving to return to a state of unity and balance. In the process of growth, the child is always attempting to regulate itself but it is this pivotal organic process that simultaneously causes much difficulty for the child. In times of change, such as starting school or during certain phases of growth or certain ages, the child perceives a gap between what it feels and thinks, a space that the child tries to fill. This void needs to be filled so that a child can deal with the new situation and restore its whole self. The *soul push* requires that we integrate both worlds of feeling and thought, rather than choosing one over the other. So, as you can see, we are always being pushed to move and grow, and sometimes this is very uncomfortable for us, as rationally we cannot see how it is all going to come together; in this way we all need some type of support until we are ready to leap.

Some of the significant transitional opportunities I see as occurring for every child are listed below. If these experiences are managed well, they help children maintain balance as they move through life in other areas too;

1. One of the most troubling transitions, besides the birth itself, is when the child realises that it is separate from its mother.
2. The emergence of language.
3. When the child sees itself for the first time in a mirror.
4. When the child starts school or permanent day care outside of the home.

When these transitional times, which are the very axis of transformation, are approached consciously it allows the child to feel they can move forward without having anything denied, restricted, or prohibited. For Donald Winnicott, the first point, the awareness the child has of being separate from the mother, is the most significant. Winnicott says, that every child when entering the symbolic world goes through a drastic shift, as they are moving on from the sensory world of the mother, and in this move they often adopt a transitional object to hold on to. This object signifies reassurance, and the child forms an attachment to this special thing and uses the object at times of transition for reassurance. This transition from unity to fragmentation or from feeling connected to the mother through one's sensory life to feeling separate when it enters the 'symbolic' world creates confusion in the child. Winnicott says the child must eventually see the 'reality' that it is not at one with the mother, or anything else for that matter. This realisation is very traumatic for the child according to Winnicott.

In part two, the *Need to Feel* you will see in the case of Tommy just how important it is to be conscious of the trauma of the child's transitions. For all children, as they grow, there will be many times when a previously harmonious state of being will be challenged. Children face constant difficulty from an often somewhat dismissive, overbearing, and/or censoring civilisation.[25] The previously harmonious and unified feelings and thoughts about self and world have turned to fragmentation and separation; in effect, the separation of feelings from thoughts, and thoughts from feelings. It is not that children should not transition from a sensory world to a symbolic one; that is, to adopt language, look at itself in a mirror or start school. Of course, we all must face the trauma of growing up. But when we can recognise that such transitions create imbalance, we can be more sensitively attuned. There is a discussion in the *Need to Speak* on how to respond to the child's needs as they form language; and in the *Need to See* when the child sees it's image in the mirror for the first time; and in the *Need to be Safe and Secure* when the child starts school.

In their natural evolution to become more independent, children must also face the fact that the mother may not always be there for them when they need. And that they themselves may not be all powerful in relation to the outer world in the same way they command this from the mother. Sometimes children need help to integrate their new experiences as they move into the world, and sometimes reassurance comes in the form of a particular item to hold onto, until the child is ready to accept the changed reality of life. We often see a blanket or doll come out in times of need, such as tiredness, stress, or illness. Then when it is assumed, it is no longer socially acceptable to walk around with a blanket in public, or when the child has to give up the object of security, the gap it filled becomes open. As the child grows it is always transforming from one way to another, and there is no going back to the way things were. The child spontaneously tries to unify through holding onto an object, or through certain activities such as fantasy, play, and dreams - which can offer the child a space in which they may attempt to integrate the fragmented aspects – to reunite the fragmented self. Sometimes the transitional state is not experienced as an attachment to an object, and it becomes hidden until it arises as a symptom or behaviour. The necessary progress required, as the child becomes 'a big boy or girl' can cause additional imbalance that goes underground until it resurfaces sometime later in life.

A very important dimension to my work has been to further Winnicott's transitional phenomena to include all of the child's symptoms, behaviours, and illnesses – as forming a way to cope with transitions. As pivotal as the major points of separation highlighted are, I have also seen that there are many times when the child feels the trauma of the separation of self. I have come to see that the child's symptoms are in fact transitional phenomenon that offers a symbolic indication that a particular need has not been attended to at a particular time in the child's growth process, and also even unmet needs within the child's family history. In other words, there are many periods of the child's development, which can occur without the body-mind-spirit (feeling, thought and action) being in harmony.

The latent meaning of childhood issues, concerns, or symptoms, seen in this way, therefore do not represent disease or disorder, but rather a fortuitous signal that a difficulty is occurring for the child. We can see that a child's behaviours, such as thumb sucking, is just a version of the transitional process, and fills a gap much like the transitional object. Then by making the link to interpret all other childhood behaviours and embodied responses as doing the same, that is: as filling the same gap, becomes much easier. These, in effect symbolically, all represent forms of self-satisfying behaviours and the child can get caught in a 'holding pattern' with their symptoms and behaviours, which are in effect an important, transitional requirement to feeling ready for life.

When a child feels blocked energetically, we will see signs and signals in the child; in their facial expressions, their reactive behaviours of diversion or avoidance, and by virtue of more serious symptoms that are often labeled as medical conditions like ADHD, which are very often treated with drugs. When a child cannot verbally communicate something, they will use body language that tells those who care for them what they need or how they feel. Non-verbal cues such as rubbing eyes, looking away, rolling eyes, or rocking back and forth, for example, exist in all children to varying degrees. All non-verbal cues are important and can manifest as disruptive behaviours; physical symptoms and illnesses, which always serve a larger purpose because they are indicating the block to the flow of energy in certain aspects of the child's life.

Children become stuck in holding patterns when they are having trouble transitioning into the new experience. It is important to remember that these blocks can emanate from either external sources (other people, dominant beliefs, and behaviours from culture, family groups, and schools) or from internal sources (lack of unified feelings, thoughts, and actions). When a child's needs are not met, remember that there will be the possibility of either excess or deficient responses in the child and oftentimes children will vacillate between polarised behaviours. When there is a lot of challenging behaviours presenting, we do not always recognise that these many behaviours actually centre on a particular need. Caregivers can observe these communications and begin to read children's underlying unmet needs, rather than focus on the behaviour. Then from a caring space they can intuitively interpret how to best proceed.

Growth is not a ladder: It's a seesaw

While we have come to believe that growth can be accelerated – that faster equates to better – it is this *adult push* that has created further imbalance. A child needs time and space to move forward, to find a way to integrate the way it feels and thinks about the new situation, and to integrate the previous way they felt and thought before the transition to the new. And we are never ready unless our nervous system is ready. If the feelings and thoughts of the child can become congruent, their transition will occur with relative ease. If there is incongruence and this persists overtime there will be an imbalance. Without any attention these imbalances will become somewhat camouflaged within certain behaviours, symptoms, and disorders.

Evoking the image of a seesaw is a great way to explain the child's need and subsequent imbalances that result from difficult transitions. The centre of the seesaw is the point of balance or unity represented by the balanced need. Within the *Need to Act,* for example, one's Power is a key theme. Imbalance in the way of difficulties arising for children can tip the seesaw in either an upward or a downward motion. The heavy end of the seesaw tips down because there is an excessive energy moving from the centre point of balance, the end of the seesaw that goes up indicates that there is a deficient energy in relation to the centre point of balance. In the example above the excessive energy of the *Need to Act*, specifically to act on one's Power, is excessive when the child forces its Power on others. When others are forcing their Power on the child, we see the deficiency of this need manifest as Oppositional Defiance in the child. Both are indicating an imbalanced *Need to Act* in the child's life. There is a needs table at the end of each Need in part two of the book that show the common excessive and deficient responses as they appear in the child.

From this locus, we can begin to look more open-mindedly at those things that occur in the daily lives of children and to help children notice for themselves when they have become disconnected from their unified state of being. When we come to see that children actually *always respond appropriately* to what they are feeling and thinking, we can resist projecting labels on the child's expressions and behaviours. When children experience symptoms or behaviours that we have issue with, they are exactly what need to be expressed, because they are indications about what the child needs. To an attentive parent, teacher, or therapist, this imbalance provides the key to unlocking information that will assist in restoring balance, unity, and, in essence, wellbeing in the child.[26]

As the child moves forward, they need to do so as a whole so they feel prepared for their next experience. The child who moves from a cot to a bed has to navigate new boundaries (the *Need to Be Safe and Secure*), as well as its relationship to self-control as a result of its newfound freedom (the *Need to Act*). If the transitions for children can happen with an awareness of the importance of every transition, then the child can move forward with a greater degree of confidence. When the adults who care for them view children's challenges in this transitional way, children seem to navigate new experiences with relative ease. From a transitional stance, we can recognise any imbalance in the child is simply an indicator that the child is transitioning from one way of being to another, from a unity of feelings and thoughts to one of fragmentation, and so the child requires some sensitive assistance with this transition.

~~~

In a way, we are all shape shifting as we traverse through life and try to manage the different parts of ourselves—the fragmentation of feelings and thoughts, the variance of truth and lies, the felt pleasure and the contrasting pain—all indicate a seesaw type of dynamic we are a part of as we try to maintain balance within ourselves and our lives. Children have a wonderful adaptability that allows them to move through life's transitions, and if they feel safe and secure in the transition from home to school (*Need to be Safe and Secure*) for example, it will be easier. Children do, however, need help with such transitions, and there are more suggestions for this assistance as we move through the second part and in part three when I offer a way to hold the space for children's expressions.

As adults we can start by becoming aware that there is a completely different energy evoked when we imagine how it feels to sit on a mat listening to stories, as to how it feels to sit in a chair at a desk being instructed to write a story about the same experience. Being aware of the energy in the household, school, or any place that children frequent, is important because children are literally absorbing the energy fields around them; that is, they absorb the unseen thoughts, emotions, and belief systems of the environments they encounter.

Individually, it could be said that the child will repeat or display compulsive behaviour to grasp a deeper understanding in attempts to merge their feelings and thoughts. Collectively, it appears we all do this to a degree. Therefore, if we can see the concerns that children encounter of a repetitive type nature, as they seek unity, we are offered a wonderful opportunity to resituate the events of the past, or to bring more awareness to the child's needs; needs that had always been present, but not recognised before. Many social problems are really symptoms of childhood unmet needs.

Assisting a child to discover the unmet need that is at the base of their concerns, starts with a shift in the interpretation or story that we often attach to such concerns. In order to begin to apply knowledge in a practical way, however, we need to situate the life of the child within a much bigger map of a much larger story than the one we have previously been given in regards to what children really need. The next chapter offers a map of the soul that allows us to appreciate and begin to respond to the *soul push* of the child. This map transcends a purely step-wise (ladder) approach to the child's growth, to include the moment-to-moment growth of our children as a seesaw, and positions us to better meet the needs of children.

Chapter Four
Mapping The Soul

How children act depends on their physical growth, especially the growth of their nervous system, a complicated web of nerve fibres, spinal cord and brain. As children's nervous systems grow, their minds develop, and their behaviours change. Because of this natural process, children cannot be hurried or pushed to act in more grown-up ways.

~ Arnold Gesell (1933).[1]

Models of human growth still interpret development as a series of steps, like tasks that must be undertaken and achieved by a certain age or within a set amount of time. We have presumed that this approach is necessary to ensure the proper advancement of the child. As highlighted in the second chapter of this book, the (inadvertently unhelpful) legacy of Aristotle sees the child, smaller in size and more dependent on adults to begin with, having to be helped and taught how to become bigger and more independent. The fear that the child may be left behind or may not be ready for something is a challenge for many adults in the home and classroom. Our children, therefore, grow up in a world that invariably requires them to improve and overcome perceived deficiencies. As new physics is challenging the old ways, one model of energy from solid-state physics, which is discussed later in this chapter, offers a different model of energy, one that is more aligned with the energy in the human body, and offers a view to an improved model of growth.

As has been expressed the human nervous system does not work hierarchically, but holistically, within fields of energy and patterns of influence. If you have seen an image of the *nadi* energies in the human body, or even the meridians of traditional Chinese medicine, you will have a visual image for what I mean. If you have not, it is simple to understand in this way: there is no up and down or lineal simplicity to these systems; they are complex webs of interdependent energy supporting the more solid structures of our human frame. The nervous system is in essence our human ecosystem. To reiterate - if the child's needs within each energy centre are cultivated at each age of their growth, it allows children to move through their many growth phases with an inner integrity. If this is possible a child will not experience extreme imbalance or challenge to equilibrium in the same way as a child who has been forced, or not given the leeway, to develop at its own inner-directed pace.

We are now at a point in our evolution where our children can stay connected energetically as they are growing, rather than wait to revisit wounds of the past as adults. The previous chapters help us to appreciate that without a theory or map to understand our dynamic human existence from the beginning of life, we can see why it has been so difficult to support children to maintain wellbeing. We can see too why it has been difficult for adults to understand their own childhood as well as their vital role as caregivers. Paradoxically, regardless of the type of maps we have had to interpret childhood and help children to understand themselves, there is that dimension of our human experience that transcends our visible existence pushing us all forward. An energetic map of the child that places them as part of a greater energy supporting their growth is necessary if we are to understand what they really need. From quantum science we now know we are part of a larger field of energy that does not discriminate based on age. As we evolve in the way we relate with children we are now ready to assist our children to cultivate the energy in their bodies from the beginnings of life.

The Energy of the Push

Utilising the Chakra map offers a way to apply this energetic cultivation of needs from the earliest of interactions and at each age. In this chapter you will come to see how the human neurology extends to all other aspects of the nervous system and the vast biological body systems, vital organs and anatomy. Consciousness as discussed has been deemed according to quantum theory to be transcendent to all phenomena and is not bound purely by neurological activity in the body's nervous system. Thereby in recognising that the totality of the child's soul is in dialogue with its extensive environment, we can begin to value their spontaneous insights and innate wisdom. The child through its body-mind-spirit is continually communicating vital information that helps us to interpret why children do what they do and what they really need.

The anatomical locations of the Chakras are based upon 5000 years of wisdom and correlate with a physical location in the child's anatomy (body), thought patterns and psychological aspects (mind), and their often-inhibited potentials as they manifest through the child's behaviours and issues (spirit). The whole child's growth, their body; sensory, biological and cellular processes, their mind; mental, neurological, cognitive, and brain approaches and their spirit: the child's actions in the form of behaviours and responses, are able to be located within these seven main Chakras. In this way, the FNM offers a critical addition to the current brain-based and behaviour-based models of the child as the FNM locates the complex interplay of the whole child's experiences and helps adults and children understand what's going on beneath the surface for a child including experiences such as, a child who is struggling with family dynamics, to a child who has a persistent rash.

In the *Yoga Sutras* and the *Upanishads* one's potential is realised by preparing and cleansing the physical body to be a clear instrument for the divine, to become an open vessel.[2] The map of the Chakras therefore is a template by which one can begin to become a clear vessel as they look to navigate the solutions to many conflicts in life, as well as use the knowledge as a guide towards optimal self-awareness and development. Gaining more awareness of the energy in the body and the blocks to the flow of energy assists one to keep the flow of energy in the body in good balance. If, for example, there is an experience of specific physical, emotional, or psychological symptom, one can look to the Chakras for clues and make the symbolic connections. By applying this map to children and in childhood we can look to the Chakra for clues every time we become aware of, or witness, imbalance in the child.

The importance of caregivers and children themselves having access to this knowledge about themselves is pivotal to how they manage their own energies and gives them a feeling of authority over the things that they experience. When the child is feeling, thinking, or acting in a way that may not be optimal for them, the energy in the Chakras is affected. In fact, everything the child feels and thinks has an effect on the body. Every emotion, fear, sadness, joy, and love for example, has specific effects on the body, and so the body responds in a particular way to a particular emotion. These emotional patterns often also lead to physical issues for the child. For example, a child with anger issues might also present with hives. A child who feels smothered and controlled may also present with asthma. There is more detail of the child common symptoms and the corresponding *Foundational Need* in Appendix 1 at the back of the book.

Chakra cultivation is gaining in popularity and is often referred to alongside the notion of Kundalini. Gopi Krishna states the evolutionary energy of man begins to awaken as the Kundalini energy passes through the Chakras that connect the body systems and all cellular structures within the human body. [3] Psychiatrist Lee Sannella (1987) says Kundalini is a psycho-physiological transformation, or 'rebirth' process, as natural as a physical birth that seems to be more commonly noticed as humanity evolves. In his book The Kundalini Experience: Psychosis or Transcendence, Sannella tells us that in 1932, Carl Jung and his colleagues observed that the rising of this force had rarely, if ever, been seen in the West. They implied that it would take a thousand years for the Kundalini to be activated by the process of depth analysis. Yet, Jung, according to Sannella, also said: "When you succeed in awakening the Kundalini, so that it starts to move out of its mere potentiality, you necessarily start a world which is totally different from our world. It is a world of eternity." Jung refers to the Kundalini as an:

> *"Impersonal force and claiming it as your own creation is done so at your own peril. The price is ego inflation, false superiority, obnoxiousness, or madness. It is an autonomous process arising out of the unconscious that seems to use you as its vehicle."* [4]

Although this process was a rare occurrence according to the Western understandings in 1932 when Jung wrote of it, it now occurs regularly, with and without training, as is shown by the growing number of cases in the files of the

Kundalini Research Foundation in New York [5]. The cultivation of energy in the human body has a purpose that both includes as well as transcends human benefits. Often Kundalini emergence or awakening is attributed to be the cause of a psychological imbalance and is often also attributed to a mental health issue. It is recognised that a resurgence of dormant energies often ignites imbalance in one's body system. Kundalini scholar, Stuart Sovatsky has pushed tirelessly for the recognition of Kundalini energy in the West, which includes the efforts of having it classified as psychological and bodily phenomena. The classification of Kundalini Spiritual Emergence can now be found in the DSMIV as a result of Sovatsky's work.[6] This classification emphasises the need for a deeper understanding of this powerful energy, and as so many have recognised already, there is something amazing happening regarding the evolution of humanity through our energetic realignment with the source of all.

Our Western inheritance of Chakra wisdom however sees to a degree, the same bias as other developmental approaches, that the child is not quite ready to express their human potential. Applying the Chakras as the FNM came with a few theoretical issues because the application of Chakra theory in Western discourse has remained largely adult-centred. Those who have adapted the Chakra knowledge to an understanding of our Western psychology, maintain Chakra development follows a vertical staged unfolding much like many of the childhood developmental theories. The knowledge of as well as the cultivation of the Chakras as the child grows plays a major role in the understanding of development because extreme imbalance may be avoided and mental health issues reduced if we cultivate the energies in the human body from the beginnings.

Embryonic Beginnings

Stuart Sovatsky informs us that Kundalini has "embryonic beginnings." The various Chakra energies within the human body have been forming since the embryonic stage and beyond. The primordial origination of all bodily life is Kundalini, the "coiled serpentine wisdom-energy." [7] Sovatsky contends that, "In each individual, then as now, Kundalini's motherly creativity is first visible microscopically in the nucleus of the fertilised ovum as, literally, the immortalising chromosomal process of cellular meiosis." Sovatsky discusses in detail in his larger work, *On Being Moved*, how Kundalini guides this process of embryological development towards a recognisable human form,

> *thus Kundalini creates a bodily home for the jiva, the "one who lives—the soul." When the fetus is fully formed, Kundalini sequesters herself at the posterior node of the spine (the Muladhara Chakra or "root centre") and becomes quiescent until she is reawakened.*[8]

This idea is also commonly supported by the Kundalini yogic practices, which acknowledge that the blockages or imbalances to the Chakras occur due to life experience, and occur over time. However, the Chakra energies, that is, those needs and capacities vital to our human experience, surface the moment we are born as subtle energies and have been influencing us even before our physical birth at the microscopic and cellular level contributing to what we call the self.

Attribution of a stage-wise approach to the Chakras always went against what I felt, and seemed decidedly counterintuitive to what I was seeing in the actual life of the child. Contrary to this common application for the child, my contention is, and always has been, that children have a vast storehouse of potential available to them in every moment and at every stage of their growth. Obviously, I recognise the form and expression of Chakra energies will invariably change over time in a maturational process.[9] The maturation of one's relationship to power for example (*the Need to Act*) will change or mature over time. However, children ought to have a certain level of authority afforded them regardless of how young they are. In part two, the *Foundational Needs Model,* there are many examples that demonstrate how the biological, emotional, mental, and spiritual are interacting and circulating around the particular energetic pattern. Whilst I recognise that the child develops across a time continuum, and also that when they are small, children need extensive adult support. Children have many capacities that are largely overlooked and unrecognised that can now be seen for the important role they play in the child's wellbeing and the evolution of humanity.

Biological Correspondence of Energy Centres

It is when we look to the embodied child and the biological correspondence of the Chakra energies; we begin to see the necessity of cultivating the child's needs from the beginning. The position of each of the major Chakras within the physical body corresponds with both an endocrine gland that controls hormonal balance, as well as a major nerve plexus. Below is a visual representation of this.

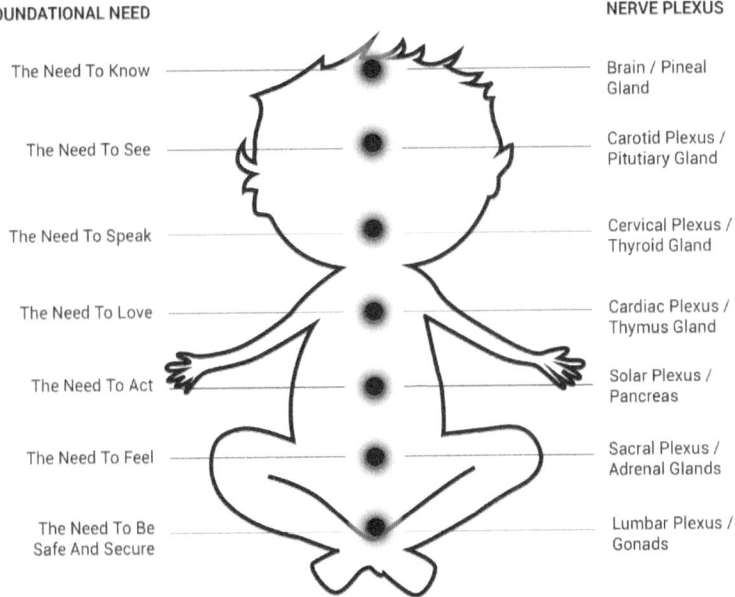

Figure 2. The Foundational Need as it corresponds to the Nerve Plexus and Endocrine Glands according to Pert (1997) [10]

The discovery of the alignment of the Chakras with the major nerve plexus was made during a meeting with Candace Pert and a Hindu Yogi when the Yogi showed Pert a map of the Chakras. After they had overlaid this map on a drawing Pert had made of the primary peptide locations in the body, she saw how the maps corresponded. Pert states that it was the first time she seriously considered her research in light of the Eastern philosophy of the Chakras, and this was in 1984.[11]

Candace Pert (1997), an American Neuroscientist and Pharmacologist, highlighted the importance of the energy of the Chakras in determining the emotional life of the individual.[12] This was not her first discovery in this regard and in fact before this, Pert suggested the idea that in bio-molecular medicine (receptors, protein, and peptides), the tiny components of our body and mind, are in fact our emotions. Pert dubbed neuropeptides the 'molecules of emotion'; those neuropeptides, she says, are the chemistry associated with our emotions. The neuropeptides are not transmitted just through the nervous system but are found in every part of the body. If you are experiencing pleasure, for example, Pert says you will find neuropeptides, those chemicals associated with pleasure in your body, and alternatively, if you are sad, you will find sad neuropeptides or chemicals in your body.[13] One of the most significant findings Pert has made, and importantly for my work, was her comparison of the position of the Chakras with the body's seven major peptide-manufacturing locations where she says nerves are gathered in interchanges.

Pert describes the Chakras as nodal points of electrical and chemical activity that perceive, interpret, and then distribute information to and from the rest of the bodymind. To recall from the soul theory in chapter three, this process of perceiving, interpreting, and distributing information corresponds directly to the process of the child's unified self—I Feel, I Think, and then I Act as a composite whole soul. The Chakras therefore serve as the nodal points of this very process and are located in the midline of the body where there is also an associated endocrine gland and a major nerve plexus.

> *An appreciation of the ancient wisdom of the chakra system, which corresponds to modern scientific discoveries about the location of neuropeptide-enriched nodal points along our bodies' longitudinal axis, can help us enter a relaxed state of mind where natural recuperation and recovery can occur. Learning new positive thought patterns is also facilitated so that we can permit conscious calm access to our "bodymind" below the neck. So often folks today are unnecessarily stressed out instead of blissed out,*

spending time and energy on subconsciously focusing on irrelevant frantic survival patterns which no longer serve us[14]

Pert claims that the more we understand about the flow of subtle energy in our lives and bodymind, the more we realise that thoughts, emotions, spirit, and physical body are interrelated. The Chakras receive and transmit energy and intersect with the physical body through the major nerve plexus and glandular systems (the endocrine system), exposing correlations between various aspects of human consciousness, the anatomy of the human body and the body systems, as well as spiritual themes that are common to all of humanity. The subtle body in the Yogic and Tantric systems of India comprises invisible channels and points understood to determine the characteristics of the visible physical form. The subtle body overlays the physical body as vortices of energy that are invisible to most human vision but which are energetically spaced on a vertical axis in the subtle body, corresponding roughly to the spinal column and brain. Each Chakra represents a particular aspect of consciousness taking care of a particular area of the body. The action or movement of any one aspect of our component self ultimately affects each of the others.

I loved reading the research where Pert claimed that the Chakras are nodal points of electrical and chemical activity that perceive, interpret, and then distribute information from and to the rest of the bodymind, and how aligned this was with my idea that our feelings thoughts and actions work together. *I Feel* (perceive), *I Think* (interpret) and *I Act* (distribute energy) all impact our physical body and determine our wellbeing. Pert declares that, "We are hard-wired for bliss", which is both physical and divine; our body makes its own natural opiates, the endorphins.

Western concepts of God, according to Pert, are the summation of how the natural laws of the universe operate; with peace and harmony.[15] I love to consider, as you might too, that the chemistry of the soul can be found within this very process, and therefore the Chakras really are the anatomy of one's soul, which is not reserved to adulthood. It is through the Chakras that the soul becomes receptive and communicates with the universal energies (God) and this is happening from the very beginnings.

Biological support for the Chakras is not just limited to the Pert Model, because we know the very lineage of the Chakras themselves accounts for this connection. Throughout the *Upanishads* and the *Yoga Sutras,* biological accounts of cultivating the energies in the body are found. Within the Indian traditional medicinal texts mentioned in the previous chapter, there is classification of these energies as they present as imbalance in the human body system. The partiality in rational Western thought concerning the validity of the Chakras can be informed by this ancient wisdom, which now is being verified by science. It appears that we took quite a detour in our route to understanding our human experience in the West because we had incomplete, partial and fragmented maps.

This detour is best demonstrated in another aspect of the biological support for the Chakras through vitalism. Don Glassey, drawing upon knowledge, experience, and expertise as a chiropractor, has researched the nervous, meridian (Traditional Chinese Medicine), and Chakra energy systems, which led him to the discovery that cerebrospinal fluid (CSF) is the physical connection that links all the energy systems.[16] To me, CSF sounds a lot like the Mother energy Kundalini and the *soul push*. Glassey's theory that CSF is the fluid of life as the life force (*chi or prana*) of the body is based upon a vitalistic principle that links us back to 17th century biological theories. As mentioned in the last chapter just as we have had difficulty mapping the child outside genetic determinism, current conventions concerning what children need and what is best for them largely discounts that the child has access to a larger field of consciousness, which contains information that is supporting their growth and expansion in the most optimal way for them, as well as for the world they are creating.

A Soul Physic

Making the biological links of the Chakra energies is important in our understanding of children' needs and yet, this alone does not really reinforce the idea that the child has access to all of these energetic capacities while moving through life. Although I was seeing profound examples in my clinical practice my determination to create a model to help adults understand such capacities was not enough to validate my intuition. The established bias about the child's growth and development that I have argued throughout (that many potentials are only available to children when they grow bigger and into adults) is deep and wide. My claim that the child possesses capacities, which are often suppressed, restricted, and blocked as they grow may seem intuitively plausible and yet for many years as I researched this principle, there was no rational logic for it, yet.

In my clinical practice I have always witnessed so many things occurring for children that by current understandings of child growth and development I could not answer. I always held out hope that one day there may be a framework to incorporate the many dimensions of the child's experience. Research truly does seem to come in all manner of ways, because almost out of nowhere, one day; I had the most fortuitous encounter that answered some very important questions for me. A synchronous informal conversation with a senior physicist about my research, turned out to be very fruitful indeed.[17] I explained in this conversation, I hypothesised (based upon the extensive experience of the child's needs according to current paradigm versus the energetic paradigm in Chakra theory) that when the child's needs were equally attended to at each and every age of development, the possibility for the greatest potential may be realised within the child. I communicated that in effect, the child's *Foundational Needs* (Chakra energies) had to be cultivated all the time, and the child was never too young to experience this.

I explained that in fact, I believed that we might be missing vital information by not attending to the child in this way. I gave a simple example of the idea to demonstrate my point and expressed that when it comes to the spiritual life of the child, (which I had spent years examining) even those evolved 'integral' approaches do not recognise certain spiritual capacities possible in the child. I have claimed elsewhere that the dimensions that Integral Theorists say we are aiming toward as our highest expression of development or evolution is already operating in the child. Due to a dominance of hierarchical developmental models within Western institutions, this has gone unrecognised. The conversation turned and I was asked if I had any idea that what I was explaining was akin to a particular law in solid-state physics called the Fermi filling law. On the basis of these comments, I took some brief notes on which to research later.

In solid-state physics, it is proposed that the filling of states of energy levels at any given temperature always occurs in such a way that states are filled simultaneously without having to occupy a lower order; there is always an even distribution.[18] This theory was indeed important because we can think of the Chakra system in exactly the same way. The human being is embodied energy that has become a solid state or mass. Remember Sovatsky's notion of the embryological, cellular origins of Kundalini energy forming the self. The Chakras are in this way akin to energy centres that occupy the space of this bodily mass; that is, they occupy specific locations in the human body. To repeat: the filling of these states or energy levels at any given temperature (exposure) always occurs in such a way that states are filled simultaneously without having to occupy a lower order. There is always an even distribution.

I imagined the formation of the embryo and I elicited in my mind's eye all the diagrams I had seen in my own research, which position the embryo at certain stages with certain development and recalled certain organs forming in conjunction with each other at the same time. Because the location of each level of Chakra energy also has a resonance with certain organs and themes that are fundamental to our human growth and wellbeing, they are all working together. The energies of the Chakras, if we interpret them according to Fermi's law, need always be filled simultaneously because energetically there is always an even distribution.

> *"The concept of the Fermi energy is a crucially important concept for the understanding of the electrical and thermal properties of solids. This implies that the vast majority of the electrons cannot receive energy from those processes because there are no available energy states for them to go to within a fraction of an electron volt of their present energy. Limited to a tiny depth of energy, these interactions are limited to 'ripples on the Fermi sea'."*[19]

The electrical and thermal properties of the self, indicates that the lower order states of the first Chakra for example, the *Need to Be Safe and Secure,* does not need to be filled first in a stepwise way or filled completely for a higher state to be filled; for example, the seventh Chakra the *Need to Know,* because there is always an even distribution. The embryo develops its body system simultaneously. The seventh Chakra theme, the *Need to Know,* incorporates and encompasses themes of unity, highest power, and universal knowledge. This need correlates with the muscular, skeletal, and skin systems of the body and is an important nerve plexus site and makes up a distinct part of the nervous system. It is unreasonable to think that these vital aspects of the child's biology are not always affected by the child's interactions in the world and would not need to be attended to at all times throughout growth, and yet we have reserved the certain spiritual aspects such as unity, highest power, and universal knowledge predominately to the adult.

Each field of energy in the human body has a specific role to play and relates to specific body functions, and these are all operating simultaneously according to this energetic law. In thermodynamics the second law states that there also needs to be equilibrium of the various energy states (that often can have an impermeable wall). This equilibrium is necessary for integrity and increases in energy. These various energy (states) themes of human life should be cultivated simultaneously to maintain equilibrium, balance or what we in human terms refer to as wellbeing. These should not have to wait and in fact, the child is seeking the variety of these expressions in every moment. The case examples in the next part of the book literally bring this idea to life. This finding although potential for an enormous field of research in itself, underlined and highlighted my appeal to look beyond hierarchical, vertical, bottom-up or top-down, ladder like approaches to energy in the human body as they do not apply and should not apply to our human needs; which clearly begin in childhood.

This law in solid-state physics contradicts the understanding of energy that we have from Newtonian science, which most of our developmental frameworks follow, where the lower arrangements need to be filled initially for a higher level to be obtained. All educators will know that Piaget demonstrated a child had hit a cognitive milestone when the child understands that upon pouring a liquid into a different shaped glass, the level of liquid might vary, but the amount of liquid is the same. Interestingly, in Piaget's constructionist model, the child is only taught about the conversion processes from a bottom-up approach. In Piaget's model as well, conversion is based upon one model of energy, but not on *all* possible models.

It is a fact that physical bodies are designed to be open and receptive, and when they are, they activate the multifaceted dimension of the child's consciousness. The child's nervous system is connected with the themes and needs of the Chakras as shown by the Pert Model. The child can only progress and move through otherwise noted stages when it is ready; it cannot be forced and, according to Arnold Gesell (whose quote opened this chapter), the child is never ready unless the child's nervous system is ready. The child's development, according to Gesell, is a genetically determined process that unfolds automatically, much like a flower. Gesell believed the timetable and pattern of human development is the product of millions of years of evolution, and that children are naturally knowledgeable about their own needs. Certain capacities in the child emerge based on heredity, temperament, culture, environment, experiences, and intelligences.[20] Gesell was quick to point out normal development can be sporadic and inconsistent and may appear to have setbacks, including negative and positive behaviours, all of which are vital in helping the child to grow and develop.

The focus on preparing the child's nervous system to be in an optimal position to learn, to grow, and to create, means children require integrity of body-mind-spirit: a harmony of feelings, thoughts, and actions. The next part of the book shows how preparing the nervous system to be ready means that we simply need to meet children's *Foundational Needs* and pay attention to their growth as they naturally seesaw in an attempt to maintain a balanced and whole self.

PART II

THE FOUNDATIONAL NEEDS

1. Children Need To Be Safe And Secure: Soothe Me

Rock-a-bye baby, in the treetop,

When the wind blows, the cradle will rock,

When the bough breaks, the cradle will fall,

~~And down will come baby, cradle and all.~~

And I will catch baby, cradle, and all.[1]

Even the smallest things that occur throughout the day in the life of a child indicate the degree to which they will be safe in the world and secure in themselves. The child is, in essence, proclaiming *Soothe Me*.

Figure 3: Physical Location of the *Need to Be Safe and Secure.*[2]

Case 1: Sally

When I first met Sally she was experiencing a high level of body pain and a type of contraction in all of her joints, restricting her from sporting activities. Sally also had difficulty with many day-to-day physical movements. Sally was six years, and for two years her parents had been trying to work out what was going on. Sally's parents, eager to find some relief for their daughter's pain, had taken her to many professionals to seek answers. After various types of medical testing, Sally was diagnosed with juvenile arthritis. By the time I met Sally, she was fatigued, medicated and very sad. Her parents were overwhelmed with their inability to change the reality of life as it was now for Sally. Sally's parents were open to exploring what else might be going on for her. They explained to me that perhaps they had missed something or perhaps there might be something else they could do to make Sally's day-to-day functioning easier. It was evident when I met Sally that she was fragile as she struggled to sit down on the chair. Her body appeared to belong to that of an ailing adult, not a young child. It looked torturous for Sally just to move. I expressed to Sally that it seemed to me that it was hard for her to move and I also expressed that I would like to know what it felt like for her. According to Sally, it was scary.

We spent some time exploring the scary feeling, after all; it was this very feeling that would eventually lead us to the unmet need that was at origin of Sally's symptoms. This process of holding the space for children is outlined in detail in part three, basically to demonstrate here, it required that Sally and I both feel the scary feeling that was present for her. You will notice that we have not spoken about the label or even concerned ourselves with thoughts and beliefs that might have been created as a result of Sally's experience of juvenile arthritis; we are more concerned with her scary feelings. On exploration with Sally, I asked what else made her feel scared, really scared and she recalled a time in which she was indeed scared. This memory of Sally's then becomes the touchstone or the original experience that allows me to talk to Sally about her feelings in a way that resonate with her. Sally started to talk about how she felt very scared when a man, who was a stranger, had grabbed her at the park and tried to take her.

Sally's mother and father were surprised that Sally remembered this experience; they had tried not to talk about it in front of her. They were also perplexed as to why this memory was coming up in regard to exploring how to support their daughter with her juvenile arthritis. They opened up, as it was now clear to them that Sally did remember this trauma. The mother told me that when Sally was three they were at a local park. As the children were familiar with the park, they often were given some freedom to explore (both Sally and her big brother). At one point about 15 minutes after they arrived at the park the mother lost sight of Sally. The mother looked to the distant swings and she saw a man was grabbing Sally off the swing. The mother ran quickly after them both, screaming and making a lot of noise. Thankfully the man dropped Sally.

The scary feeling that Sally experienced at three was connected to the theme of feeling unsafe and insecure and she expressed words such as, taken and grabbed, in relation to her being scared. Of course, at three, one does not have the capacity to express the depth of how this experience might feel, or even know what one might need after experiencing such an event. So, the trauma of feeling scared often remains in the biological body system as it had remained for Sally. This feeling was held in Sally's body and had set in motion an autonomic response of protection within her immune system, sending various signals about her need for protection. In fact, incidentally, after this event the father expressed that both he and the mother had also become rather protective of Sally limiting her freedoms and surveying her movement, just in case something else might happen. The juvenile arthritis spoke for Sally, as it was Sally's way of communicating that she needed to be protected from feeling the original scary feeling of being grabbed and taken without any warning. The symptom also reinforced the energy of extreme protection coming from the parents, as they also held unprocessed energy (fearful feelings and thoughts) surrounding the same experience.

The pathway of both the symbolic and energetic interchange in the child's life pertaining this *Need to be Safe and Secure* is the 1st Chakra energy (*Muladhara*). These energies represent a sense of feeling connected and safe in one's body as well as the physical world, both of which were disrupted for Sally. Specific themes include; being connected, grounded, trusting, prosperous, secure, nourished, and having boundaries between self, other, and world.[3] You can see in the case of Sally that she experienced a symbolic and real threat to self-preservation, trust, and boundaries in this situation. These feelings then transpired to Sally activating a response in her biological body system setting in motion the autoimmune response. The associated anatomy and body systems of the *Need to Be Safe and Secure* (1st Chakra) are located at the base of the central nervous system; the physical body support, the base of the spine, bones, legs, rectum, and immune system.[4] (See the A-Z of common ailments associated to this 1st Need in Appendix 1.) Of course, not every child will experience such a response when they face a threat to their safety and security in the way Sally did. This is just one example that allows us to see the physical and real response that a child may experience from the unprocessed feelings and thoughts tied to the specific theme of safety and security.

Issues that present in children based upon the *Need to Be Safe and Secure* will vary among individuals, families, and cultures, although there are certain themes that could be considered the same for all. Boundaries, for example, as a theme may be seen to exhibit at one end of the seesaw as a child who clings to others constantly (deficient energy regarding healthy boundaries) while, at the other end, a child not wanting to be touched at all (excessive energy in regard to healthy boundaries). A clingy child is communicating a *Need to Be Safe and Secure,* just as a withdrawn child is also communicating a *Need to Be Safe and Secure.* It is the same original unmet need with a different presentation. The needs table at the end of this section shows a variety of excess and deficient responses in the child if the *Need to be Safe and Secure* is not met. Knowing that the unmet need to have *Safe* and *Secure* boundaries is at the origin of the child's behaviours in this way, we can in effect pay more attention to ways that we might encourage affirmative thoughts and responses to meet the need if a child expresses such imbalance, rather than using reactionary measures or responding from our unhealed past.

Of course, as Sally's case demonstrates, we cannot always protect our children in the ways we would want, and therefore we may become over protective or have an excessive energy of safety and security in our relationship with them. However, if we can see the energetic impact our own unresolved issues are having on the child, we can offer a clearer energetic space to support them to express the very real feelings that they experience when unexpected or troubling things happen. If we do not address the feeling beneath the issues for the child or for ourselves when such experiences occur, these feelings remain stuck and will naturally seek another way of release. This is how feelings become transformed into a physical symptom such as Sally's. When we can return to the origin of the patterns of energy that are creating disharmony in our lives, we can attend to them with more awareness. Sally's parents also had recognised that they had been contributing unconsciously, to the child's symptoms due to their overprotection. Sally's parents worked with the feelings, thought and beliefs that arose for them in regard to protecting their daughter and as a result gained much self-awareness about the patterns of safety and security that were unhealed from their own childhoods.

Sally, thankfully, overcame her physical restrictions and six months after her first visit with me, (her parents also worked through some of their residual emotions with me as well), she was in what is medically referred to as a remission. Sally no longer had to express through her pain and restricted movement that she needed to feel safe in her world and secure in herself. Once the link was made that both daughter and parents were responding from the same unmet need, it could be healed. Sally, with support, has found another interpretation and expression for the original trauma, and one which is much more connecting and supportive compared to the pain of disease. Sally is now secure and feels safe to move with ease and enjoy her body and her life.

> **Need to be Safe and Secure - Common Themes**
> - *Attunement - Attachment*
> - *Maternal Deprivation*
> - *Stress*
> - *Trauma*
> - *Anxiety*
> - *Secure Transitions–Separation*
> - *Physical Body Awareness*
> - *Nourishment*

Attunement – Attachment

Children's initial attachment relationships are responsible for all of the child's future relationships; with themselves and the world. [5] The attunement of feelings, thoughts, and emotions between the child and its primary caregivers influence the way the child feels and thinks about itself, as well as the emotions they come to experience. The child's ability to focus, its awareness of feelings, its self-calming capacity, as well as its resilience are all related to a secure attachment. *Attachment Theory* conveys that a mother who is secure in her parenting will encourage a securely attached child who trusts others and feels worthy of others' attention. The secure child can then build attachments to other objects and people that become a surrogate for this original connection. This type of surrogate attachment is seen in the case of transitional objects where the transitional phenomenon serves the purpose of commanding smoother transitions for the child.

There are four patterns of attachment in Attachment Theory (avoidant, ambivalent, secure, and disorganised), each pattern has varying levels of feelings of safety and security. A child who does not experience a secure attachment with the mother but rather an avoidant, ambivalent, and disorganised one will be more likely to exhibit excess or deficient responses and behaviours (rather than a balanced approach) to themselves and others, and will seek objects of security by way of other satisfiers (a transitional object). The mothers' sensory bond with the child is vital. In many cases, children can and do develop a secure attachment with the father, a sibling, grandparent, or aunt or uncle, who becomes the surrogate for a lost mother bond. In fact, many men make better 'mothers' than some women. However, regardless of the quality or shape it takes, we know there is an attachment (positive or negative) happening at each and every moment.

Given that the role of mothering has been devalued culturally in the West (especially in the last few decades), many women have sought to be recognised as more than just mothers, and thus, children have become somewhat devalued as well. From the earliest moments, the growing embryo perceives (feels) and interprets (thinks) if it is or is not safe to be welcomed into the world. The neural and hormonal interactions between mother and child are establishing strong bonds.

> *"High oxytocin causes a mother to become familiar with the unique odor of her newborn infant, and once attracted to it, to prefer her own baby's odor above all others. Baby is similarly*

imprinted on mother, deriving feelings of calmness and pain reduction along with mom. When the infant is born, he is already imprinted on the odor of his amniotic fluid. This odor imprint helps him find mother's nipple, which has a similar but slightly different odor. In the days following birth, the infant can be comforted by the odor of this fluid"[6]

The mother-child exists as the one organism for the period of gestation, and for nine months they work together healing (and even creating disease) in each other. The unborn baby sends the mother's organs healing in the way of stem cells if she needs it. This unique energetic conversation is seen most tangibly in women with autoimmune disorders who experience a submission of symptoms and illness whilst the baby is being carried, and in many cases, it continues even after the birth.[7]

After childbirth, the cells of the baby remain and protect the mother in a variety of ways, and decade's later traces of the child's cells can still be found in the mother. The child's cells that remain in the mother then fuse and interact with any subsequent child the mother will carry.[8] The youngest child of a large family actually holds and stores cells from every sibling that predates them, so in a way the youngest child is a combination of all of the past and the most recent gift of the generations of the family line going back and further back. The baby is the newest and most recent evolution of this lineage and therefore in effect is the most evolved. No wonder the babies of the family are so loved or so resented, depending on the family dynamic. This knowledge presents parents with a whole new perspective to consider in regard to sibling rivalry, sharing, and birth order theory. Sibling rivalry is discussed in more detail in the *Need to Love* part of this *Foundational Needs* section.

In the physical birth process itself, the level of care coming from those assisting the mother and child in the birthing process has been seen to be paramount, resulting in many improved measures and policy for better birthing practices. Welcoming the child into the utmost secure environment for the first 3 months of life outside the womb is said to optimise the nervous system's ability to cope, which in effect allows for a sensory integration of the child's complex body-mind-spirit. This need for integration and smooth transition from the womb has been recognised in what is often referred to as the 4th trimester. Many cultures practice confinement of mother and child after birth. This tradition dates back thousands of years in China and India and is said to promote the wellbeing of both mother and child. [9] Keeping the mother and child in physically close proximity is supportive to both.

The birth and subsequent trauma (of course, some births are more traumatic than others, however; even the most natural birth can be distressing) occurs because the world of the warm, sensory experience of the womb inside is severed by the harsh, cold reality of life on the outside. The disruption to the physical relationship between the fetus and mother creates a birth trauma, and this is theorised to be the original trauma that all humans experience. This trauma becomes a central, unconscious force in adult life. One may not remember their birth experience, but it has become embodied, and thus, although not consciously recalled, it directs much of one's life. It is reported that there's no way to tell what kind of pain a baby feels when he travels through the birth canal, but research shows that in the case of the mother's felt pain the birth process can be so traumatic that a mother disengages from the child emotionally. This, of course, has a subsequent impact on the child's ability to feel connected and safe in these earliest experiences. Postnatal depression is linked with traumatic birthing experiences for the mother, especially in the case of the loss of child. The severed bond with one's own baby is perhaps the most severe trauma a mother can experience and in the next part the *Need to Feel*, there is more discussion of how one might cope with such trauma.

Outside the womb, safety and security can be established quickly in most cases with bonding as the mother breast-feeds the newborn. From the mother's milk, the child receives colostrum, which contains biologically active molecules and properties in the way of immune factors and growth promoters. These assist the child's biological processes immediately to deal with the transition into the world and guard against health-related issues; not just in childhood, but also for the remainder of their life. A child who is breastfed, however, from an ambivalent or disoriented mother will not get the same nourishment as it would from an emotionally welcoming one. In such cases, the wisdom of 'breast is best' will depend on the mother's emotional attitudes about the baby, just as much as the biochemical content of the milk which mirrors each other. Bottle-fed babies are still, of course, able to experience the most positive attachments.

The emotional attitudes toward the child become evident through the relationship we hold toward ourselves as well as our ideas of mothering or fathering (familial, social, and cultural), which all have an impact on the type of relationship we develop with our children. [10] A critical aspect of the child-carer relationship is based on the quality of the nonverbal communication processes that occurs between children and adults. Even to entertain the idea that we would not be seen or felt to be all-important to the primary caregiver is very distressing for a child. Children need to bond and feel like they are important and wanted. Research that studies newborn direct skin-to-skin contact with its mother confirms that the child receives many positive physiological effects from direct touch alone, such as weight gain in preterm babies, and a rise in the baby's body temperature with improved oxygen levels in the blood. In line with the ideas presented earlier, the child's nervous system is organising itself to provide the best foundation for life; a feeling of safety that results in a trust of life, and the intuitive readiness necessary for solid and sustained growth that leads to an open, healthy, self-awareness.

Maternal Deprivation

Sometimes the child does not get what it needs from the mother. Childhood neglect and abandonment are related to interpersonal safety, anger, and emotional needs that underlie such feelings are said to precipitate dissociative episodes, self-destructive behaviour, and self-harm. Insecure attachments affect the child's development, leading to difficulties in learning and being able to form relationships later in life. What is referred to as the 'working model of the self'[11] (how we come to feel about ourselves as we grow) is at risk of being geared toward self-sabotage when the child is neglected and not given a secure and safe start to life. As expressed previously, even the perceived idea that we might not be all-important, or holding the feeling of not receiving the total attention of the primary caregiver, is distressing for a child. Statements such as, "I wish I had never had you," or "You don't know the trouble you cause me," will not just wound the child psychologically and emotionally, but also damage the child's physiological functions. A child who is told they are not wanted will assume deep insecurity issues because the hurtful words interact decisively with the physical counterparts of the body, resulting in a measurable difference in the way a child feels, thinks, and acts toward themselves and the world.

The child's wellbeing is threatened through maternal deprivation, as chronic violation of their bonding needs can potentially have an impact on life-long HPA regulation (stress), and thereby can impair important biological and psychological function.[12] "In the complex and dynamic ecological system in which the child develops, such a need can be realised (or violated) by the caretaker, and a child's access to resources and their combined capacities can avoid or prevent threats to wellbeing." Studies of Romanian children and infants living in state-operated residential institutions, otherwise termed orphanages, have provided a unique, yet tragic, insight into childhood deprivation, and are a telling display of what happens when a child is not regarded, and in effect, is dehumanised. The denial of nurturing caregiver–child relationships is said to be responsible for "delays in most major domains of development in institutionalized children." Not being connected to the mother is traumatic for the child but it is never too late to re-establish bonds. Studies show that feeding and stroking children who are experiencing maternal deprivation reverses stress levels. Even when these same stress levels do not improve with drugs that are specifically designed to reduce them.[13]

In the case of the Romanian children, they experienced custodial care in which their medical and nutritional needs were met, but their social and psychological needs were not. In fact, none of the child's obvious need for connection was met, and they were without any opportunity to develop caregiver–child relationships. The Romanian children were observed to have many developmental deficits based on the UN's general approach to needs and capacities of children and youth and the near universal acceptance of its principle. The children in Romania did not get social or psychological recognition, and the lack of touch, which affirms a child's realness and meets an internal plea such as, I am here and I need soothing, were all denied.

Stress and Trauma

Stress and trauma informed research are critical fields of research helping us to understand why children do what they do. Both stress and trauma are often unrecognised in the child; the effects, however, will present in a variety of ways over time. Stress hormones released in pregnancy in the case of chronic anxiety can also lead to prematurity, complications of birth, miscarriage, and stillbirth. Some researchers suggest that even though we know stress is an adaptive response and thus appropriate to a degree, it may also be the reason our children are so open to having so many issues at this point in history. "It is suggested that extra vigilance or anxiety, readily distracted attention, or a hyper-responsive HPA axis may have been adaptive in a stressful environment during evolution, but exists today at the cost of vulnerability to neurodevelopmental disorders. [14] The impacts of stress may not even be evident until there has been a significant space of time[15] between the original stress and the presenting problem, so it is often harder to see the link. Stress in the mother is connected with anxiety; ADHD and lower cognitive development in children, which are categorised as neurodevelopmental issues, largely associated with the brain functioning. The same prenatal stress responses noted above are associated with physical problems such as asthma. [16]

Many children experience trauma; however, the notion of what even constitutes trauma in a child is largely misunderstood. In traumatic known experiences, such as abandonment or violence, it is easier to see how these will cause an imbalance in the child's feelings and thoughts, and the subsequent and real threat of safety and security. And perhaps Sally's case allows us to see this most poignantly. Yet, the same physiological reaction to stress occurs in a child who is disregarded, avoided or treated ambivalently as a child who is physically harmed.[17] The same response also occurs even if the child has not experienced the trauma itself but is surrogating the energy for a parent or grandparent through the epigenetic transference of memory as we see in the research of epigenetics. The energetic build-up of emotions and sensations in the child's body from trauma is an entirely appropriate response, because it is a tension that has not been able to find release, and so becomes activated in the child's body and life. Often however, the source or the origin is not as evident as it is in Sally's case.

The abuses children experience in the form of rejection, belittling, deflating, and shaming can mark the beginning of a fragmentation of the unified state of being. In other words, the child becomes split in how it feels and what it thinks because the trauma (the traumatic event) involves the need for a child to protect itself from this attack to its security. Having to cope with such assaults produces feelings of alarm, which is best understood as the automatic stress mechanism and is connected to a very real survival process called the *fight or flight* response. Questions are in a way automatically and unconsciously asked as the child's body is deciding the most appropriate physiological response; "Do I stay and face the threat and fight, or do I flee and find a more secure place to be?" The child's body releases the most appropriate neurochemicals to act in the best way for its need for security and safety, which is, in essence, its survival.[18] The most appropriate response may be to bite or scream or run away. It is hard for a child to feel connected to their own body and the physical world when the security, trust, and boundaries are not there for them in a tangible way, particularly if these have been taken away or if they are unstable.

Behaviours in children that indicate trauma might be excessive rocking, scratching, or biting themselves or others, and these responses indicate that the child is trying to integrate their sensory environment or transition more fully into the world. When we view sensory processing disorders in children as a problem, we are forgetting that not only are children integrating their sensory information, they are also doing it for the adults in their lives as well as their ancestral lineage. These energies are often no longer visible and remain unseen and so we fail to account for them in our interpretations of the child's responses to life. Practically, we can see that sensory overload in children will lead to meltdowns and problems with daily tasks, and not just for the child, these occurrences also affect the adult's ability to cope. The lack of understanding of what is actually going on for the child means that often the child is still punished or treated as odd, and therefore does not get the support they need, or have the space for the emotional process needed. The sensory integration of the child, although largely established in early growth, can be supported in a variety of ways at each and every transition in their growth. There are tips at the end of this section that help with integration of the *Need to Be Safe and Secure.*

Anxiety

Anxiety in children has risen significantly in the last decade. The reason why a child becomes anxious and what the anxious child is responding to is an area of great interest. The idea of stress, trauma, and anxiety in childhood are all linked to the *Need to Be Safe and Secure.* One of the first people to consider anxiety in the child seriously from a therapeutic position was Sigmund Freud. His *Analysis of a Phobia of a Five-Year-Old Boy,* also referred to as the case history of Little Hans details a child's angst.[19] I examined this particular case in my honour thesis and this case was pivotal to Freud's ideas about anxiety. Of course, we have clearly moved on from the Freudian model, nevertheless Freud's thinking is still latent in many of the models we have to understand children, and also in how we understand our own childhoods. It is important then to visit Freud's thinking on anxiety for a moment. Freud actually had two theories of anxiety. In the first theory, he attributed anxiety to birth trauma, and in the second theory positioned anxiety as a signal. In the case of birth trauma, Freud said the original birth separation created an energetic store of motivation within the human being that is unconscious, and therefore was largely unknowable until it became manifest as a symptom. Both the instinct (feeling) and the symbolic interpretation of the instinct (thinking) from birth trauma was said to be the main influence on the development of the personality.[20] For Freud, development of personality was sexually motivated and occurred in a series of psychosexual stages that all derive from the original birth trauma. This staged theory has shaped psychoanalytic practice.

It was Freud's second theory of anxiety that came to light from his work with the child Hans. It is important to pay a visit to this case history, so we may obtain a deeper understanding of the child Hans' anxieties. Hans had a phobia of a horse, and Freud attributed the phobia of the horse to the child's transferred fear of Hans' own father. The idea is that the boy wants to get rid of the father to be the mother's 'special one' and this creates anxieties.[21] Children's behaviours and responses to life, for Freud, were seen through the model of the *Oedipal Complex*, which views, in short, that all boys have a fascination with the mother and want to get rid of the father. From the case notes itself, we know that Hans has a phobia of a horse and he had witnessed a horse fall down and this frightened him, which set in motion many questions about life and death for the child. Each time Hans feels scared or his many questions are not answered, his body responds by foot stamping, a funny feeling in his tummy, sore throat, and constipation.[22] Hans was worried the horse would bite him, and Freud said the horse was a symbolic representation of the boy's father.

Releasing the worldview of Freud for a moment (which has historically been difficult to do) we might be able to see that the phobia actually speaks for Hans; Hans, like all children who experience anxiety (or as Freud would have it, a phobia) is stuck in an automatic response and they do not know how to transition through the experience in a way that feels safe to them. Petrified by the trauma, a phobia (anxiety) develops; the child's energy gets stuck, either literally or symbolically, repeating the same cycle (a feeling of fear) every time they are confronted with the object of fear. The child's body continues to feel the physiological response to the fear without any way of understanding the purpose of it (thinking and interpretation). Of course, the case of Hans is very detailed, but in essence, we can say that the phobia keeps the child stuck in a cycle; the body responds by signalling danger every time, but without any satisfying interpretation. In my thesis on Hans, I concluded that the phobia marks a signal for both parent and child that the child is having trouble transitioning from where it is currently (feelings and thoughts) to where it has to go (action). The phobia offers relief from Han's over-censoring adults and their inability to assist the child. The phobia becomes Han's safe space and signals to the adults that the child cannot move forward without leaving a significant part of himself behind.

Looking to a common childhood issue or experience, Separation Anxiety we might say is not a problem at all, but rather a signal that the child needs help. Separation anxiety is a common response as we transition from one environment to another. As discussed earlier the environment of home and school can often have a different feel to children. If children are not yet ready to separate from their parent (mothers, generally) because they feel unsafe without them, they will be resistant to change. The child may feel that the new environment is not able to meet their needs in the same way they are met at home. There are many ways that separation anxiety will present in the child, from clinging to being rigid, having fears, exhibiting insecurity, and unstoppable crying. Separation anxiety is an opportunity to recognise the unmet need for safety and security in your child; it is not a problem to be fixed.

Freud's attribution of the child's fear of the father to the Oedipal complex was in effect limiting, not just for Hans but also for humanity. All children need a bigger story about themselves and their lives—one that makes sense; not a reductive one that placates the child, as children can feel patronising energy at a distance. Hans needed a different representation of why his fear was presenting compared to the one that he held prior to the phobia. A new story and a new model by which to interpret Hans' phobia is needed in order to release the holding pattern activated by unknown energy within the child. This need for a bigger story becomes more apparent when we are enlightened as to Han's cure later in the book. Many things can activate instinctual response systems of anxiety in children. Conditions of isolation for the child (separations) tend to activate and remain activated until the child is in close physical proximity with the parent (caregiver) or when the child feels safe. The security of this comfort soothes the body's response for some time, but it is necessary for the child to learn to do this for him/herself.

The body responses can be difficult for children to feel, because they seem to come from nowhere. The degree of intensity of the anxiety equals the degree of defense, what we see as the child's reaction. Hans too articulated the experience of the intensity of his body responses when he calls his foot stamping 'nonsense'. Helping children to understand that the unknown feelings (their nonsense) is communicating important information has many benefits. In part three, the relational approach *Being in the Question*; you see that children can be helped to know their own body's signals. Many children experience uncertainty in response to their feelings as they work out what is appropriate and what is not. They need help to do this in unfamiliar places, as it is often frightening and stressful for them. Children can instinctually view certain feelings as a problem to be avoided. Many times, I have heard an adult ask a child, "What is wrong with you?" whilst at the same time unaware of the signals the child is sending about their need for reassurance. All anxiety could be said to be both separation anxiety and signal anxiety and a failure to reconnect with the things that make one feel safe - the change one feels when feeling connected and unified switches to feeling separate. Every child could be viewed to be balancing between the idea - that at any time I could be disregarded or separated from my safety and security when all I wish to be is safe, loved, and cherished. Simultaneously, they also have to cope with a body that is physiologically responding to trauma. We can perhaps feel the importance of the need of a child who is proclaiming *soothe me*.

Freud actually went on to change his position on birth trauma, arguing later that he considered it fairly unremarkable in its effect on psychological life. This was because Freud always stopped short of believing that there was active mental life in the child, so he considered birth material from psychoanalysis to be fantasy rather than memory; a position held by the majority of psychotherapists to this day. The fact that we have for so long not really believed that the child has a complex inner life, one that is complete in body-mind-spirit, has been detrimental to our understanding of them. Thankfully, neuroscience and other scientific discoveries are confirming the child's psychological life as very active from the earliest of moments. All anxiety is a result of trauma—we just need to recognise the trauma. All separation from the feeling of being whole is very traumatic for any child.

Secure Transitions

A major transition and challenge to separation in early childhood is starting school. Successful transitioning into school in a social sense as well as intellectually is indicative of further progression of achievement. Aline-Wendy Dunlop and Hilary Fabian in *Outcomes of good practice in transition processes for children entering primary school* state that the extent to which a child feels successful in the initial transition to school, is likely to influence future experiences at school and other social transitions. Emotional support within families results in the majority of children having a positive transition from home to school. Some research, however, indicates that starting school might cause stressors, such as anxiety, that can affect some children's emotional wellbeing. This, in turn, can affect the child's long-term social adjustment, which translates to problematic future learning. [23] Sound transitions are noted to enhance emotional wellbeing (*Need to Feel*) and feelings of capability (*Need to Act*), which in turn will result in fewer difficulties in later schooling.

It might be helpful to question how your own early transitions from home to school were for you. This recollection might remind you of what a child could possibly be experiencing in this change. Situations of separation anxiety bring with them an opportunity for adults to *push* themselves to reconnect to their own unity that had been fragmented from their own childhood. We can begin by asking a question such as, "Am I truly looking forward to reconnecting with my child, or am I feeling overwhelmed and need a break?" If the latter is the energy under the outward reassurance that you give the child, then this is what the child will feel. The child will not feel the words of connection, but the underlying energy of disconnection and separation. This is confusing because the child is hearing one thing or being told one thing, but feeling another. One cannot hold the space and process feelings with a child if they are rushed to get to work or emotionally imbalanced due to another issue that is taking the focus away from the present moment needs of the child.

This transition can be navigated in a way that secures the child and even the most fragmented or disconnected child will be less stressed by any transition or feared separation when given comfort and reassurance. The child who feels that their caregiver has a genuine desire to be with them, (as they have already discussed a way to reunite with them), will have a smoother transition. This is generally the case when a special plan is put in place for how long the separation will be, as well as awareness about the assured reunion, which settles the child's stress response. The proactive management of such transitions by communicating the reuniting plan well before the drop off time, allows the child to enter the period of separation when it happens in an open, receptive way, rather than being closed, combative, or resistant when the event happens. This approach is counter to much of the advice given that suggests it's better to just leave the anxious child without saying goodbye, as they will settle in time. My professional and personal experience in such situations shows that the child becomes very good at hiding their disconnected feelings, which may not initially manifest as separation anxiety but will manifest in some other form at some other stage. There is much more detail on emotional processes in the next section, the *Need to Feel*.

Repeated separations of vital attachment ties in children are seen in extreme ways with foster children. Children in non-permanent foster care frequently suffer from developmental delays and severe behavioural problems, which then lead to recurrent movements between carers and, in turn, increase the risk for attachment disorders, which constitute severe trauma. The expression of trauma in foster children is evident in suppressed immune functioning and autoimmune disorders as an activated defence.[24] Like for Sally, this supports the idea that when feeling insecure in this way, the child's defence system has to be vigilant and protective at all times. These responses communicate security issues and children are often on high alert in these cases, and will most likely continue across childhood and into later adulthood. The continuity of care in the case of permanent foster care is said to enhance the children's feelings of safety compared to those not placed in permanent care. When children are placed with their 'forever family' highly activated defence systems actually go into arrest. The felt sense of security from the forever family supports the other dimensions of development that occur with a level of hope *(Need to Love)* and confidence *(Need to Act)*.

The consistency of presence of care during childhood will vary for all children, but at each point in development it is important the child reconcile the dilemma of trust versus mistrust, as Erik Erickson noted in his work. There is nothing like feeling like you belong, and finding your home of belonging. If this *Need for Safety and Security* is not met in the child there is an underlying tension, apprehension, and uncertainty in self, such as difficulty sleeping, impaired concentration, edginess, and irritability that can be carried through to all other growth phases if continually unmet. Consistency then in the approaches used with children also establishes a solid sense of safety and security in the child. The more consistent the adult is, the more secure the child feels. Routines in this sense are good for assisting the child's feeling of security, especially children who need reassurance that they are safe.

Physical Body Awareness

The more we allow children to tune into the wisdom of their bodies, the fewer imbalances they will experience. Body awareness and a reverence and respect for one's body by self and others has been correlated with a positive effect and satisfaction with life, as well as decreased negative effects.[25] Adults can support children to have healthy body associations and trust their own felt sense of knowing. Teaching children to respect their bodies and to listen to the messages of their bodies actually sets the foundations for a body dialogue to be as valid and reasonable to listen to as are any verbal or thought patterns. In fact, as you know by now, I believe that the child's body wisdom and body knowledge is the basis from which the child comes to *know thyself as* discussed in chapter three. Anything is interpreted (thought) after the initial perception (feeling) of the child's body ought to be from a model that supports the unity of the child's *soul push*.

Children will hide, hang on, cower, or run away if they feel their body risks being violated, and that they cannot stand up for themselves against a dominant adult. On the spectrum of mistreatment of the child's feelings of safety and security is the impact of sexual abuse, which leads to the widest range of imbalances within the child. Sexually abused children have more symptoms than non-abused children. Fears, post-traumatic stress disorder (PTSD), behavioural problems, sexualised behaviours, and poor self-esteem occur most frequently among a long list of symptoms noted, but no one symptom characterised a majority of sexually abused children.[26] The energy of such traumatic childhood sexual experiences left untreated create further imbalance. Adult symptoms of repressed sexual trauma range from physical complaints such as headaches, reproductive issues, sleep disturbances, sexual dysfunction, and distortions of body image seen in anorexia and self-mutilation. Adults who experienced sex abuse as children may not be able to make a clear judgment in regard to what is going on in the lives of their own children. Or they may have repressed such memories in order to cope. Amnesia in certain periods of childhood is common for many adults with a history of sexual abuse in childhood. Repressed memory is said to be an adaptive necessity so the trauma can be forgotten, and yet the body holds and stores it until it can be released in other ways.

Body movement therapies are allowing many adults to work through trauma from childhood, as the past seems to arise spontaneously given nurturing conditions. The *soul push* to unify is a powerful force. As mentioned in chapter four the energy of the biological body as found in Kundalini; In yoga studies, both men and women with more frequent yoga practise have been recognised as having increased body awareness and satisfaction. Yoga and other Chakra based modalities offer people a deep understanding of how energy gets stored in the physical body as illness. Researchers acknowledge that there are exciting policy implications of such research that point to the particular importance of teaching yoga in schools to increase children's body awareness and body satisfaction.[27] Meditation also has a wonderful way of connecting the child to their body and body wisdom. The positive outcomes for children learning more about their physiological responses and the functioning of their bodies are immeasurable. When children come to know that the symptoms they experience are connected and correlated to their emotions and/or body organs and how these are affecting the way they act, they can make sense of why they have acted in certain ways. With awareness adults too can come to see that any child who is exhibiting what we term disorganised, disordered, or problematic behaviours is simply responding as a result of the unmet *Need to Be Safe and Secure*.

Spending time in nature and play are both paramount for secure children, yet when deciding policy for children there seems to be a need to continually justify the importance of such natural aspects of children's lives to be considered. The point is that children need activities that help them to get to the central locus of their body. We can all benefit from taking a few deep breaths when we are overwhelmed, and such an exercise, practiced daily, actually calms both child and parent at the same time. (There is more detail on the importance of play and movement in the next part, the *Need to Feel*). Connecting to nature has demonstrable results to children's wellbeing and vitality. Spending time in nature (or just being in the back yard!) supports resilience to both physical and viral stressors, which translates to being less vulnerable to illness. Children exposed to images of nature (not actual nature) have also shown a measure of improved wellbeing. The idea that one's imagination elicits the same physiological response as really doing something is discussed in the *Need to See*. Vitality (physical and mental energy) is improved in children exposed to nature; being outdoors was associated with greater vitality, a relation that was mediated by the presence of natural elements. Research that asks for self-reports of vitality, has seen vitality felt in nature linked with specific brain activation and positive stress response mechanisms, as well as behavioural changes, better coping, and greater health and wellness.[28] Restricting children from having a relationship with the natural world restricts the child in these same ways. Regardless of the geographical location of where we reside, we can assist the child to connect with the earth by grounding, or earthing, as it has been termed, which can be achieved even in small ways, like digging with hands in a bucket of sand or planting seeds in egg cartons. Such activities, as Maria Montessori realised, reconnect the child and allows for the integration of vital energies. Children will always to a degree need reassurance and grounding to help them come back to a centre and balance when they are fragmented. Initially, however, the primary caregiver has to model this balance in order for the child to anchor it in. Assisting children to ground themselves and feel like they belong is paramount to their feelings of security.

Nourishment

Food and nourishment make one feel safe, and we can perhaps all identify with how a solid warm meal grounds and settles us. Alternatively, our children will feel deprived if there is no food available when their body is sending signals that they are hungry. Eating behaviours evolve during the first years of life; children learn what, when, and how much to eat through direct experiences with food and by observing the eating behaviours of others. Studies conducted on children's eating habits revealed that, children "ate more carrots when they believed that other children had eaten a lot of carrots, compared to all other conditions."[29] So if you want your children to develop healthy eating habits, you don't have to continue to feel irritated about the fact that they are not; just eat lots of carrots and make it fun, and they will do that too! Of course, we need a balance of nutrients, and the carrots analogy was only used to bring light to the idea again that if we wish to instill good eating habits in our children, we have to look to all the messages we as adults are sending to them about food. The food we eat has been said to be our medicine or conversely our poison. There is much concern about food choices in the developed world, concerns about how food choices have adverse effects on health[30] The importance of gut microbes on the child's mood and overall wellbeing is discussed more in the *Need to Act*.

Some of the messages our children receive about food, eating and nourishment, we might realise, belong to the past. The beliefs surrounding these are often carried from the past and appear in the child via epigenetic inheritance as discussed in chapter three. Overeating sends a symbolic signal that there may be a perceived shortage of food in the future and it is best to hoard the food rather than risk starvation. The energy of deprivation, lack, and famine can continue in the child's energy system. As a parent, when we cannot be bothered about mealtime, we send a clear (albeit silent) energetic message that nourishing our family is a chore. One of the most significant family rituals and potential for connecting is during meals. What messages about the importance of home, family, and connection are your children inheriting at breakfast, lunch, and dinner? Do you all eat separately, or is there a requirement for a shared experience, a welcomed ritual in which everyone has a special role and is valued for their contribution?

Summary

As a child grows in age, they do not stop requiring the *Need to Be Safe and Secure*; they just demand a different type of comfort and reassurance, just as we all do when facing an uncertain new environment. The ability to deal with change is a foundational requirement, not just in childhood, but also in life. Soothing your child even after they have learned to meet the need for themselves is also an important part of helping them to maintain balanced wellbeing throughout their growth. This kind of support is different from so-called smothering and perhaps it is most imperative in the teen years when the child still needs a level of comforting but might also reject it. Teenagers often face fear or uncertainty when they are called to explore new horizons. Being able to push their parental limits and still be safe and secure in the home is important in helping them to feel assured. Telling children, they will be grounded or restricted if they explore or push their boundaries overlooks this vital need. Yet many children's security is threatened by the words, not whilst you live under my roof. We all need to know what our own boundaries are, but if we are continually surveyed and restricted in our physical identities and in finding our own way forward, we will not feel secure in ourselves and instead will feel flighty and resistant. Or alternatively, we will simply leave home at the first opportunity we get to seek out our own sense of home. When we know that children need to push so they can learn how to establish what good boundaries are for them, we are better able to support the push. After all, it is the natural push of the soul to explore what might be the most solid ground for us, and our own way forward, rather than what someone else feels is secure for us.

Tips To Cultivate The Need To Be Safe And Secure

At any age, in any situation, you can encourage your child to feel safe and secure in the following ways:

- Be mindful of the energy that you hold when attending to your child's physical needs and nurturing them. This will change depending on the requirement and health of the child. Pay full attention to this task (be disconnected from social media whilst feeding or bathing the child, for example).

- Be present to your children and be mindful that you are not rushing them or shushing them. Directives like, "Hurry up!" or "Get a move on!" all make the child feel anxious and rushed. Allow for a schedule that considers them too.

- Consider ways that you can encourage a sense of belonging with the children. All children need to feel like they belong and that they are part of a family tribe, which is a special type of belonging. Perhaps you could consider giving each child a special role or a ritual at mealtime. Having specific rituals that you stick to and known boundaries help children thrive.

- Be open to helping your child explore different foods and different ways of preparing and eating that promotes a love of food as nourishment and fun.

- Allow your child the space to do what they need for themselves and make some space each day for non-structured activities. Let children know what it feels like to be bored. The value of children being able to process their experiences in their own time and having the space to do what feels best for them is immeasurable.

- Ensure that your actions toward your children are reassuring rather than rejecting. When your child is scared or uncertain about life or themselves you can assist them to understand their feelings by making the time to help them ground in nature or through simple breathing meditation.

- Find ways to encourage the connection your child has to the physical world as well as to their body. Bring the child to you physically and rock, hold, or soothe them so they learn to trust they are safe in life and secure in themselves.

- Let children go barefoot or carry a rock/stone in their pocket; it helps them connect to the earth's support.

- Breathing slowly connects the child to itself as well as to its environment and relaxes the child. Meditation and breathing prompts work wonders to soothe an unsettled child.

- Become more self-aware. When you begin to listen to the inner messages of your own body and what these messages may be telling you, you are able to support your children to do the same. Know when your body tells you it's aching or tired, in need of something, or getting sick.

- Offer to the child ways to voice their worries or concerns as part of a ritual in quieter times (not when you have to rush out the door). Writing the worries down helps release the energy in the child's body. You might put them in a worry jar or on a worry tree. Journaling the things the child is grateful for shifts the focus of energy.

- Don't push a child away and expect them to deal with their uncertainty or fears on their own. This leads to them feeling more insecure, which results in many other common childhood issues. Cuddles and hugs work wonders for confusion and fear.

- Nest—make your home a place of rest—a safe space. Reading stories that promote belonging, home, tribe, and different cultures are all wonderful supports for the child's feelings of safety and security.

- To promote secure sleeping use heavy bedding so the child feels the weight and protection.

Needs Table 1 – Safety and Security
Potential of need as the centre point of balance

Deficient	Balanced	Excess
Fearful	Safe	Bold/Unflinching
Lack of confidence	Secure	Over confident
Insecurity	Security	Taking risks
Doubtful	Trust	Gullible
Erratic	Grounded	Rigid
Pushing Limits	Routines	Obsessive
Open	Boundaries (physical)	Pushy
Over pleasing	Boundaries (enforced)	Disagreeable
Listless/fragile	Healthy	Acute/Forceful
Underactive	Physical Activity	Over active
Frozen	Movement	Flighty
Disregard	Physical Body	Over focused
Separation anxiety	Survival	Over protective
Lacking	Possessions	Coveting
Exposure/gamble	Protection	Defensive
Damaging	Preservation	Hoarding
Purge/Rations	Food	Binging/indulgent
Malnourished	Nourishment	Overweight
Fussy eaters	Eating	Mindless eating

2. Children Need To Feel: Free Me

"The best way out is always through"

~ Robert Frost [31]

Children need to feel the full spectrum of their human experience. The child's body-mind-spirit will more likely be aligned when their feelings are acknowledged as a guide. The child is, in essence, proclaiming *Free Me*.

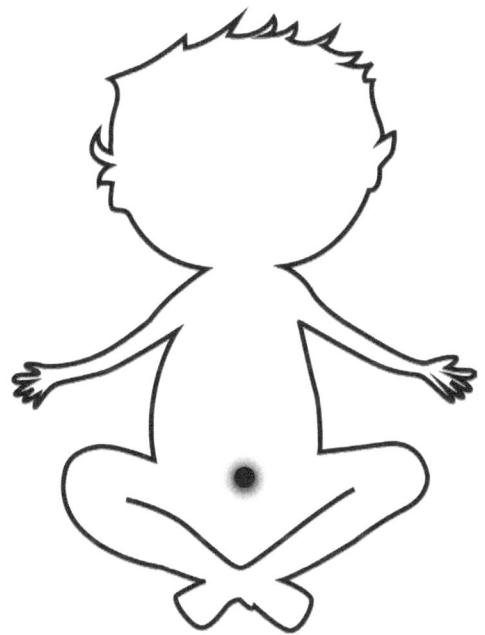

Figure 4: The Physical Body Location of the *Need to Feel*.

Case 2: Tommy

Tommy is 4; he is affectionate to his mother, and strokes her arm as she sits talking to me, he seems relaxed and open. His mother says he is not always like this. Sometimes, Tommy has extreme tantrums, which have over time become unbearable for his mother. She is often frightened to go out in public as she tries to avoid any possible triggers that may set Tommy off, as she calls it. Most children at some point will experience tantrums, and I discuss tantrums in more detail soon as they are one of the central themes of this *Need to Feel*. Tommy's tantrums see him kicking and screaming and always revolve around him wanting something or having to possess something. "If he wants something and if he can't have it, he goes off", his mother explains. For Tommy however, there is a much deeper message of healing in his tantrums beyond the projected battle of getting his own way.

Tommy who is playing with the toys in my office, looks up as his mother speaks about his behaviour and he stares at me with a curious, but kind of dissatisfied look - almost like a look of shock. Tommy's look indicates that he objects to his mother and I exploring his inner world without his consent. I immediately ask Tommy directly, "What happens for you Tommy when you feel that you really want something but cannot have it?. The reason I ask", I continue to tell him, "is, because your mum is trying to understand why you need to respond by kicking and screaming when you do not get what you want?" Tommy got up from the floor and went over to his mother; he grabbed her by the hand and started stroking her arm. Confronted perhaps with the realisation that he was required to talk about his feelings, Tommy sought reassurance from his mother. Tommy's mother pushed his affections away, not in a forceful way, but she did remove his hand and gave it back to him, so he wasn't touching her. Tommy then went back over to the toys he was playing with and almost immediately became fixated on wanting to take one toy that he was playing with home. "Can I have this?" He asked me. I looked to the mother rather than respond to Tommy straightaway. She looked uncomfortable but she did not say anything. I asked Tommy why he wanted to take the toy home with him. He said simply, "Because I want it." Tommy had raised his voice as he expressed this, and then he gave me the same stare that I had seen earlier.

So here we were, at the beautiful transitional moment, which is the axis of transformation. If I had denied the child the toy there would most likely have been a tantrum, yet without denying or negating the child's request. I was curious to find out more about his wanting. "What will you do with it if I give it to you?" I asked him in curious way. I was very eager to know why he felt the need to possess things. "I want it because I'll have it," he said declaratively. "How will that feel to have it?" I re-joined. "Good," he said, and almost without pausing to breath, he added, "let me have it or I'll scream." Tommy's behaviour appeared to seesaw between looking for the affections of his mother and demanding that he have something for himself - that he possesses something just for him. I asked the mother if she knew of any reasons why Tommy might be swinging from one end of the emotional spectrum to the other, in this almost dualistic way. This question to the mother was to give language to the polarity of behaviours I had witnessed in Tommy in the short time I had been with him. The mother then stared at me in almost the same way Tommy had earlier, before expressing that she felt exactly like that, especially since the loss of her unborn child 12 months prior.

There was a complication with Tommy's mother's second pregnancy that was undetected and the baby had died at 21-weeks. Whilst recounting the story, Tommy's mother started to cry and said, "It was the most horrible thing having to birth a baby, whilst knowing I would never get to keep it." Listening to the mother, I was acutely aware that I could not even begin to imagine the pain the mother must have felt, nor how hard it must have been for her to continue to find a way to carry on for Tommy. The severed bond with one's own baby is perhaps the most severe trauma a mother can experience and as mentioned in the last section in the *Need to be Safe and Secure,* postnatal depression is linked with traumatic birthing experiences for the mother, especially in the case of the loss of child.[32] Tommy's mother had not been able to have something that she wanted and the pain was so extreme it was difficult to feel. The *Need to Feel* in this situation could not be met for either the mother or the child because such painful feelings often require a numbing of sorts, as this is often necessary to temporarily begin to deal with the shock, loss, and grief. This numbing was occurring for both mother and child. Even though, it is much more obvious that the mother is grieving, Tommy had experienced a loss too. Tommy still needed his mother's affection, and, in a way, he wanted to be her possession. When he didn't get the affection, he needed from her due to what she was experiencing, he chose something to fill the gap. When Tommy did not get the thing, he wanted to feel safe; a tantrum resulted. The tantrums became his way of coping with overwhelming emotions that could not be processed. Both the transitional behaviour of the tantrums as well as the objects themselves, helped Tommy to cope with the loss of the bonds of affection that had left his relationship with his mother at the very same time that his little brother had died.

When Tommy and his mother were supported to see that their affection for each other had been damaged when the baby brother had died, it made sense to them. The trauma of this event had fragmented their connection to each other. They were both so sad at that time as they had both lost something that they really wanted and they could not integrate the feeling of wanting something and not getting it. Both mother and son were essentially proclaiming 'free me' from the feeling that I want something that I cannot have. The meaning was different for mother and child, but the feeling was the same. A sense of feeling connected to others through one's feelings and emotions is represented in the 2nd Chakra (*Swadhisthana*) the *Need to Feel*. The disconnection that Tommy experienced set his emotional life on a seesaw moving from one extreme to the other. Every person's emotional life can feel like this at times. Movement, confidence, celebration, spontaneity, pleasure, process, and emotional acceptance are all themes that are specific to the *Need to Feel*. The anatomical position of the 2nd Chakra is found in the reproductive glands of the gonads and ovaries and the body systems of the lower vertebrae, appendix, reproductive system, hip area, pelvis, urinary system, colon, large intestine, bladder, and endocrine system See the A-Z of common ailments associated to this 2nd Need in Appendix 1. Even though Tommy did not have any physical issue, we can see that this energy centre governs the reproductive system - and the mother's loss of the child and her subsequent emotional turmoil is tied to this energy centre.

Not every child will experience a challenge to its *Need to Feel* in the way Tommy did. The *Need to Feel* will have a different meaning for individuals, families, and cultures, and yet there are certain aspects of our *Need to Feel* that are considered shared. Pleasure as a theme for example, may be expressed in a child as jealousy toward others (deficient energy regarding pleasure), and in another child at the other end, self-indulgent behaviours in the child (excessive energy in regard to pleasure). A jealous child is communicating a *Need to Feel,* just as a self-indulgent child is also communicating a *Need to Feel*. It is the same original unmet need with a different presentation. The needs table at the end of this section shows a variety of excess and deficient responses in the child if the *Need to Feel,* is not met. Knowing that the unmet *Need to Feel* pleasure is at the origin of the child's behaviours (such as jealousy or self-indulgence) means that we can pay more attention to ways in which we might encourage affirmative thoughts and responses when a child expresses imbalance.

There is a degree to which everyone has difficulty interpreting and understanding the reasons they feel the way they do, no matter how emotionally aware we claim to be. As Tommy's mother shows us that sometimes even as adults it is difficult to be fully present to our children's emotional life, especially if we have a traumatic experience occurring for us. This too is just a natural part of adult growth as we transition to a new way of being after being fixed upon a certain outcome. Neither Tommy nor his mother had done anything wrong. It can be a real challenge to allow our feelings to be fully felt. If we as adults are not able to access the *Need to Feel* then we may not recognise children's behaviours that centre on this unmet need, simply because we have not known how to activate a strong energy in this aspect of our own lives. A sense of being able to feel the full emotional spectrum is important for children, as it allows them to process their experiences in an optimal way, and move through life with ease rather than feeling restricted. A large part of feeling at ease is developing acceptance of all of the feelings, thoughts, and emotions that arise without judging them as good or bad. Emotional acceptance brings ease, confidence, spontaneity, pleasure, and celebration into life.

Need to Feel - Common Themes

- *Feelings or Emotions*
- *Feelings as Inner Wisdom*
- *Talking about Feelings*
- *Emotions*
- *Emotional Control and Self-Regulation*
- *Tantrums*
- *Pleasure and Pain*
- *Play*
- *Sexuality*

Feelings or Emotions

One's feelings are defined in this book as the things we perceive in our environment that come firstly through the sensory body. Because there is much debate about the difference between feelings and emotions in approaches to children, this section discusses both feelings and emotions. Although feelings and emotions are words that are used interchangeably, there is a distinct difference between them. My distinct definition of feelings is that they are our perceptions and the felt energies that we sense before we make an interpretation about those same feelings. Emotions are an unconscious instinctual response to ones sensory experience. The emotional response is unconscious because it has been carried over from the collective past; such immediate responses have allowed us to react quickly to threats and rewards. Children have been understood as either reacting to a painful type of threat through fight and flight, or they are seeking a reward -- a pleasurable something they want. This is the very idea behind behaviour modification strategies, which state that the child's emotions can be trained away. There is no space in these approaches for observing what the feeling of the child is indicating about what they need when they act out. Emotional reactions are implicit in our genes and as epigenetics and morphic resonance validates are encoded into one's life. Supporting the cultivation of the energies of the *Need to Feel* in children means that we are supporting them to move through their feelings in a way that allows them to be as free flowing as possible.

Emotions vary individually and according to one's circumstances as well as ones past generations' responses to life. Emotions are also universally similar across all humans and even other species. Emotions, at a biological level, are the receptors, protein, and peptides, the tiny components of our body and mind. Pert tells us that the chemistry associated with our emotions are the neuropeptides which are transmitted through the nervous system and as such are found in every part of the body. Recall Pert says if you are experiencing pleasure, for example, neuropeptides will be found in your body, and alternatively, if you are sad, you will find sad neuropeptides or chemicals in your body.[33] It is by changing the thought patterns that permits conscious and calm access to our bodymind, which changes the emotional response in the child rather than them having to spend time and energy on subconsciously focusing on irrelevant frantic survival patterns which they no longer need.

The emotions indicate a false interpretation, which has already been transmitted energetically to the child based upon how things have been interpreted in the past. Emotions are automatic as such and often not the most accurate interpretation of what is occurring now. *Being in the Question* and making a space to be in the present moment with children allows us to explore what the meaning of a feeling actually is, rather than continue to react to the child based upon the past. To better understand this concept, I return to the idea of what feelings are. Consider for a moment most people have a degree of physical sensitivities to certain environments, people, and things, and these feelings come firstly through our bodies. The sensory pathways are the primary mode of experience, and knowing more about the subtle energies in and around us is vital for our own self-development as realised beings. Yet this mode of innate perceiving has largely been reduced to secondary, childish, or naïve in comparison to the thinking, rational mode of being. Children learn early what is not appropriate. Being a good child often means we have to go against what we feel because of the dominant culture of adult expectations since Aristotle. For a long time, it has been considered that the child ought to be conditioned away from its feelings, which have mostly been attributed to instincts. Like the tantrums of Tommy, one's feelings if misunderstood or unaddressed will transform into some other imbalance in life. These inhibitions and unprocessed feelings from childhood will keep recirculating if we do not move through them fully felt. They will not go anywhere until they are realised for the message they contain. (So by allowing all of the child's feelings to surface, and by having a deeper understanding of the message of the feeling, we are closer to supporting them as a whole.)

If you can recall for a moment, you may have had feelings as a child that were confusing, complicated, unclear, and difficult to express to someone else. Or perhaps you were a child who just wanted to have everything. You know that feeling when you feel like you want more of the good stuff, and ask, expecting to get it? This is often a joyful and pleasurable energy of not holding back on desiring anything or considering expressing what you really feel; the type of energy that arises easily and spontaneously. When a child asks for what they want or desire they are not spoilt; the ways we respond to the child can be a projection about how we may have been responded to as a child when we may have asked for something we really desired. We may have been made to feel embarrassed by our desires. Quite often children's feelings are reduced to the type of temperament the child has, and are duly dismissed or trained away. I have heard many parents say, "Oh, that is just the way they are," when the child is expressing an important unmet need. If Tommy and his mother did not realise the unmet need beneath his tantrums, it could have set up long standing imbalance, which would have been assigned or justified as just the way he is.

All children are sensitive and some have their sensitivities recognised and supported and some do not. If you know a child who sniffs the cup before he drinks out of it, or smells her clothes before she gets dressed, these children are not odd; they are just sensitive souls who are utilising all of their sensory capacities to move through life with as much ease as possible. Every child perceives their environment in a unique way that is necessary for both the child's individual growth, as well as for the survival of the species. This is not a survival of the fittest mentality, but rather an evolution of consciousness, which as discussed earlier will result in human beings actualising their full potentials as divine vessels. Tommy's behaviour was directly linked to his mother's unhealed past, and shows the degree to which supporting the child in an enhanced way also supports the mother and the evolution of all involved in this experience. Children's feelings ought to be explored beyond the temperament of the child, because they are a guide; the child's *soul push* that comes firstly as a body-based knowing, one that is usually referred to as intuition or instinct.

Feelings - Inner Wisdom

The word intuition is defined as the ability to acquire knowledge without inference or the use of reason. The word comes from the Latin word *intueri*. Sri Aurobindo in *The Synthesis of Yoga* translated this to mean to look inside or to contemplate, and describes intuition as knowledge and awareness of our existence that transcends individuals and extends out to the broader fields of consciousness. [34] Some people refer to intuition as an inner knowing or an inner wisdom and I have even heard it referred to as innertuition. We can get a feeling of what intuition is like for ourselves if we are asked the following questions: "Have you ever felt something that you cannot know with certainty, or thought something was going to be said before someone uttered the words? Have you ever felt a strange feeling in the company of others that you don't usually feel when you are on your own? Can the smallest thing in your physical environment cause discomfort or challenges your equilibrium?" If so, these are an inner knowing that indicates that there is something important for you to pay attention to. This knowing is present for us all, from our beginnings. You may remember or you may have forgotten, but this is what it feels like to be a child.

Because our intuitive function provides us with perceptions that we cannot always justify or interpret just yet, we often deny these feelings. It is difficult to relate with others when something cannot be justified or if a person demands justification. It is hard to bring attention to the smallest of details about something that is making you uncomfortable when someone is in denial about their own emotional life. When someone does not want to open emotionally, it may be because they may have had to close down to what they really felt, because it had been necessary in order to survive as we saw with Tommy's mother. Often, as we all know to a degree, those things that are too hard to justify or that are not acknowledged as important by others because of their own trauma get judged as wrong or at least are seen as problematic. Trusting that all of the feelings we have are purposeful, even if a meaning of the purpose cannot be known just yet, is one most important thing we can encourage our children to appreciate. We can affirm with a statement such as, "You should never have to apologise or feel bad about what you feel." But so many children do, and so many adults continue to live out emotions such as shame and unworthiness based on these childhood patterns of feeling bad about their important feelings.

Human sensitivities cannot really be understood if we don't know more about our own feelings and use these to help us to interpret why children do what they do. The idea that traits and behaviour of children happen in isolation of the environment they inhabit, which includes the environment of the past, ought to change. Children feel deeply about the world and themselves; they worry about many things from the state of the environment, animals, and plants to other human beings. Children are highly sensitive and highly sensitive people, (HSP)[35] is a term attributed to people who process sensory data deeply and thoroughly due to a biological difference in their nervous system.

Talking about Feelings

Leo Tolstoy poses the question in the book, *Anna Karenina*, "Is it really possible to tell someone else what one feels?" If we grew up in families that avoided talking about or sharing feelings because they did not know how, or to do so led to more grief and pain, then we might agree it can be difficult to tell someone else what we feel. The funny thing about feelings is that sometimes we are not even aware of why we feel what we do. Therefore, we can often hide our feelings to protect ourselves from being judged. The flow of energy in the body, however, is restricted if there is no awareness of the underlying feelings. In such cases, the lack of awareness keeps trauma circulating, as seen in the section *Need to Be Safe and Secure*. In my experience of working with families, I see that no family consciously wants to create destruction. But if we are not aware of a destructive pattern of relating and cannot begin to find a way to express our feelings in conscious ways, then we cannot see it and thus it will play out almost beyond our control. These emotional patterns are the result of denial, avoidance or projection and become embedded and we do not even realise they exist.

Consider for example if a child has a question about something such as, "Why does my mum sleep all day?" or "Why does dad throw things at mum when he drinks?" they often have to come to a conclusion for themselves, because to ask about such things can be dangerous. A child who wants to know answers to questions about the things that they feel, therefore, are often not able to get an answer that resonates or gives them meaning. The conclusions that are drawn by the child as to why these things happen or why they keep occurring often have a path back to themselves; that is, children often feel that perhaps the reason for someone else's imbalance has something to do with them. In order to transition through such difficulties requires that we need to acknowledge, talk about, or even seek help for the limiting patterns of relating in families; otherwise, any natural movement that a child wants to make within such situations may become further impaired. And yet, as you can see, it is hard for a child to do this without help.

Children never encouraged to have a positive regard for themselves, may be assaulted further by being blamed for the family dysfunction. It seems a terrible load to place on a child, but sometimes we do not know better. Additionally, many children actually take it upon themselves to try to understand or fix family dysfunction. Children cannot break the cycle; try as they might, because they are dependent on the family for so many things. Perhaps also because of this, children will not confide in anyone, less they risk getting their family in trouble. It is natural, then, that children internalise the blame and take responsibility for the reason things are not harmonious and happy. Because of the pain associated with relating in families like this, any genuine connection is sacrificed at the expense of hiding the truth (albeit mostly unrecognised, as it is unconscious) of the unhealthy patterns that are circulating in the family. When this happens, we tend to consider the feeling as wrong, rather than trying to understand the meaning of the feeling first.

When we can objectively know more about emotions, their role, and the degree to which they become stuck in the child's energy and life, we become acutely aware of how the link between the emotions and feelings needs to be included and incorporated in childhood approaches. The pain children feel does not go away, and somehow, somewhere, it will always surface. Underlying, unresolved emotional tension leads to many symptoms in a child, such as persistent bedwetting. The needs tables at the end of each section support the awareness that when a child's needs are not met there will be a response that is either excessive or deficient. A child, who persistently wets the bed for example, may not be able to emotionally express and often holds feelings that they are not good enough regardless of their achievements or behaviours. Even the bedwetting itself can keep this negative feeling circulating and often children are hard on themselves because it keeps happening. [36] The energy block that has been established due to the child's lack of emotional expression thus creates a physical symptom in the bladder, which indicates the child is not able to hold on any longer without some form of expression. The bedwetting, then, becomes the language, which communicates that the child needs help with this unmet *Need to Feel*. This plea for help can go unheard because of the tension it can create in the house. Unfortunately, there is a further requirement for the child to hold onto emotions, only to find that the unconscious need to release occurs each evening and the emotional patterning is caught in a loop.

Emotions

I define emotion as an instinctual response, a habitual reaction to a feeling. Emotions can restrict the flow and movement in our bodies and lives, and when things are hard to feel we can get stuck. So, we can see as children push to grow, and when they are moving from one experience to another or one environment to another, they can get trapped and caught in the emotion of it all. The advantages of understanding our emotional life are immeasurable, and yet teaching about the emotions is not actually as helpful as demonstrating them. When we can understand that children's emotional life is not dependent on what we say or do, but is transmitted unconsciously to them. We need to be aware that emotions only get us stuck when one's feelings and thoughts are conflicted. This is a process that happens so quickly, it is no wonder we become so confused. A caregiver's emotional stability or lack of will be reflected in a child. Many caregivers, who seek to understand and transform their own emotions, as well as support children to do the same, have trouble doing so because of the pervasive misunderstanding and misappropriation of emotions generally, especially in regard to children.

Emotions are signals that there is an imbalance in the system as a whole (body-mind-spirit) and also speak more directly to that imbalance. It is the feeling and thinking struggle, the struggle I have spoken to throughout the book, the same struggle that Plato recognised in the chariot soul; that of keeping the opposing horses running in the same direction. Emotions, like the many symptoms of the child are alerting the need to try and right the imbalance, like we see in the phobia of Hans, or in a child's transitional object. The emotions serve as a way of feeling whole temporarily until we can be whole in actuality. Perhaps this makes it easier to see how some people become addicted to unhealthy emotional patterns, as it actually makes them feel together or connected, albeit unhealthily; that is, in a way, falsely connected.

We embody all our experiences, and the emotions indicate a response to how we are feeling about these experiences. Research at the HeartMath Institute found that intuitive information (feeling) is received before the brain makes sense of it (thinking). The feeling nature is our first order of being, and when we deny this we run into all manner of issues. Additionally, the research at HeartMath highlights that the heart sends more information to the brain than the brain sends to the heart.[37] The sensitivities the child feels in their body are linked to a subtle energetic field that contains information about objects and events in space and time. The child's thoughts are formed and shaped dependent upon their experiences and memories of these past experiences, also called conditioning, training, education, programming, or beliefs. The emotions, in turn, form and shape thoughts too. The feelings, however, are felt first, and in the present moment. Then, based upon the interpretations (thoughts) of those feelings, they get a story attached to them (emotion).

Emotional Control – Self-Regulation

The reason for the focus on feelings and emotions in detail here is to allow you to begin to support a strong *Need to Feel* in the life of your child, and to understand that your own emotional responses are a simple, but often problematic, disparity between your feelings and your thoughts. If our children's feelings are met with neglect, denial, or indifference children will not learn to honor their feelings as a valid guide in their lives. When we try and control our feelings, or have our feelings controlled, we have an emotional resistance built within us. The frustration a small child feels at not being understood, or the anger a child displays at being told to change the way they are feeling (to be more compliant), is the beginning of a disparity between what is actually felt and what is allowed to be felt. Consider for a moment that children seem particularly perceptive to the colours, sounds, and many other sensory experiences that adults may have neglected over time. Imagine, too, that an overstimulation of such sensate experiences, such as a noisy shopping centre or classroom or a busy road, can be overwhelming for the child to integrate. In order for children to become emotionally literate, it is very important that adults mirror the child's feelings back to them, as this helps them to situate their feelings.

An affirming responsive approach to a child's cries and expressions of rage, fear, or confusion is one that does not judge the child for the resulting emotion, nor negates them, but reflects or mirrors them back. For instance, when observing the child's anger, an adult can express and mirror back, "Are you feeling angry? What do you need?" When children have the space to express what they are feeling, even without verbal language, it is possible for them to communicate what they need or want. As adults, we have to become more attuned to the reactions we have, and the parts of our own bodies that tense and respond to stress and to things that do not feel good. Sometimes experiencing an emotion (such as sadness) is unavoidable and yet it is also very natural (especially as a part of processing pain, either in the moment or in response to a past pain, or both) can be uncomfortable and make children, and even adults, feel like they are losing control.

Working with emotions can be confusing, too, because when we begin looking for the source of the emotion, the disparity between how we feel and what we think can seem destabilising at first, and it appears instinctively best to avoid such an inquiry. However, the avoidance of getting to the origin of the imbalance means we will remain disconnected. This is why in so many cases we can see that there can be a resistance to getting to the actual *cause* of the pain, because of the subsequent emotions, which are so hard for many people to deal with.

As mentioned earlier, as adults when we can begin to become aware that there is a completely different energy evoked when we sit on a mat listening to stories, as opposed to sitting in a chair at a desk being instructed to write a story about the same experience. The energetic field of all the situations children find themselves in has subtle variance in those unseen thoughts, emotions, and belief systems in different environments. The degree of emotional stability in an environment has a direct impact on the emotional stability in the child. Research has shown that positive emotions and interventions can bolster health, achievement, and resilience and can buffer against depression and anxiety. Positive psychology, and its offshoot, positive education, headed by Martin Seligman, articulates that having positive approaches, as well as cultivating certain character strengths, results in the wellbeing of children. Seligman suggests that cultivating character strengths, which resonate with Aristotle's virtues, will lead to wellbeing. These character strengths can then be used by the individual in his or her relationships at schools, in their hobbies, and with friends and family. Results from empirical studies suggest that whole schools can be imbibed with a positive approach in which wellbeing is the result for all staff and students.[38]

The virtues and character strength approach to wellbeing, however, still looks to putting virtues *into* a child versus bringing forth their inherent capacities. My contention is that fixing children by putting information into them, does not allow a child to evolve according to their own pattern of unfolding, which sometimes, in all honesty, does not feel very positive at all. Martin Seligman contends that while considerable research in neuroscience has focused on disease, dysfunction, and the harmful effects of stress and trauma, little is known about the neural mechanisms of human flourishing.[39] The aim of cultivating energy in the body according to eastern yogic practices and Chakra theory seems to fill this gap. Research into emotions is beginning to look to the neurobiological correlates, as well as the psychotherapeutic impact of emotions. Scientists have identified the location of biological correlations or neurobiological pathways of pleasure and other emotional pathways that may be informed by a deeper understanding of the child's needs, and the location of these in the physical body. Having access to the locations of the complex interplay of the body-mind-spirit, and how these impact and support the whole self, means we are now ready to apply this to the life of the child. The brain-behaviour relationships, neuronal circuitry, and functional neuroanatomical, as well as biochemical factors, can all be considered from the FNM.

Tantrums

As difficult as it is sometimes to experience, the full spectrum of the human emotional range is very purposeful, as it allows us to come to know contrast. Some say we could not know joy without its contrast of sadness. As true as this might be, there is still resistance to feeling the negative emotions, preferring only the most positive ones. We cannot disregard or gloss over negative emotions either, because emotional patterns of unexpressed feelings do affect the child's life, and present as symptoms in both the child and the adult as we noted with Tommy and his mother. Anyone that has seen a toddler have a tantrum, at first glance may see what appears to be an irrational self-assertion; the child definitely wants to assert itself, and we might say this is an evident control issue (*Need to Act*). My contention, however, is that the child who loses all control when they are denied what they want, has an unmet *Need to Act* in accord with their own direction and that an unresolved emotional issue is driving the behaviour. Frustration then results in the child, and, as expressed in the last section this is when the stress and trauma responses get activated. The activation of the biological responses then blocks anything else getting through to the child. To reconnect with the child who is distressed, it is important to know that a tantrum is not a conclusion of a future uncontrollable child. It is present moment awareness that the child needs reconnection. The child is actually proclaiming *Free Me* from the conflicting and overwhelming disparity between what I feel and what I am being restricted from feeling. In order to support the child in that moment, it may require leaving the shopping trolley in the aisle at the supermarket and finding a safe space to regroup (both the child with itself and the child with the adult) as a unified force. Tantrums as we saw in the case of Tommy are the result of a child's big, overwhelming feelings and emotions that they have no words for. We can see, then, that the child is simply proclaiming *Free Me*. If we as caregivers feel judged by others for our children's responses, we will be more occupied with that, and therefore we cannot give attention to the child to support them to process their feelings in the way they need.

We have all perhaps heard the interpretation that tantrums are just an act on behalf of the child to get what they want, and this may be true, but it is often never what we think it is. Unless we can truly connect with the child and meet them the way they need us to, we will not truly know what they need. The child learns early on how to navigate the parent's emotional landscape. Conflict-ridden and aggressive relationships that are cold, unsupportive, and neglectful create vulnerabilities and/or interact with genetically based vulnerabilities in offspring that produce disruptions in psychosocial functioning (specifically emotion processing and social competence), disruptions in stress-responsive biological regulatory systems, and poor health behaviours, especially substance abuse. [40] Parents who are in greater emotional and somatic distress often have a lower threshold for children's misbehaviour and may react more punitively to it. [41] The need for expression of feelings in an open, supportive, and warm environment is vital for children.

Often, too, there is a disagreement between the child's views and the parent's views. Children thus need to navigate a dual reality, both the adult's emotional state and their own. There is often dispute as to the degree of the emotional damage that is felt within the family environment; both child and adult often feeling wounded. Research supports the notion that parents have a tendency to disregard the child's emotions, and sometimes even the child's physical pain. Perhaps this is because they fail to understand what is occurring for the child, or more importantly, perhaps it is because they have never been offered a space in their environments to feel their own pain. In one study on children's physical pain, it was demonstrated that parents tended to underestimate the level of their children's pain. The study states, "Parents are often the primary source of information regarding their children's pain in both research and clinical practice." [42] Yet, this study found that the parents demonstrated "low levels of sensitivity in identifying when their children were experiencing clinically significant pain." The authors concluded that this underestimation might have been due to inadequate pain control of the child, rather than purely due to parental insensitivity. But even this conclusion demonstrates the adult tendency to take the adult's perspective over the child's, and not to see the child's experiences as real, reducing it in an obvious way by projecting the child's inadequacies. The child's experiences as well as the covert power relation between child and adult often still discount the child's information about their state of emotions, health, and general wellbeing. There is more detail about the power dynamic between adult and child in the next part, the *Need to Act*.

Pleasure and Pain

The significance of having a deeper understanding of what is actually going on for our children means we have to look to cultivating our own self-understanding. The pain of life can often be hard to deal with, and as a natural response we can deny, mask, or deflect our inner emotional life. It is important to work through this pain in ourselves so as to support our children when they, too, may respond by denying, masking, or deflecting their emotions. Many adults are not able to take responsibility for their unhealed and destructive patterning. The importance of stopping the cycle means that at some point we have to face the situations in our own lives that may have caused pain, so our children will not have to carry it further. Children who grow up in families that have relationship and intimacy issues are more likely to develop an addiction. Substance abuse disorders, as well as sexual addictions, are seen to come from a family environment in which family members are detached, uninvolved, or emotionally absent.[43] A lack of ability to deal with feelings and emotions leads to compulsive and addictive behaviours.

Such behaviours have been researched from Family Systems Theory and Attachment Theory models that provide a framework for understanding how the family relationships and family relational processes impact addiction. Studies also show that experiences of emotional abuse from parents and verbal victimisation from peers contribute to negative changes in children's inferential styles, as well as increases in their depressive symptoms.[44] If a child grows up in a family that cannot manage distressing emotions, and in fact in many cases doesn't realise the extent to which they are perpetuating distress, the child can look to the addiction as a means of escaping the pain that is felt from the family dynamics. Of course, the child would not seek addiction in this way with a strengthened energy centre that allowed for feeling all of their emotions (if their *Need to Feel* was met). If this need is cultivated and activated, one will not need to look outside themselves for pleasure and release from pain in the form of addiction.

Obsessive Compulsive Disorder (OCD) is the acting out of a symbolic feeling of having to compulsively repeat behaviours in order to find relief. The thoughts about the feelings get stuck in a type of loop; as Robert Frost recommends in the quote that introduced this section, "The best way out is always through." This is, however, sometimes a challenge, as it is difficult to see outside of our own conditioning. Long-term behavioural therapies can also cause more inhibition than they release in many situations. Such approaches just stop certain behaviours because children get better at hiding them; they will, however, pop up as another symptom, highlighting the idea that if the source of the unmet need is not met, it will continue to manifest within the child and the child's life in some way, shape, or form.[45] Viewing one's life responses in light of trauma-informed research gives a much bigger picture as to why children may do what they do, and in fact, why any of us are motivated to do what we do.

Play

Play is an important part of the child's life, but it may be lacking from the adult's life, hence the reason for the absence of fun or happiness. Through play, children develop and demonstrate improved communication and verbal skills, high levels of social and interaction skills, intimacy and friendship bonds where they are establishing a sense of give and take and patience and perseverance. Play allows for the full spectrum of emotions to be experienced. Play can provide the need to feel pleasure and joy; it can also engage a child to feel hurt, upset, or discouraged. According to Lev Vygotsky, sociodramatic play in early childhood contributes to the child's ability to self-regulate. Research in this field has demonstrated that impulsive children (with no specific label of disorder) benefit from sociodramatic play. The findings are consistent with Vygotsky's theory and suggest that sociodramatic experiences may be especially advantageous for impulsive children, who are behind their peers in self-regulatory development. [46] Imagining, dramatizing, and creating play-based activities when we are experiencing distress is an amazing relief, and actually transforms the energy in the child's body.

The sensory integration activities recommended for children with sensory processing disorder actually look much like what we would have called play twenty or thirty years ago. These sensory integration activities are said to improve daily functioning, intellectual, social, and emotional development, the development of a positive self-esteem, a mind and body which is ready for learning, and positive interactions in the world.[47] This raises the question, Are our children experiencing sensory integration issues that affect the full range of their capabilities over their complex whole system (body-mind-spirit), simply because we have pushed them too early to integrate set learning that has taken them away from being children? The need to integrate the sensory world cannot be forced; it is an organic process that evolves according to each child's nervous system, which knows when it is ready, itself.

Research on brain development shows that the physical movement that is necessary for an adaptive way of being in the world is strengthened by play. Play, with its active exploration and open-ended possibilities, is noted to strengthen brain pathways. Play creates a brain that has increased flexibility and improved potential for learning later in life.[48] Techniques used in Gestalt play and play therapies such as drawing, imagery, music, movement, fantasy, storytelling, the sand tray, photography, the use of metaphors, and games are all recognised as having a healing effect on children, as they release emotional blocks. Techniques have been used throughout history and across cultures to move energy and immobilise latent potentials.

> *"Play in all its rich variety is one of the highest achievements of the human species, alongside language, culture, and technology. Indeed, without play, none of these other achievements would be possible. The value of play is increasingly recognised, by researchers and within the policy arena, for adults as well as children, as the evidence mounts of its relationship with intellectual achievement and emotional well-being."*[49]

Yet, there is still a continual effort required to justify the importance of play in children's life and learning. The inclusion of play within policy for children is now becoming an important main focus for educators. A report on the value of children's play in a series of policy recommendations conducted by University of Cambridge found that even the type of place we grow up in (urban environments) affect the playfulness of children. A comparative study looked at the play and attitudes toward safety while playing outdoors between children living in Nicaragua and the UK. While the children in Nicaragua enjoyed a high level of independent mobility, and developed self-reliant attitudes towards safety while swimming in lakes, climbing trees, etc., the children in the UK were much more closely supervised and did not generally experience these opportunities.[50] Parental over-supervision and over-scheduling of children were marked as an important issue in this regard as they halted important processes in the child's body and life. The value of free-range parenting has been noted as offering the space for independent exploration in this regard.

When children partake in unstructured play, they are making sense of their world in a way that feels right to them. The degree to which any child can follow his or her own rhythm is often restricted as soon as the child is required to follow a familial rhythm, a school rhythm, or a cultural rhythm. The freedoms of children to follow their own rhythms either individually, in groups, families, and communities, are not as readily available as they should be in order for children to develop a sense of self which sees them resilient to the many emotional challenges of life. The next section speaks to dynamics of control and surveillance of children when I address the child's important *Need to Act*. Many of the pleasurable experiences of childhood and what we might call a happy child is tied to being a creative being, imagining a world beneath a blanket or looking for treasures in a pile of dirt. Such free-flowing, simple activities become somewhat prohibited as we grow.

When Freud was developing an understanding of children, he proclaimed that the child's inner life is different to the adult psychic reality. Freud's material reality (matter, body) and psychical reality (intellect, mind) are both active for the child, and as the child grows and becomes an adult there is a tendency to operate primarily from the latter reality. The child is able to switch more easily between material reality and psychical reality, and as Freud recognised, this is due to different functions operating in the child's mind as opposed to the developed adult mind.[51] The movement between these two states is found within Freud's idea of play, fantasy, dreams, and "The Uncanny". We are, in effect, always moving between these two aspects of self, and thus we need some transitional holding space whilst we integrate. This movement between the body and mind, the feelings and thoughts has been deemed to be a problem—and as we see in the emotional responses that result—are very inhibiting.

Children traversing the worlds in play is symbolic and literally a microcosm of the macrocosmic family, social, and cultural worlds. Many play therapies are created for this reason; to enable us to reconnect to a fluid transition that allows us to rewrite the past imbalances with more awareness. Violet Oaklander said that in the process of growth the child faces many difficulties, and through the use of sand play, the child's fragmentations become apparent in the stories they tell and the words they use to describe their play. There is more discussion on language and the role it plays, in both fragmenting and reuniting aspects of the self through speech, in the section, the *Need to Speak*. The fluid movement between different aspects of the self offers our imagination an opportunity to rework existing mental structures. This is why we see so many adults welcome childish but nourishing activities as their children are growing, and building cities out of boxes, or making mud pies in preparation for the tea party. Adults who do not otherwise activate their creative aspects or feel connected are offered another opportunity to reconnect to the aspects of their childhood that brought a sense of joy. And as we regress as the parent and teacher of children with each of the child's experiences, we are offered an opportunity to rewrite our perspective and rework the existing mental structures, so that we may become whole again.

Sexuality

Children's freedom of movement between feelings and thoughts often gets stuck when they begin pondering certain topics such as sex. When is the best time to talk to children about sex? As with most matters in life, children will begin asking questions about sex when they are ready. Parents and teachers have worried that they have to try to discern when it is appropriate to introduce information about sexuality and reproduction, as well as gender issues to children. This is often attempted without any true recognition that the child has already absorbed all of the family, social, and cultural beliefs about sexuality and gender.

A parent's sexual life, repressed or even overt, has an effect on the child. The ways adults project and even play out destructive sexualised patterns with children has been seen evident historically in the sexual abuse within families and other institutions in charge of children. Children have been maltreated in so many ways because of their vulnerability and many adults have a tendency to hijack the child's life and attempt to occupy the child's inner world in many ways as well in regard to how the child comes to understand itself and its sexuality. Children are often seen to be objects of adult pleasure, which means that many children become overtly sexualised. The sexualisation of children is said to be the result of the earlier loss of childhood or growing up too quickly. But many adults treat children like objects, which leads to harmful self-constructs including body surveillance, body shame, self-sexualising behaviours, and appearance-contingent self-esteem.[52] Media and advertising is often targeted as the site for change in these attitudes, and yet perpetuate the same, especially social media. Families also often encourage the sexualisation of children, and often before the child is emotionally and physically ready.

Adult models of sexuality are readily applied to the life of the child and have been for decades, which can be directly traced back to Freud. In *Three Essays on Sexuality*, Freud espoused the notion that children have a staged sexual development. Depending upon the child's sexual desire either being recognised and gratified or repressed and denied at each stage, it will play a role in adult personality because these functions form a symbolic meaning for the child. This meaning holds a certain type of gratification based upon the need that assists the adjustments and adaptations the individual makes in coping with the anxieties and stresses of life. The insistence that a child's behaviours become the adult personality is not reserved to Freud, in fact, it permeates most child theory and yet as we have seen throughout the book, the child's behaviours are not just allowing an adult to forecast the child's future. Nor are they simply the result of nature, nurture, but come from an often-misunderstood past. Remember earlier I expressed that children decide purposefully if a pattern of behaviour or habit will be left behind or kept dependent upon its usefulness, and so every new generation will consciously or unconsciously question every aspect of its patterns and habits of sexuality.

When an adult can adopt a relaxed curiosity when a little boy wants to breast feed a doll and a little girl wants to play trucks, they are supporting the child to flow and explore, not get stuck and set. These early play orientations speak to a deeper need of the child and therefore should not be analysed by adults as indicative of the child's future gender and sexual preference, nor for parents' surveillance measures. Gender fluidity is seen amongst even young children who are seeking to integrate the opposing and dualistic notions. Conditioning of the past in regard to fixed gender ideals is up for review. The family beliefs and attitudes about the difference in the sexes are seen very clearly in the ideas about what a boy's role is and what a girl's role is and these are all shaping the child's sexuality. Children dressing or expressing themselves in a gender neutral or gender specific way seems to be something that emerges from the child. Focusing on children being valued for the essence of who they are, without worrying too much about gender assignment, means that the child will not be as likely to be objectified. Boys that value girls as friends, sisters, and girlfriends do not tend to see them as objects of sex, and girls that value boys, brothers, and friends, tend not see them as sexual objects.[53] Furthermore, they will be respected and understood for their need to what feels right.

Summary

Of course, the *Need to Feel*, like the *Need to Be Safe and Secure*, is a need that will have a different meaning for each child. The variance of the *Need to Feel* will also depend on the situation, the people, and the event the child is experiencing. One child, for example, may feel that they can express their emotions in a school environment, where another child will have difficulty knowing or understanding why they are feeling a certain way. Some children might get their *Need to Feel* met one day, but not the next. As a child grows in age, they do not stop requiring the *Need to Feel*—they will just demand a different type of emotional process. The ability to deal with one's emotional life is a foundational requirement, not just in childhood, but also in life. Children and adults that are in balance with this need, move freely through experiences and are confident. They know how to process their emotions in healthy ways through play-based activities, and are generally what we might refer to as happy. There is a real sense of freedom when one has mastery over their emotions. Part three assists adults to relate to children with an emotional awareness. There are many examples given to assist the flow of energy in your child's life to be supported so they may follow their own natural push and deeply attuned sensitivities.

Tips To Cultivate The Need To Feel

At any age, in any situation, you can encourage your child's *Need to Feel* in the following ways:

- Let children participate in activities that make them happy. Encourage your child to trust what feels happy to them without having to explain why.

- Take some time to enjoy activities that make you feel good. Take a moment to appreciate the movement and ease when it is present, and notice when things are uneasy or rigid. The contrast helps to have deeper understanding and acceptance of emotion.

- Support your child's play; even in team sports, the contrast of winning and losing supports the child to flow through challenges with ease. Winning at a game might feel better than losing, but both winning and losing are necessary.

- Try asking yourself a question and listening to the first answer that pops into your awareness. This answer is your inner direction. If you are having trouble making a decision or you feel off balance, focus on what feels best to you. This will bring balance back into your life.

- Encourage a child's creative gifts as these are different from anyone else's. Encourage your child's special blend of unique talents.

- Try to incorporate play into your relating with children with music, movement, and creative expression. Model a playful approach to tasks that might otherwise be mundane. Hanging out the washing can be so much fun with a little helper.

- Do not control the flow of the child's money (pocket money). If you give and then tell them what they can spend it on you are missing out on a great opportunity to see if their relationship with money is the same as or different than your own.

- Promote attitudes about sex as a sacred act that values the people who partake in it. Be open to helping your child explore differences in sexual feelings, and be open to gender fluidity.

- Allow your child the space to do what they need for themselves. Make some space each day for non-structured activities. The value of children being able to process their experiences in their own time and having the space to do what feels best for them is immeasurable.

Needs Table 2 – The Need to Feel

Potential of need as the centre point of balance

Deficient	Balanced	Excess
Scared	Confidence	Pushy
Unresponsive	Emotional stability	Hyper sensitive
Numbing	Sensations	Pleasure seeking
Guilt	Celebration	Making fun of others
Jealousy	Desire	Greed
Regulated	Creativity	Irrational
Inflexible	Spontaneity	Impulsive
Secrecy	Intimacy-closeness	Deceitfulness
Insecure	Self-assured	Boastful
Sorrow	Joy	Frantic
Fearful	Sexuality	Over sexual
Unenthusiastic	Enthusiasm	Over excited
Displeasure	Pleasure	Pleasure seeking
Self indulgent	Pleasure	Spoilt
Desensitised	Sensitive	Hyper sensitive

3. Children Need To Act: Allow Me

"Your soul knows the geography of your destiny. Your soul alone has the map of your future; therefore you can trust this indirect, oblique side of yourself"

~ John O'Donohue.[1]

Your child inherently knows what is best for their growth. How children act, therefore, is a wonderful indication of their inner world of feelings and thoughts, and a register of how integrated they are. The child is, in essence, proclaiming *Allow Me*.

Figure 5: Physical Location of the *Need to Act*.

Case 3: Jeremy

Jeremy is what most might call, a troubled teenager. His parents have a restraining order (protective order) against him. This was a necessary step, they say, because his violence had become uncontrollable. Jeremy is 15 and the incident that led to the restraining order, involved him punching his mother in a fit of rage. The mother went to hospital to have stitches and the hospital staff urged the mother to file a charge against the son. The thing is, Jeremy is not totally aware why he did this and what led him to violently strike his mother? Jeremy has shut down from talking about the incident and when I met him, at the enforcement of his father, he appeared broken. Jeremy was stooped and his shoulders rounded. Whatever is underneath this situation it seemed apparent to me that Jeremy is feeling ashamed. It is natural to question what might have led a child to respond in this way and physically assault his mother? We might be quick to judge the character of the child as a bad seed. James Hillman in *A Souls Code in Search of Character and Calling,*[2] says the notion of a bad seed is indicative of the ingrained belief that some children are just born bad, thus allowing any parental responsibility to abate. Perhaps we might ask what might have led to a parent enforcing a restraining order on the child placing the child fully responsible. The source of the problem in this case has clearly been attributed to Jeremy, and by all appearances; it is his burden to carry.

Jeremy's father told me about his son and spoke as if he wasn't in the room. As he spoke, he started to berate his son's behavior toward his own wife (the child's mother) and replayed all of the various details of the incident to me in a way that further appeared to shame his son. "This behavior is not acceptable and he needs to learn that we are tired of feeling threatened by him," the father declared. The father himself admitted that he had grown up in a violent household, and he felt the same threat from his father and it was the last thing he was going to tolerate in his son. I acknowledged the father's feelings and expressed that the hostility that must have been felt in the home environment for the father (when he was a boy) was still happening now to a degree. Similarly, it was a clear issue of conflict and power within the family repeating with his son. I asked the father if he could see that the pattern was in fact the same? The father seemed perplexed and Jeremy looked interested.

I asked the father to describe the ways that they as parents of Jeremy had dealt with conflict since he was little. "We have rules in our house', the father said, "and breaking these rules results in punishment". Often, it was admitted by Jeremy's father, the punishment would include physical punishment. The father justified that "this is not the same as domestic violence; it is discipline and necessary, because how else do your children learn right from wrong." I watched Jeremy become uneasy, and because I advocate for a better way, I suggested to the father that there were many other ways of supporting the moral development as well as the motivation of children. In fact, much research indicates that children know right and wrong for themselves, are highly motivated and directed towards certain goals and achieve without any external enforcement. Of course, if one grew up with disciplinary and punishment measures then one may lose a degree of one's own self-motivated and self-directed actions; they have in essence been beaten out of us. This type of parenting may have worked in the past, and as you will see further in this section it was a common measure in the industrial era, but we have evolved from this rudimentary way of enforcing children to activate their *Need to Act* in a moral and motivated way.

It is not, however, always easy to shift embedded power dynamics between adult and child, and much of this section examines the theme of power more broadly. The realisation of this out-dated power dynamic in families often leads to much healing for parent and child because if we can recognise it and see the bigger pattern, we can seek better ways of understanding what each family member needs to maintain their own power. The bigger pattern emerging for Jeremy and his dad was the level of power the father held over the child and his unresolved anger from his own childhood where he recounted how he could not say what he needed to his own father. You will notice the same feeling was directed at the son and the father "This behavior is not acceptable and you need to learn that we are tired of feeling threatened by you." The family patterns of influence are strong and the son has become the unconscious projection of the father's own childhood because the father also expressed that he wanted to find a better way of dealing with the conflict in his own family when he was a child, but obviously could not. The cycle continues until we realise it and bring it to a stop, when we can see the energetic loop, we have been stuck in, we can start to do things differently.

The aspect of the child's life pertaining to the *Need to Act* is the 3rd Chakra, (*Manipura*) which is linked to one's will, power, self-control, confidence, self-esteem, self-definition, individuality, and motivation. The anatomy and body systems correlated to the *Need to Act* are the adrenal glands, mid-spine, digestive system, stomach, upper intestine, liver, gall bladder, kidney, pancreases, and spleen. See the A-Z of common ailments associated to this 3rd Need in Appendix 1. The adrenal glands are the bodies fight and flight centre and when imbalanced will set in motion archaic survival reflexes and responses that often are of a violent nature. Not every child will respond to domination and control through physical force toward others, and yet the situation with Jeremy is a case in point for us to consider even if we justify aggressive actions toward children as discipline, without considering our own relationship to power and violence these actions will affect the child and the child will carry them as their own. When this happens we may also appreciate in the child a seesaw of responses from being ashamed of themselves to forcing their will and power on others because in essence Jeremy was acting on the unresolved past of his father and his father's relationship to power.

If we look to another aspect of the *Need to Act* the theme of Motivation we can recognise that motivation will differ between individuals, families, and cultures, and yet, there is certain motivations that we all share. The way one child feels and thinks about what motivates them will vary to that of another child. When the *Need to Act* is not met, there will be an energetic response on one end of the spectrum, with a child showing little interest in anything and being despondent toward taking action (deficient energy regarding motivation), to the other end of the seesaw, where a child may feel they have to get everything done and achieve externally (excessive energy in regard to motivation). An inactive child is communicating a *Need to Act* in a way that is unmotivated, and an over-achieving child is *also* communicating a *Need to Act* and being motivated. The needs table at the end of this section shows a variety of excess and deficient responses in the child if the *Need to Act* is not met. Knowing that the unmet *Need to Act* is at the origin of the child's behaviours such as despondency or excessively striving means that we can pay more attention to ways that we might encourage affirmative thoughts and responses about motivation if and when a child expresses such imbalance.

Need to Act- Common Themes

- *Power*
- *Discipline and Punishment*
- *Autonomy*
- *Agency*
- *Toilet Training*
- *Self-Motivation*
- *Freedom*
- *Will*
- *Stomach Aches*

Power

One of the biggest challenges to the child-adult relationship is allowing the child a level of authority over their experiences. We can only parent from the level of awareness we hold, so if as adults we still feel the need to ask for permission, even subtly, we will expect our children to do the same. If as adults we feel controlled by life and life's circumstances, we will find it difficult to allow our children the opportunity to express and act from their own locus of control. This leads to a defiance and determination in our children to get their own way, and then we get upset and react defiantly to them when they act against us. When we can allow children control over their actions each day, they develop confidence in their direction, and improve the capacities to follow it when they need to. The *Need to Act* according to our own motivations, to act like we are the leaders of our lives, is something we seem to have to work toward. In this way, we all require the authority to navigate life in our own way; in a way that is directed by our *push*. Children, however, are not often afforded the *Need to Act*, and many adults presume to know what is best for them without giving them an opportunity to act for themselves. Many adults continue to control and dominate children in order to make children comply. In this way, adults largely enforce their own will over the child's will. Of course, children need guidance, protection, and help from adults, and when they are very little, a parent needs to make decisions based on what they feel is best for the child, I know this very well, but as children grow (and today it seems to be happening faster than ever before), they need much less of this way of relating and much more space to unfold. Ultimately, children must learn to feel and know what is best for them, according to them.

Many adults' direct children to be, act, and even think in certain ways. This direction is often justified because of the idea that the child must fit into certain social structures. It was sociologist Margaret Mead who called this "the generalised other." This term means that children act and learn in a social world where more mature partners guide and add supporting structures to the child's learning. Whether these supporting structures are positive or negative to the child's wellbeing is questionable, and many adults will justify it with, "This is how we grew up, and it was ok for us," and inevitably pass the same power imbalance on to their relationships with their own children and often do not recognise it as such. The degree to which the *adult push* directs children and the mode in which they do so (mostly unconsciously) will have an impact on the child's ability to be self-directed or, in social interactionist terms, their capacity to balance the demands of the "generalised other" (the normative demands of the current milieu) with the development of the *I* (the child's unique self, including their ability to reflexively interpret their environment and thus maintain their own safety and wellbeing).[3]

From the beginning, children learn about life and relationships based on the ways they are responded to by others. The child learns management of emotions, how to resolve disputes, and how to engage with others, not only from their experiences, but also from the way in which their reactions are responded to. For younger children especially, the primary source of these experiences is in the context of the parent–child relationship and the family environment.[4] The importance of a child's independence and the acknowledgement that the child is an active agent in its own life is somewhat underappreciated.

Discipline and Punishment

The power relationship between adult and child is not just evident in families, but in schools and the wider social world of many institutions that involve children. In fact it is part of our collective consciousness. Parenting models, for example, which have largely tended to be based on social learning theory, have a cultural and historical emphasis on discipline and on altering negative, aggressive behaviour in children. These approaches have tended to emphasise parental conflict, coercion, and consistent discipline of the child by enforcing a set of rules, rewards, and punishments administered to teach self-control, increase desirable behaviours, and decrease undesirable behaviours in children.

Even though social learning theory does not advocate corporal punishment in its disciplinary measures as a behaviour modification strategy, it seems that this form of dominance and violence toward the child continues in many families. The UN Committee on the Rights of the Child defines corporal punishment as, "any punishment in which physical force is used and intended to cause some degree of pain or discomfort, however, light."[5] Corporal punishment of minors within domestic settings is lawful in all 50 of the United States and, according to a 2000 survey, is widely approved of by parents. In Australia, the smacking debates often get heated, and seem to resurface annually. Dr. Gervase Chaney, the head of Australia's peak paediatric body, has called for parents to be banned from disciplining their children with physical force. He said it was no longer okay for parents to argue, it never did us any harm, and called on colleagues to stand up for children's rights.[6] While many may argue that the purpose of child discipline is for children to develop acceptable social behaviour, the degree to which the child develops and maintains a level of self-directed discipline based upon these (corporal) ways of relating is questionable. Punishment is not at all effective and does not assist children to understand why they do what they do. When children know the deeper meaning of their actions they do better.

When such a way of relating to children has been present for centuries, and we have all grown up with some degree of punishing measures within the families we belong, it is easy to see why people argue that there is nothing wrong if they want to tap their child for being naughty. Smacking certainly has a long history of human thought and action. In the 3rd millennium, however, it is important to note that we are still relating to children based upon things developed in the industrial times and before. The industrial era saw an interest in and focus toward a rationalised society, and the prevalent school of thought was utilitarianism; that is, the idea or philosophy of the greatest good for the greatest number or the greatest amount of happiness for the greatest number of people.

In the Charles Dicken's novel, *Hard Times,* set in the industrial era, the adult's happiness is placed over and above that of the child.[7] Dickens brought forth a subject of great importance, which is still present in our education and social systems today, that this way of being may lead to great misery. In Dickens' interpretation, the prevalence of utilitarian values in education and institutions promoted contempt, competition, and master-slave relations between mill owners and workers. This way of relating to self and others according to Dickens not only created "young adults whose imaginations had been neglected, due to an over-emphasis on facts and education of economics at the expense of more imaginative pursuits that continued into adulthood", but also gave the authority to the adult to decide what was appropriate punishment for the unruly child.

Even though this way of relating comes from a distant past, it is still present in many respects. The revisiting of the past is helpful to gauge the lineage of why we relate with children the way we do. To look at the power dynamic between adult and child requires we look to the theme of power more broadly and situate it within a paradigm. Jeremy Bentham, a political philosopher and utilitarian, may be part of the reason we still approach children like they need to be controlled and dominated. Bentham is most famous for creating designs for the Panopticon, which was his idea for the prison system.

The panopticon was established upon the idea that there was a need to have an all-seeing surveillance of prisoners. Most of us can evoke images of towers in courtyards and inside buildings, set up in such a way as to keep watch of those that needed to be 'surveyed'. Bentham's model was adopted as a way to watch over the unruly. Of course, prisons are not the only message from utilitarian thought, but they are the most obvious. We can see as an extension of this thinking, the modes and methods of surveillance that are still applied to children almost unconsciously. Children are still treated in many cases as slaves or prisoners, and most certainly this is evident when adults insist on controlling the unruly. Even today, many adult-child relationships appear to mirror the master-slave dialectic.

In the 1970s, philosopher Michael Foucault was deeply interested in looking at the history of the different modes by which human beings have been, and still are, dominated. He says the prison is a form used by the disciplines as a new technological power.[8] This power according to Foucault can be found in schools, hospitals, and the military. The fact is that even in many classrooms today there is a parallel design of the panopticon, with a common passage between the desks to allow teacher access to survey each student. Adult power relations with children, therefore, could be said to be a similar discipline, with overt adult interference in the life of the child. Sometimes adult-child relating can go beyond the necessary, justified care and concerns around safety and best interests. Sometimes adult power is intrusive and damaging to the child who feels they cannot do anything without someone watching them or someone ready to punish them. Because we have all to some degree grown up with such conditioning, we do not see the incremental damage it is doing; or perhaps we do not see the damage at all. It often takes a shift in perspective to begin to realise how archaic some of the ways we relate to children still are.

Autonomy

Even the ways that we convince or persuade children to do things to be compliant can be harmful. The way adults' direct children is important to consider as often these directives are unconscious and energetic in nature. Research on adult directives with children has historically looked mainly at spoken language or verbal directives in social interactions. More recently, however research, as well as theory on social interaction, has accentuated that interaction is embodied and embedded in the social world. This embodied understanding of power has resulted from communication practices emerging within the field of linguistics that include embodiment. Many studies have demonstrated that directives rely on both verbal and embodied resources. In one study on directives of parent-child interactions, researchers looked at routine family tasks in which directives such as 'take a bath, brush your teeth', and so on, were observed alongside distinct formats of embodied actions. Embodied actions that parents used in the study were body twisting, tactile and non-tactile steering to get the desired compliance.[9] The embodied facets of participation are important communicative patterns that shape the child's development. The same multimodal influence on children is found when a child is forced, manipulated, or coerced through both verbal and embodied practices such as violence, even in the subtlest forms, which transpires to negative outcomes. The costs children pay for such negative conditions of forceful childhoods are often neglected, because they are not perceived as a direct threat to wellbeing in the same way as other factors. The important point here is that even the unspoken directives we give to children are paramount as they are felt deep within the child's body.

We may notice that sometimes we ask the child to do a task with words and simultaneously we are pushing them or shoving them in the direction of the task. The embodied directive of the shove will stay with the child, and they hold onto this energy long after the words about the direction have gone. Many children withstand the demands placed upon them and overcome negative social conditions, often in ways that seem as justified as the parental role, but there are limits to what children can do without acknowledgement of their autonomous needs. The child's symptoms and imbalances of forceful directives are often embodied and misread until it is too late. On the spectrum of embodied actions of adults on children are the forms of physical violence. Children respond to experiences of violence on many levels, and studies have measured the neurological and physiological effects of violence and trauma on individual arousal and stress reactions, and the results show debilitating dissociative results. The trauma of violence influences the pattern, intensity, and nature of sensory perceptual and affective experience of events during childhood.[10]

Agency

When adults value the child's agency as co-creators in forming foundational skills, children learn not only a positive self-narrative but also a healthy interdependence. Yet, often the *adult push* sees adults make decisions for children without consulting them, and take actions toward children based on their past, or how things have always been done. I have certainly made choices for my children founded upon what I thought were the right choices at the time. It is not just parents, but many adults in social and cultural environments involved with raising children who take the lead in deciding for the child; they rarely allow the child to be directed according to what feels best for the child, in their own way. It is always a difficult awareness for adults to face that we may have made a significant decision with the best intentions, but that it conditioned the child to have beliefs about themselves and the world that are not as expansive as they could be. When and if we have this realisation, we can either feel guilty about placing a particular worldview or model on a child, or we can support them in continuing to ask questions in order to express their feelings, and no longer reduce their feelings to our own justifications no matter how much this may challenge us.

In sociology, a person's agency is defined as, "one's independent capability or the ability to act on one's will", and this will is almost always in contrast to the external factors that limit one's agency. There is a complex interplay between the factors that influence human agency. For example, disagreement on the extent of the child's agency causes conflict between parents and children (adults and children) and often has a metaphorical and embodied language. The *Need to Act* from a strong sense of power is rarely afforded to children. Paradoxically, the opposition that mostly results from this lack of recognition of the child can be problematic for adults. Many adults, therefore, try to control and dominate children so as not to battle with them; a little like the *might is right* argument. Empirical evidence from studies that link parental psychological control to aspects of child and adolescent development reveal consistent findings to disturbances in self-processes, increased internalised and externalised problems, and decreased academic achievement in children. [11] Not all pressure is harmful, and of course, our children will always be exposed to some level of stress and pressure, but learning to cope with smaller stressors is said to make one resilient.

Resilience is a concept that is widely used to explain why some children cope well with many transitions in life and others do not. Social competence, problem-solving skills, critical consciousness, autonomy, and a sense of purpose are all necessary for resilience, and yet many families, schools, and communities fail to afford these competencies to the child. If these environments do offer caring relationships, high expectations, and opportunities to take part in the many life situations that a child encounters, then the child will show resilience. However, stress becomes harmful when it is unpredictable or out of a person's control. In response to violence, dissociative patterns of decreased responsiveness have been found that contribute to feelings of helplessness and depression. [12] In supporting children's autonomy, competence, purpose, and will, it is obvious that adults cannot relinquish all control. Studies show, too, that severe punishment teaches aggressive behaviour and fosters shame[13] as we saw evidently in the case of Jeremy. Children are highly sensitive to parental approval, and yet, some of the negative psychological changes associated with adolescent development, are said to result from a mismatch between the needs of developing adolescents and the opportunities afforded them by their social environments.[14]

Toilet Training

Control issues are perhaps best demonstrated through a stage that we all have to navigate in our civilised world, toilet training. Toilet training is both an important milestone for children and a common parenting challenge. In toilet training, the child has to be an active participator and co-operate voluntarily for this stage of growth to be mastered. Most parents realise that they need to employ strategies in which to convince a child that using the toilet is a good thing for the child. If the parent takes an approach the child does not like, then there may be some resistance from the child. Battling with a toddler often leads to frustration (more likely for the parent) and will not achieve the required result. Symbolically, this is a great opportunity for a child to show control over their environment and not comply with the toilet requests.

Children hold onto their bowel motions for many reasons, but in my experience, it is mostly a matter of exerting control. The child is expressing, albeit symbolically, that they are in control of their environment. 'Holding' as a metaphor for the ways in which children get stuck and have difficulty processing their emotions.[15] Often, a child holds when the parent or caregiver does not allow the child's opinions, feelings, ideas, or suggestions to be validated. Often when the child opposes what is asked of the child (even if it seems like a rational demand, such as asking them to use the toilet) it is because the child is feeling powerless due to other situations that they have no control over. Situations, including starting school, moving to a new home, the birth of a sibling, or a parent returning to work, can often feel forced upon the child. Every child *Needs to Act* in a way that embodies a healthy balanced relationship to control. Many of our children's experiences, such as those mentioned above, are chosen for them or decided without regard for them. It is not that the child should not go to preschool, not move to a new home, not have siblings, or expect that parents will not work. However, the degree to which the child's unity is considered in these situations will be the degree to which the child feels the need to oppose or have control over the other occurrences in their lives. The child has to be an active participator and co-operate voluntarily for this stage of growth to be mastered. Underlying unresolved control issues can lead to toileting and bowel issues. The energy block that has been established due to the child's lack of control has created a physical symptom in the bowel of holding, which indicates the child, needs to be in control of something. The toileting resistance then becomes the language, which communicates that the child requires help with this unmet *Need to Act*. Often, however, this plea for help may not be heard, and we then see a battle develop.

Toilet training is a poignant example of the balance between children having control over their environment and the adult expecting compliance are on-going for many people, and transpires in all human relationships, regardless of age. Oppositional stances occur more when the child is feeling powerless because of other situations over which they have no control. By offering choices to our children and discussing what might be possible and what might be unsafe for them to do, they are empowered to feel that they are free to make decisions. This consideration also allows them to feel the consequence of taking the lead. When it comes to everyday decision-making, rather than just giving directives, adults can ask the child what they feel they should do. In my experience, children always have an answer that is specific to their best growth. In the asking of this question, we recognise that children can give an indication of the best way forward for them. By acknowledging the child in this way, they feel there is no need to fight so hard for what they want, and power struggles often diminish because, in essence, you have heard their declaration of *Allow Me*.

Self-Motivation

When we look at the power dynamics between adult and child, we notice that most of the tensions results in what I term the *adult push* on the child. As if it is our task to motivate and thus adults have had a tendency to try and shape and mould the child according to what the adult wants, not what motivates the child. Children have a motivation toward their own happiness (and this has not generally been afforded to the child); a motivation that has nothing to do with what the parent desires, but an innate force of the child's soul.[16] If a child is unmotivated, we can assume that they are not interested. If we simply look to what interests a child, you will see what motivates them. If you have ever tried to teach a child something, you will have noticed that the level of the child's engagement will be a good match with the degree of motivation. Research into motivation shows how many regions of the brain are associated with the themes that relate to drive and motivation, and how these connect directly to one's actions in the world. This field of study is called the neurology of motivation.[17]

Many people adopt a 'learned helplessness' narrative in childhood from a perceived lack of control over their lives and the dismal outcomes of particular situations. A person with a learned helplessness narrative will feel a lack of control specific to one situation and may at other times extrapolate the lack of control across different situations.[18] Although not all pessimists will develop a learned helplessness narrative because all individual responses are unique—not just to adverse events and trauma, but also to life in general. Pessimism in children is paramount to learned helplessness and is represented by statements such as, it will never change, it's all my fault, and I can't do anything right. This type of destructive belief about self and life leads to ill-health and depression. Looking into studies of children who are motivated, Research indicates they are motivated largely based upon a need to have a degree of power in their lives. Despite being identified as above average in ability at school, children still reported experiencing a lack of competence (those less certain of their abilities) or a lack of autonomy (being externally motivated) when asked what a high score on a test meant to them. These same children also reported more negative effects and withdrawal behaviours than children who perceived themselves as having innate ability (they felt good about their abilities), or who perceived themselves to be autonomous, and yet, did not score as well.

The findings thus indicate that balance of power in homes and school is an important influence determining the child's self-esteem, motivation, and sense of perceived power. When the child is empowered to act autonomously, it leads to self-esteem and wellbeing.

Children who fight for control in their lives will engage in what we call power struggles as demonstrated with the toilet training issue. They are, in effect, trying to push to have their need for control recognised. A child who is allowed to experience control for itself and is given mastery over their own experiences becomes less interested in fighting for control, and as a result, is more powerful in their sense of self. Studies reveal that children who did not do well on test scores still maintained wellbeing if they had a deep sense of autonomy and belief in their abilities.

Respecting a child's expression of individuality is important from the beginning of life, and is developed by encouraging a child's feeling and thoughts to be shared by asking questions rather than giving answers. Allowing a child to feel what their internal motivation feels like aside form external motivation. It is also helpful if the adult-child relationship is interactive rather than dominating. (There is more detail on the interactions of child-adult in part three.) If we can keep in mind that children are always in the process of the formation of the self, and this process is not a stage one reaches, but rather a guiding force, or steering wheel, throughout the lifespan we see that how children express themselves is always changing. The many identities and trends that a person goes through will change many times over a lifetime. Looking to the other end of the spectrum of parental control and not allowing children to activate their own will, we see clinical reports compiled concerning adults indicate that, "depressed patients report that when they were children their parents were insensitive, unavailable, or overly intrusive, and unable to tolerate the child's autonomy and independence." This suggests that dominant parental relating is a central dimension in depression and levels of motivation.

Will

A Theory of Human Motivation was the title of the paper that revealed Abraham Maslow's Hierarchy of Needs, which was later outlined in his subsequent book, *Motivation and Personality* (1954). Human motivation, for Maslow, was geared toward the highest human need of self-actualisation or realised individual potential, and to reach this end goal, a series of other needs must be met. Maslow emphasised the importance of self-actualisation, which he says is a process rather than a state of being. Individual potential and power in the sense of the *Need to Act*, however, may not be something we grow into, and like happiness, it may be possible that individual potential is latent and available to be activated at every stage of development. An example of this idea comes from one study by the University of Illinois, conducted over a five-year period, called, "Needs and Subjective Wellbeing Around the World."[19] This study discovered that while fulfillment of Maslow's needs was strongly correlated with happiness and wellbeing, people from cultures all over the world reported that self-actualisation and social needs were more important to them, even when and if many of the most basic needs were unfulfilled.

The individuals Will to Meaning as Victor Frankel's *Logo Therapy* mentioned in the first chapter, seems to be important in our understanding of this motivational force. And yet, the child who is in the search for meaning at each and every stage is still usually being told what their meaning is, or that they will understand their meaning when they get older. The eternal wait for meaning can wait no longer, nor can the eternal recurrence of adults presuming that children have no meaning other than that which is ascribed to them. If we also look to Freidrich Nietzsche and a concept that he attributed to human beings as a Will to Power for our children, we might begin to serve them better. The Will to Power is, in essence, a revolt against the models of the past that we have adopted, and that are in large part, the beliefs and values of those before us. Nietzsche tells us that people always adopt perspectives by default, knowingly or not, whereby the concepts of their existence are defined by the circumstances surrounding their individual perspectives.

> *It is our needs that interpret the world; our drives and their For and Against. Every drive is a kind of lust to rule; each one has its perspective that it would like to compel all the other drives to accept as a norm.*[20]

There is for Nietzsche a Will to Power within us all. We may call it achievement, ambition, motivation, or striving, but it is a human drive to claim the authority of our existence. Individual psychology was even imbued with the Will to Power when Alfred Adler incorporated this idea in his works. Each of these Wills teaches a very different essential driving force in human beings, and yet, there remains a common theme in them all, that there exists a force driving the human being forward. If our children's natural push is recognised, we may begin to work with this force rather than against it.

Freedom

When children are controlled and dominated, we are depriving them of their self-competencies, and lessening their ability to manage life on their own. As mentioned previously, often adults who are depressed have come from homes where freedom was restricted. If the freedom of children to follow their own will is restricted either individually, in families, or in communities, it impacts the flow of children's confidence and challenges the child in developing a strong sense of self. The degree to which any child can follow his or her own will is often restricted as soon as the child is required to follow a familial, scholastic, religious, or cultural direction. The idea that we need to protect and direct our children in the dominating ways of the past, means we are seeing anger and fear in children that results from being surveyed and controlled. Any person that feels restricted unnecessarily will naturally push against the restrictions. This is an appropriate response to feeling controlled, and yet, our children end up experiencing negative outcomes if they display this natural response.

It makes sense that the more we encourage our children's freedom when they are little, the more we can support them if and when they need it before they are out on their own, so to speak. However, many adults are almost too afraid to even try. If we can surrender to the *child push*, we find that they do find their way forward, and the challenge for adults is in allowing them to do this for themselves with guidance, rather than control. When childhood potentials are not recognised, they go underground, and when children's self-direction is disregarded, they are disempowered. Self-reliance, self-regulation, and resilience all result when children feel they are free to do what they need for themselves. In my own journey, I have looked to many cultures to see how they care for, heal, and educate the child, to ascertain how children who are self-directed and free may offer some insight into the importance of the *Need to Act*.

On a visit to a Krishnamurti school in India, I learnt more about the philosophies of Krishnamurti because I saw them in action. The curriculum at the school provides a context that encourages the development of the already expansive potentials within children but without reward or punishment, thus empowering children to feel and think on their own. It also sees creativity and play as paramount for children, as it is more pleasurable than structured learning. In creative play, children are watchful and responsive to things that are meaningful. I was told by the teacher drawing on the work of Krishnamurti, "If you dominate a child, compel him to fit into a pattern, however idealistic, will he be free at the end of it?" And, "Merely to stuff the child with a lot of information, making him pass examinations, is the most unintelligent form of education."[21]

When the children left the classroom to walk to the lunch pavilion, I noticed they took a variety of tracks. In fact, there was no clearly delineated track from the classroom to the lunch pavilion. I noticed that many of the children diverted on the way to lunch to interact with nature. Some of the children sat in the grass, some of them climbed a large tree that was on the way, and some of them appeared to talk with the birds. They made their way in their own time, enjoying the space between activities. When it came time for me to walk toward the pavilion, I asked my guide if there was a track I should take. She looked at me and smiled. She told me that when the school was constructed there was a path made between the buildings, but over time there had become little use for it. She continued, "What use is a track, really, when these children find their own way?" At this moment I was struck by the metaphorical connection between children's self-direction and finding one's way physically. My guide must have felt this, and she added, "What meaning does that track have when children make their own meaning?" Yes, I thought to myself, children are meaning makers. The children made their own way to the lunch pavilion, a way that had meaning to them personally.

Stomach Ache

If we look at the case of a common occurrence such as stomach ache, we can see, there is so much more going on for the child than just the "symptom". Perhaps we might imagine that a child may have a stomach ache because they feel conflicted about going to school for a variety of reasons, yet the child is most likely not even aware of why this is occurring. The stomach ache is an unconscious or bodily response to the child's need. If we look to a case of a child, aged seven, who has a stomach ache at 8.45 am in the morning, we might realise that the stomach ache may not just be a physical problem (genetic, dietary, or environmental), but has to do with the child's feelings about going to school, because 8.45 am is when a large majority of seven-year-olds in the Western world attend school. According to the *Foundational Needs Model*, the stomach ache is the result of an unmet emotional need (the disparity between feeling and thinking). The anatomical location of the stomach is in the third Chakra. Stomach problems are metaphysically deemed to be a manifestation of a failure or refusal to stomach a person or situation.[22] There may be something hard to tolerate going on in the child's life. Often a stomach ache alerts a resistance to new ideas or changing habits. A child who experiences stomach aches needs to feel that they have the confidence to cope with change, and have a sense of self-control. Each child will manifest a different response to the unmet *Need to Act,* which is the first cause of the stomach ache.

In a study titled *Somatic Complaints and Psychopathology in Children and Adolescents: Stomach Aches, Musculoskeletal Pains, and Headaches,* researchers examined the links of somatic complaints of stomach ache, headaches, and musculoskeletal pains with DSM-III-R defined depression, anxiety disorders, conduct disorder, oppositional defiant disorder, and ADHD in children and adolescents. The findings indicated that somatic complaints were strongly associated with emotional disorders in girls and with disruptive behaviour disorders in boys:

> *For girls, stomach aches and headaches together and musculoskeletal pains alone were associated with anxiety disorders. For boys, stomach aches were associated with oppositional defiant disorder and attention-deficit hyperactivity disorder. Musculoskeletal pains were associated with depression in both girls and boys.* [23]

The stomach aches in girls were seen as the physical manifestation (body) associated with anxiety disorders (mind). The stomach aches in boys (body) were associated with oppositional defiant disorder and attention-deficit hyperactivity disorder (mind). This variance in itself is interesting, as the girls appear to respond to an unmet *Need to Act* by becoming anxious as per the DSM-III-R defined anxiety disorders, while the boys appear to respond to the unmet *Need to Act* by exhibiting oppositional defiant disorder and ADHD as per the DSM-III-R definitions. Obviously, cultural norms played a part in the physical dimensions of the presenting imbalances, but the point remains that there is a strong correlation between bodily manifestation and underlying emotional imbalances, that through the FNM a clinician and parent can identify and remedy. The need then is, in essence, the recognition of the composite whole in the concerns our children are faced with. In the case mentioned above, if the clinician had been given an opportunity to speak to the children, it is likely they would come to see that the *Need to Act* had not been met.

Of course, to draw a causal link, major research would need to be undertaken in order to test this relationship empirically. My experience working with children using the FNM has seen this apparent connection. For instance, the boys have a tendency to resist power and the girls have a tendency to submit and withdraw, as these studies concur. Therefore, I argue that any study that aims to understand the lived reality of children would necessarily commence with the children's perspective of themselves and the world, which goes right down to the cellular level, and includes an account of the whole.

The multidimensional interactions of the child's composite whole are perhaps no better demonstrated than in the case of the stomach. When we look at the function of all the aspects of this *Need to Act*, we notice that when it comes to the physical body aspect of the stomach, there is even much more awareness. There is an increasing interest in the role of bacteria and how this can impact and affect anxiety in a person, as well as the impact on our brain, mood, and emotions. For this reason, the gut is also referred to as the second brain. Interestingly, germ theory, Western medicine's approach to illness that culminated in the discovery of penicillin in the middle of the 20th century, is also being challenged by new science. A mechanistic explanation for nutritional disease, autoimmune disease, genetic disease, and cancer can all be justified, in part, with mechanistic explanations; however, these are reliant upon a worldview that supports the separation of body and mind. With epigenetics, we see a whole new model to account for the body-mind, past-present, nature-nurture understandings that propose the self is being shaped, as well as shaping, the larger field in which we exist. Again, this dialogue goes right down to the microscopic level of our existence.

Studies that look to the relationship between gut and behaviour have made the following remarkable discoveries:

1. Gut microbes are part of the unconscious system influencing behavior.
2. Microbes majorly impact on cognitive function and fundamental behavior patterns.
3. Disorganisation of the gut microbiota can negatively impact on mental health.
4. Psychobiotics are probiotics with a potential mental health benefit.

Researchers studying what is termed the gut-brain axis say, "The evolutionary formation of a complex gut microbiota in mammals has played an important role in enabling brain development, and perhaps sophisticated social interaction."[24] Here again, it is important to point out that as Pert's research highlights, the Chakras are like mini brains and every organ in the body contains the molecules we once thought were contained to the brain.

Summary

As a child advances in age, they do not stop requiring the *Need to Act*. They will, however, demand a different type of relationship to the dominant culture, as we all do when facing an uncertain, new environment. The ability to deal with change is a foundational requirement not just in childhood, but also in life. Allowing your child to act on their own direction, even when they are little, communicates a healthy relationship to power. Meeting the *Need to Act* for themselves is also an important part of helping children to know how much they can do on their own, which means they will not excessively seek control over others. The *Need to Act* means we have to allow children to act according to their own direction when possible. The various symptoms of the child resulting from the unmet *Need to Act* might range at one end of the spectrum as the presentation of pleasing, indecision, or withdrawal, and at the other end of the spectrum presenting as demanding, aggressive, and dominant behaviours. Children (and adults) that are free to act in accord with their own direction have a deep confidence and autonomy; they are highly motivated, self-directed, and resilient. Children with a strong sense of power can approach unfamiliar environments and new experiences with an inner balance. When we become aware that at the root of the unmet *Need to Act* are energies of defiance, over-activity, indecision, withdrawal, powerlessness, and shame, we are offered a great opportunity to transform these energies by exploring ways of relating to children that make them feel recognised as active agents in their own lives.

Tips To Cultivate The Need To Act

At any age, in any situation, you can encourage your child's *Need to Act* in the following ways:

- Allow your child to lead the way in some activities. This allows the child to establish its own degree of competency and feel capable.

- Ensure that your actions toward your children are reassuring rather than dominating.

- Talk about the reasons why a certain decision has been made and encourage the child to express how they feel. (This does not mean that you have to negate your decision. Rather it allows for communication so the child may come to know why you have decided what you have, and that it is okay if they do not always agree with your decision).

- Become more self-aware. When you begin to listen to the inner messages of your own body and what these messages may be telling you, you can support your children to do the same. When your body tells you something is wrong, trust it.

- When your child feels motivated to do something, help them to follow through, even if watching the disappointment or pain challenges you.

- Encourage determination and try to direct the child to get to know its soul push—this is a powerful force. "Sometimes there will be things that you do not think you can do. When this happens, try to feel why you think this is so."

- Allow a child to be the motivator. Follow their direction at times while doing shared activities—make it a game and encourage them to use their inner guidance.

- When it comes to everyday decision-making, rather than just giving directives, adults can ask the child what they feel they should do. By acknowledging the child in this way, they feel there is no need to fight so hard for what they want, and power struggles often diminish.

- Remind the child of their power within and that they can work through anything. When they honour the power within themselves, they will not need other people to praise them all the time.

- Give a choice, and when a child does not want to do something that you ask, you can look to your own energy first. The concept of *fixed* and *flexible* is a clear and fair directive. This approach is good for children that dislike authority. For example, you might say that we all have to brush our teeth (fixed), but when we brush our teeth is more flexible.

- Offer the child ways to feel they are doing great. Instead of praising your child, use affirmative truths. Writing affirmations or saying them aloud helps release the stuck energy in the child's body.

- Don't push the child away and expect them to deal with their uncertainty or fears on their own. Time out is harmful and results in many other common childhood issues. Time together is a much better option.

Needs Table 3 – The Need to Act

Potential of need as the centre point of balance

Deficient	Balanced	Excess
Indecision	Power	Impulsive
Overwhelmed	Self-control	Regulated
Withdrawn Lethargy	Self-confidence	Extrovert
Insecure	Self-respect	Arrogance
Giving Sharing	Self-esteem	Demanding
Submissive	Autonomy Personal boundaries	Dominating
Destructive	Will	Defiant
Wounded	Pro-active	Calculating
Dishonour	Honour/Courage	Empty promises
Blame	Self-acceptance	Self-promoting Attention seeking
Easily manipulated	Self-discipline	Dominant Aggression
Co-dependence	Independence	Aloof
Indecisive	Agency	Pushy
Shame	Pride	Conceit
Victim	Responsibility	Manipulating

4. Children Need To Love: Love Me

"All you need is love."

~ The Beatles[25]

Children naturally seek loving and harmonious relationships with themselves and others—extending out to animals, natural environments, and the whole of the world. Children love to know how things fit together and who belongs to who. The child is, in essence, proclaiming *Love Me*.

Figure 6: Physical Location of the Need to Love.

Case 4: Ella

To love and be loved as poets, philosophers, musician and artists have portrayed, is one of the supreme human needs. The Beatles, of course, captured this sentiment beautifully in this section's opening quote, "*All you need is love.*" Supporting children to feel loved and to love others is only possible to the degree that we feel love for our lives and ourselves. There is a common saying that suggests we get the love we think we deserve. Do you know the feeling of being loved unconditionally? Maybe you have felt this from a parent, or in a personal relationship. This quality of love is without condition and is never hurtful or unkind. Some people can only feel free to express this type of love in relationship to a pet, where they freely give and receive love. The necessity for love in our lives is often under-rated, and every person seeks and also deserves love, no matter what stage or age they are in life, no matter how unlovable they may perceive themselves to be.

Ella had always perceived herself as unlovable and it was a big issue for her. Ella's parents by all accounts appeared loving, they embraced parenting approaches that might better support their daughter to feel loved, but she did not. "My parents don't love me", she would tell people when she was feeling sad, and "my parents don't care about me", she would say if she required something she didn't have. Her parent's lack of love became the default reason for anything that was going on for the 9-year old. During one of her sessions with me we discovered something interesting in regard to Ella's feeling about not being loved. We were exploring the idea that even though these feelings were not supported by anything we could see in her life, that they were real, and we needed to explore where they came from.

We embarked on a body-guided journey together, to see what the message of these feelings was trying to communicate. We started to explore Ella's past and we discovered that Ella was an only child just like her mother and her mother's mother too. There was a family history of single female children dating back three generations. The grandmother had actually had a very traumatic childhood in which she had lost a sister to a childhood illness and had become an only child as a result. Her mother was an only child, because the grandmother had not been able to conceive more children. The mother herself had made a conscious choice to have one child and so Ella represented a very special gift of love.

The child herself however did not feel this sentiment and was plagued with feelings of not being loved. In our exploration of Ella's feeling we went on a journey what I call a type of time travel, back three generations to play a game with Ella. We wanted to go back to enquire about what Ella's Grandma might have to tell Ella about why she feels the way she does. Even though Ella's grandmother had passed away, I told Ella that she could still communicate with her. Ella nodded her head as she told me that her grandmother came to her in her dreams. "What do you think your grandma might have to tell you about not feeling loved Ella?" I asked. Ella's awareness was beyond her years, what ensued was an imagined conversation with her grandma in which Ella was gifted the wisdom she needed to understand her feelings and in essence to heal. In this process, Ella began to tell me what her grandma was saying. "Grandma says she knows what it fees like not to feel loved because when grandma's sister died suddenly as a child she felt this way. Grandma said after this sadness her mother stopped noticing the things that grandma did and if she did notice she would cry and say – your sister would never be able to do that, when grandma did anything to bring attention to herself. Grandma said she was sad that the sister had died, and she was also sad that she couldn't do anything to make her mother happy. Grandma didn't feel that anyone loved her. Grandma said her father had left them as well after the sister had died and she never saw him again. Ella continued with much detail "When grandma had her own child (Ella's mother) she felt delighted to be able to give her all the love she never got."

So, the feelings that Ella held about not being loved were actually passed on from grandma's own childhood, because she had never healed the hurt she felt toward her own mother for not giving her the love she needed after her sister died. Ella conveyed more about the story with her grandmother and Ella said that grandma had told her how proud she was that she had carried this feeling and that because of the love in the family that had been created it allowed for this past to come up again to be healed. Ella's grandma had also asked Ella to hand those feelings back as she didn't want Ella to feel unloved nor carry her feelings anymore. Something happened for Ella in that encounter and she never spoke about feeling unloved again. She did however make many more visits to her grandma's past; in her dreams and quiet times - after all, they shared so much, it was a bond that would never be separated. The general theme of this 4th Chakra (*Anahata*) energy and the pathways to embodying love in all its forms, is found within the specific themes of unity, self-love, empathy, compassion, forgiveness, devotion, service to others, unconditional love, and integration of opposites. The anatomical position of the 4th Chakra is the heart. Associated anatomy and body systems of the *Need to Love* are the heart, shoulders, arms, circulatory system, respiratory system, thymus, diaphragm, and lungs and issues of asthma and breathing. See the A-Z of common ailments associated to this 4th Need in Appendix 1.

Self-love as a main theme of the *Need to Love* will differ between individuals, families, and cultures; however, there are particular types of self-love that we all share. The way one child *feels* and *thinks* about self-love will vary from that of another child. When the *Need to Love* is not met through self-love there will be an energetic response; on one end of the seesaw, with a child being self-punishing and hard on themselves (deficient energy regarding self-love), and on the other end, a child may be self-obsessed (excessive energy regarding self-love). These responses to self and life are appropriate, as they arise according to what the child needs but is not receiving. A self-punishing child is communicating a *Need to Love*, and the self-obsessed child is also communicating a *Need to Love*. The needs table at the end of this section shows a variety of excess and deficient responses in the child if the *Need to Love* is not met.

~~~

> **Need to Love - Common Themes**
> - *Care*
> - *Recognition*
> - *All You Need Is Love*
> - *Sibling Rivalry*
> - *Bullying*
> - *Empathy*
> - *Mirroring*
> - *Heart Coherence*
> - *Gratitude*

Care

In Western philosophy in the latter part of the 20th century, there was a deeper focus on the ways in which we might truly care for others. This thinking arose from feminists who were challenging dualistic thinking, particularly concerning the mind-body discourses in their bid to resituate the idea of women's value and the value of the body. Feminist philosophers have been instrumental in shifting many entrenched ideas about how we understand the self. Luce Irigaray points out that just as it has been seen to be a 'category mistake' to think about the mind as a thing, it is also a category mistake to think about the body as a thing. When we think about the body as a thing, the body is turned into a concept, and we lose deep, personal relating with others. In essence, this thinking means we largely continue to see and talk about other people as abstractions. A large part of the stance of the feminists at this time was to gain recognition of the unhealthy dominance over women by men and the cold hard approaches to philosophy. There was another important, often unseen, agenda transpiring; that was to recognise and value the woman for the gifts that she had in the way of deep emotional insight, which included mothering and caring for children, and to have these equally honoured in the human experience, at least as much as one's rational capacities were honoured.

The *ethics of care* in philosophy, therefore, arose from the argument that caring should be a foundation for ethical decision-making. The question, "How should we respond?" became a central one in this moral philosophy indicating the moral importance to human relationships and one's dependencies in human life. Children, therefore, are in need of *care*. Carol Gilligan's book, *In a Different Voice: Psychological Theory and Women's Development* (1982), actually changed the way we view how people care, and in sum, showed that Lawrence Kohlberg's stages of moral development did not represent the full scope of children's moral lives.[26] A student of Kohlberg, Gilligan disagreed with her teacher over his stages of moral development, particularly as they apply to male and female (these stages were actually conceived from Piaget's *Stages of Development*). The assertion from Gilligan is that there are types of morality, not stages, and this assertion also shifted thinking about women's ways to be acknowledged in contrast to the dominant morality found within the thinking of the time.[27]

Another significant feminist philosopher in the ethics of care is Nel Noddings. In her book, *Caring*, she argues that care is basic in human life, as all people want to be cared for. How we are cared for becomes how we care. [28] Attachment theory, discussed in the *Need to Be Safe and Secure,* also supports this caring aspect of the *Need for Love* as well. The feelings, thoughts, and emotions that arise in caring relationships influence the way the child feels and thinks about itself, as well as the emotions it comes to experience. (Historically, this care has come predominately from women.) Of course, it might seem obvious that children ought to have all the moral and ethical considerations that adults have access to, and yet this has not always been the case. *The Moral Life of Children* and *The Political Life of Children* are two books that resulted from research psychoanalyst Robert Coles completed during the 1970s, travelling with his own family and living in different communities, with the aim of learning how children around the world obtain their values and their sense of right and wrong. Coles recalled moments he had with children, "A remark, a picture drawn, a daytime reverie shared, a dream or a nightmare reported—all of them in some fashion having a religious or spiritual theme." [29]

The child's moral life and political life, according to Coles, had a distinct connection to the child's idea of how they were cared for, and how they became informed through an inner knowing. There is a broader discussion of the spiritual capacities of the child in the section of this part entitled, the *Need to Know,* as the 7th *Need*. However, the point is, that children draw on their own unified ideas of self to make decisions about what is right and wrong, how they should care for others, and how to be most loving in the world. These ideas are not always from other people, as they also draw on nature and their concept of God (children's concepts of God are also discussed in the *Need to Know*) when making decisions. Children make decisions centred on the idea of activating their best potential, which is innate to the soul. Deciding what are the right and wrong choices seems in part at least natural, and when shamed or made to feel they are bad by adults, children are presumed to be devoid of moral behaviour, from adults who often hold a moral highroad with children.

Belittling, shaming, and making children feel guilty about being a good and caring person is damaging. After all, self-blame and guilt arise naturally as an internal moral compass to some degree (we might call it compassion in this sense, but feeling bad about hurting someone else seems evident in even the smallest of children), without any need for added enforcing. Even small children feel guilty if they hurt another child's feelings, independent of others' imposed opinion of the situation. If the child is shamed, it can leave lasting scars. Accounting for a deep level of care and compassion when dealing with children (and others), Noddings says we ought to bring this ethic of care both inside and outside of schools, and that, "It is possible to include social, emotional, and ethical learning in all curricular and extracurricular activities." According to Noddings, schools produce, "many highly proficient people who commit fraud, pursue paths to success marked by greed, and care little about how their actions affect the lives of others."[30] Noddings, however, is well aware that her suggestion of demanding more from school often incites the counter argument: that schools are structured to focus on academic goals, and therefore pursuing aspects of the whole child is the job of other institutions. The whole child pedagogy is paramount for our children, particularly concerning the *Need to Love* and it is evident that women philosophers have paved the way for the children in their ethics of care and recognition of the whole child.

Recognition

As we grow, we are always receiving energies that either support or deny how lovable we are. We are always attempting to integrate the way we feel and think about ourselves, while at the same time integrating what we believe and make assumptions about concerning what others may feel and think about us. According to philosopher Georg Hegel, a person's identity is formed in the context of the recognition that others, initially parents give to that person. The human need for love is deemed primarily a recognition that sustains us and grounds our development as children. The desire within the human relational dynamic therefore is to seek recognition, which has also been characterised as the 'desire for fame' by Alain de Botton. De Botton says a driving force for humanity is our need to be noticed or feel recognised. In his book, *The News,* de Botton stresses that the infatuation with fame in modern society will depend on the type of parenting you received and the type of culture in which you grew up. A society that sees everyone wanting to be famous is one where mediocrity, or in de Botton's words, "being ordinary has failed to deliver the degree of respect necessary to satisfy peoples natural appetite for dignity."[31] It seems that we are all, to a degree, seeking recognition and love externally, instead of knowing internally that we are worthy of loving and caring relationships as a natural consequence of human flourishing. If one does not have loving relationships in one's life, it seems to be that one still feels there is at least the possibility for that special love, so often one will go seeking recognition of ones worth in any way one can.

This seeking seems more evident today with social media stardom, but to a degree, it has always existed. Long before the advent of social media Sociologist Guy Debord wrote the book, *The Society of the Spectacle* in 1967. In it he states that there is, "a social relationship between people that is mediated by images," which he called, "The Spectacle". This way of relating to the child, you might already have deduced, is in line with deMause's definition of *The Projective Reaction*—, the reaction that sees the adult use the child as an instrument for the projection of his/her own unconscious. In our own attempts to make our children feel the love we wanted or the recognition we desired as children, we idolise them. I have seen many children related to as somewhat of a spectacle, and this can happen from the beginnings of life. The idea of parenting can also be seen to be somewhat of a spectacle. Consider for a moment—the birth is captured on film, the first smile is posted on Instagram, and videos of the child's life are uploaded on Facebook. Granted, these mediums are just a contemporary version of the 'family album' it appears however that the need for love and recognition appear to go hand in hand with public demonstrations of love. And yet, however we do it, we all in our own way seek love, because we all seem to know its power. When a child feels loved, especially in the eyes of the parent, they are fortified with a strength that sees them happy and secure even without any public recognition.

Alain de Botton beautifully tells us that a decade of parental love can fill a person so much that it will enable them to cope with fifty years of insignificance.[32] If we have not received the recognition and love we needed as children, then as adults, if we have not become aware of this need within ourselves, we may seek fame (regardless of whether we attain it or not). If we have children, they will carry this projected desire and want fame too. The unmet need motivating this desire for fame is recognition, and de Botton sums it all up in one sentence:

> *"This analysis has a side benefit of providing us with a litmus test for how good a job we may be doing parenting our own children: we have to ask whether they have any wish whatsoever to be famous."*

This quote brings us back to Carl Jung's idea in section one, chapter three, that states, that in trying to be perfect as parents, we are often deferring the reality of our own fragmentation, which gets passed onto our children and our children's children. In trying to be perfect or seeking approval for perfection, many parents forget that the child wants recognition too. After all, a child that is recognised for its soul brilliance will never seek unconsciously for recognition outside itself. If they do obtain recognition, it is accepted that fame does not define their sense of love. A simple remedy for adults is to try and remember that the child has its own aspirations that may have nothing to do with the adults, and if we cannot see this, we may fail to ask the child a direct question such as, "What do you need?" When was the last time you asked a child what they needed?

All You Need is Love

When you ask a child what they need, it may surprise you to hear what they express. I learnt this early on in my own mothering when asking the question. "What do you need?" to be met with a response of, "Just love me." Of course! It seems so simple and yet not always easy. The Dalai Lama says the human need for love is based upon the idea of interdependence, which he says is a fundamental law of nature.[33] The codependent ways of loving and relating are being transformed and moving us collectively into a more advanced type of relating that is based upon unconditional love, of which compassion is a big part.

> *"Not only higher forms of life but also many of the smallest insects are social beings who, without any religion, law or education, survive by mutual cooperation based on an innate recognition of their interconnectedness. The most subtle level of material phenomena is also governed by interdependence. All phenomena from the planet we inhabit to the oceans, clouds, forests and flowers that surround us arise in dependence upon subtle patterns of energy. Without their proper interaction, they dissolve and decay."[34]*

This is why compassion is so necessary. The requisite, human contact and deep relationships are a foundation for empathy and a caring, healthy society. This *Need for Love* extends to the need to see the harmonious relationship in everything, in practical terms; children like to understand how everything relates to everything else. When we are simply aware that we are an interdependent soul in communion with others and all of life, we seem to open our hearts to a source of love that is naturally a part of a field of energy supporting our highest potentials. The *Need for Love* is something that starts in our embryonic beginnings, and as Stuart Sovatsky tells us, the *push* is there microscopically in the cells of creation that bring us into existence in the first place.

Even the smallest child likes to believe that they were conceived in love. This very idea itself gives us a sense that there is a meaning to why we are here, and that we were actually loved into being which could, according to de Botton's analysis, sustain us for decades. If we grow up with the idea that we are connected and in a relationship with everything, and that our existence is crucial to the interdependence of all things, then we understand that what someone else says on the other side of the world can decisively impact our own feelings and thoughts about ourselves. We also come to understand that even saying something behind someone else's back, that being mean, can affect others in very subtle, yet significant ways; we cannot help but try to be more compassionate and loving. Of course, for many, this is a far removed idea. Many people have been born into environments that lack love, and there are many effects of such an existence. A closed or cold response to others from a child may indicate a child who has had experienced cold and unloving environments. Many children withdraw from loving environments if they are not accustomed to them, and tend to be distant as was discussed in the *Need to Feel*. A child's heart is a tender thing; children feel everything very deeply. If a child's heart is guarded, or they are protecting their heart they may respond in a variety of ways that don't seem very loving at all. Yet, as you become more aware you will see that even an angry child is just responding to an unmet *Need for Love* and the anger is a proclamation of the child who is asking just love me.

In my work with parents, I ask them to consider their own energy when they are responding to their children. I guide them to feel into their heart centre, and place the focus there (the heart centre is both the metaphorical as well as the literal anatomical location for the *Need to Love*). I then ask them to tell me what it feels like. The answers vary and it's often both powerful and challenging for parents to realise that when they are closed-hearted toward their children, they see more angry responses coming from them, and when they are open-hearted and loving, the child softens and opens up too. As researchers are becoming more aware of the literal energy of relationships, it is palpably evident that the child internalises adult behaviour (especially that of the primary caregiver) as a part of him or herself. If a parent is angry, then a child learns to be angry in his relationship with himself and others. Social relationships are largely guided by identification and imitation and parental identification is important when children are small as this allows children to feel that their parents are with them even if they are not physically present. It also speaks to the idea of connectedness and belonging that is so important in the human *Need to Love*.

Sibling Rivalry

Often adults do not realise when they are setting up an emotional distance between themselves and their children or between their children. This happens too when adults compare children, or make them compete against each other, which is hurtful to one or both, and retracts the flow of love. When we become aware, however, that at the root of the unmet *Need to Love* are emotions of anger, grief, sadness, irritability, jealousy, and hurt we are offered an excellent opportunity to transform these energies by exploring ways of relating with children and encouraging them to relate with each other in ways that make them feel loved and loving. Children (and adults) who feel love towards the self and others have greater self-acceptance and harmony, compassion, and empathy. Sibling rivalry is reduced if parents ask children to feel and think about whether their actions are loving or hurtful toward another. In doing this, you are helping them cultivate empathy, which allows children to feel the power behind making loving choices.

When it comes to everyday sibling rivalry, you can ask a child what they would feel if they had that thing said or done to them. By acknowledging that regardless of the situation, we all deserve love, there is a gentle knowing instilled in a child that everyone matters. Self-love can be cultivated easily and is not a difficult aim at all when we hold the belief that, "I matter as much as you." When we think someone or something is more worthy of our affection than we are, we will not feel worthy of receiving love, and may self-sacrifice and realise we are constantly heart-broken. The impact of a loving relationship is profoundly evident in the child's energy and life. Children, who have had loving interactions modeled to them daily, exhibit less social problems, less violence and mental illness, and improved physical health. Twins studies have been a rich resource for researchers, especially in regard to the nature-nurture concerns, mentioned previously, when asking the question why children do what they do. In one twins study, mothers were asked to separate the twins into categories in which one would be related to with more maternal positivity and warmth, and one would receive more maternal negativity and less warmth. The twin that was nominated by the mother to receive more maternal negativity and less warmth had more antisocial behavioural problems than the one that was regarded positively. Why mothers treat their children differently was one of the questions posed by the researchers, but the evidence was undeniable that the maternal emotional attitude towards children plays a causal role in the development of antisocial behaviour.[35]

Bullying

Bullying is the manifestation of the unmet *Need to Love*. It is actually the result of seeking love and approval, in most cases from a dominant male figure. Children who bully are in fact, looking for the acceptance and love of the central person in their lives.[36] Bullies try to use force to emotionally, verbally, or even physically coerce, threaten, or intimidate others, because they are looking for love. The implication of this kind of expressive behaviour is that if a child does not feel they are being treated with love, or the type of love they receive is dominating, it can be interpreted as the child never having learned that love does not dominate. A study of boy's bullying behaviours amongst football players found that the strongest predictor was the perception of whether the most influential male in a player's life would approve of the bullying behaviour. The importance of positive role models that do not intimidate or coerce others to receive love is immeasurable in terms of coming to understand how we love others.

Domestic violence is also referred to as a form of bullying, and the effects of such ways of relating in families, as well as possible supports, was discussed in the section *Need to Feel*. Part three provides relational approaches to assist when dealing with unmet love that presents as dominance and aggression. Love does not dominate and force, so a *Need for Love* is the foundation or first cause of bullying or any oppressive coercion. In reality, it is often hard to see the wound underneath of why someone would need to intimidate another, emotionally, verbally, or even physically. But in recognising the unmet need we get closer to understanding what the child is communicating, and at core they are proclaiming in a very real sense love me.

Empathy

Of course, it is not always easy to tap into the feelings of empathy that we know are possible when we are experiencing emotions such as hurt and betrayal, and yet, this is the healthiest response. Empathy has been defined as the ability to love and to share the feelings of others.[37] I would add to this, that empathy is also the ability to understand how another is feeling. The relationship between mirror neurons and empathy is attracting a lot of attention in many disciplines. A recent study on the relationships between mirror neurons, imitation, and empathy asks the reader to consider that the evolutionary process has actually wired humans for empathy. According to the author of this study, this means a major revision needs to be considered of widely held beliefs around empathy. Traditionally, self-serving individualism has been considered to be the foundation of our biology. Research on mirror neurons, imitation, and empathy, in contrast, tells us that our ability to empathise is a building block of our sociality[38] and morality, and has been built bottom-up from relatively simple mechanisms of action, production, and perception.[39] Researchers focusing specifically on the positive health implications of interpersonal flourishing argue that it is important to map the emotional configurations of quality social relationships so that more awareness can be made regarding expounding their physiological substrates.[40]

Problems with empathy are said to be major factors in many of our social problems, from violence to mental illness and even physical health, inferring that the quality of our relationships with others is central to optimal living. With empathy, children learn what the other is experiencing, which plays an important role in relationships, especially between siblings. One study measuring empathy looked to the adjustment of siblings of children with cancer. Empathy was found to be a significant predictor of externalising problems that the sick sibling experienced after diagnosis. Children's empathy meant they were able to feel for their siblings in these extreme circumstances, almost as if to help the one with cancer to cope better. The shared feelings meant that the experience is also shared, to a degree.[41] In effect, one child is giving to the other what it needs, if it cannot do this for itself.

Mirroring

Neuroscience gives us another clue to this phenomenon of mirroring in its research on mirror neurons. The mirror neurons help us comprehend the idea of imitation and mimicry. Research shows that people have a strong propensity to align their behaviour with others during social interactions. These forms of imitation and mimicry are both persistent and automatic. Additionally, they are said to function on a complex level.[42] The science behind the function of mirror neurons is vast, and not able to be explicated in full here.[43] Suffice it to say that the role of mirror neurons is important in the recognition and imitation of both the seen and hidden actions of others. Additionally, you may have also made the link between this mirroring and the idea of morphic resonance, which is further discussed in the *Need to See*, the 6th *Need* in this part.

The connection between mirror neurons and motor neurons is equally significant. Electrophysiological data confirms the existence of neurons that respond to both motor and sensory events in the macaque brain.[44] These mirror neurons respond to both specific actions performed by the self, as well as matching actions performed by others, providing what some are terming a potential bridge between minds.[45] While there is substantial evidence for a human mirror system, there are weaknesses in the attempts to localise such a system to the brain. It is suggested that there is strong evidence for a human mirror system in the central nervous system, which appears to originate from the motor system.[46] Others are attempting to research evidence of mirror mechanisms in humans and discuss their anatomical localisations in the body.[47] The child's imitative capacity is not restricted to those things they see, but significantly, also to the unseen but felt energetics, emotional dynamics, and interactional tensions of their environments.

It is important to recall here Rupert Sheldrake's idea of morphic fields, those energy fields that establish and unify the activity of the nervous system, inherited through morphic resonance.[48] Sheldrake sees this resonance as transferring a type of collective, instinctual memory, and states that in tangible, although mostly unseen ways, the child acts as a direct mirror for the total of the past as well. The child also contributes to the collective memory, affecting other members of the species in the future.

Heart Coherence

For decades HeartMath Institute has been researching the connection between body and mind, specifically the connection between the organs of the heart and the brain, as presented in *Science of the Heart: Exploring the Role of the Heart in Human Performance*.[49] I first became interested in the research being done at HeartMath about 20 years ago. As mentioned in the section the *Need to Feel*, HeartMath has conducted studies where they found intuitive information (feeling) is received before the brain makes sense of it (thinking). Additionally, HeartMath have found the body organs (their particular interest is the organ of the heart), sending more information to the brain than the brain sends to the organ.[50] The HeartMath Institute is actually one of the leaders in what is being called emotional physiology and heart-brain research. The heart and brain maintain a continuous two-way dialogue; each influencing the other's functioning. The signals that the heart sends to the brain can influence perception, emotional processing, and higher cognitive functions.[51] Neurocardiology researchers view this system and circuitry as a 'heart-brain'.[52] The interest for HeartMath has centered on the brain and magnetic field of this wonderful organ, the heart. Implications for researching the coherence between all of the body's organs, as Pert's Model suggests, is rather exciting in light of the energetics of our human experience, and how we send out signals and receive information back in through what we call our human consciousness.

If we can understand practically how my heart speaks to your heart, then we are better positioned also to be more loving in all of our relationships. If we know what happens to the respiratory system and the lungs in a state of grief, we can focus more awareness on the emotional pathways that lead from the brain to the many other organs in the body, and then from these organs back to the brain. The exciting research possibilities in this regard are immense. Practically, too, we can apply new ways to support children to know what their hearts really thrive on, what feels best to them, and so then, we can cultivate those potentials. Love, is a very dynamic, multidimensional interaction that appears to transcend individual love to relate to a force that has a vast potential in us all. To cultivate the *Need to Love*, however, we require a good dose of gratitude.

Gratitude

My childhood association with St. Thérèse taught me about a gratitude ritual that accompanied a set of beads. Ten little beads with a cross on a little piece of string, carried in a pocket, helped a child count ten things for which they were grateful. The beads are used to count the acts of love or sacrifices a person makes in a day (for God), and are also said to help a person to grow by increasing the acts of love they perform each day.[53] Did St. Thérèse know as she was making her way through her day, cultivating gratitude, that she was also supporting her wellbeing? I have a strong feeling she may well have known this, but she would not have called it wellbeing; rather, she would have called it devotion or love. Giving really is receiving, being open to receiving requires that we are grateful for the things we have in life. Small children can always find something to be grateful for, especially when we offer suggestions. Children, who think about, or write about gratitude, are more likely to be empathetic.[54] Robert Emmons, a leading researcher in the field of wellbeing, best known for his term, *Ultimate Concern*, has conducted multiple studies on the link between gratitude and wellbeing. Emmons' research confirms that gratitude effectively increases happiness and reduces depression. In one research study, *Counting Blessings versus Burdens: An Experimental Investigation of Gratitude and Subjective Well-Being in Daily Life*,[55] Emmons and McCullough found that conscious focus on blessings may have emotional and interpersonal benefits—increased well-being was recorded across several measures of "people's moods, coping behaviors, health behaviors, physical symptoms, and overall life appraisals."[56]

Summary

As a child grows in age, they do not stop requiring the *Need to Love*; they just cultivate a different type of relationship to it. The feeling we get when we feel we are lovable is wonderful at any age. Finding ways to communicate with your child in loving ways strengthens your connection to each other. The various symptoms of the child resulting from the unmet *Need to Love* might range at one end of the spectrum, as the presentation of self-punishing, self-rejection, or hoarding in the child, or at the other end, self-obsessed, fault-finding, or blame oriented behaviours. If a child is not supported to feel loved, then they will most likely not be able to experience the potentials that come from a stable, loving energy. Children (and adults) who feel loved and loving are open and accepting, they feel compassion for others, they are kind and caring with themselves and others, as well as the world and earth they are part of. Children with a strong sense of love are able to approach unfamiliar environments and new experiences with an inner balance.

Tips To Cultivate The Need To Love

At any age, in any situation, you can encourage your child to feel loved in the following ways:

- Encourage children to keep gratitude journals and write down those things for which they are grateful. Maybe make some gratitude beads and tell your child the story of the little saint that used to count ten things she was grateful for every day, so they can do this too.

- When the child can be reminded daily about gratitude in simple ways such as a discussion of gratitude, this helps a child to look for more things that they can be grateful for. Watch how this becomes a wonderful ritual after a short while.

- Encourage children to send loving thoughts to nature; the mountains, forests, and oceans as well as to animals, plants, and people.

- Mirror the child's love back to them in simple ways—thank you notes in the lunch box, positive affirmations on the bathroom mirror in an erasable text, or whatever you believe they might find meaning.

- Role-play with children allows them the opportunity to see how someone else might be feeling. When children reflect if their actions are loving or hurtful, it cultivates empathy, which allows children to feel the power behind making loving choices

- Ask children to feel their heart centre when they settle down after being angry—do not ask them while they are angry or they might act out in anger (timing is everything).

- If something makes your child feel upset or disappointed, assist them to express how they feel. By doing this with love, magically this mood will disappear.

- If the child is holding a grudge or being hurtful, ask them to think of new ways of being more loving with others, their brothers and sisters, or parents. There is an opportunity every minute to be more loving to yourself and others.

- Hug someone you love. When you do, all the love in your heart goes into their heart like a beautiful surge of energy between the two of you. Can you feel the love?

- See if you can name all the places where you can feel love in your home, in the garden, or in the busy city. Notice how much love there is around you, inside you, and how much love you can give to others.

- Occasionally have a day to do nothing but follow your heart for the whole day. This can be so much fun.

Needs Table 4 – The Need to Love

Potential of need as the centre point of balance

Deficient	Balanced	Excess
Self-punishing	Self-love	Self obsessed
Self-rejection	Self-acceptance	Fault finding/Blame
Hoarding	Sharing	Extreme giving
Lack of empathy	Empathy	Extreme worry for others
Cold, heartless	Compassion	Vulnerable
Withholding		
Timid	Self assured	Judgemental
Victim	Service	Martyr
Hurtful/Hate	Loving	Over seeking
Withholding	Affection	Co-dependant
Retract	Devotion	False idols
Grief	Forgiveness	Anger
Inhibited	Harmony	Assertive
Shy/Timid	Peace	Pushy
Suspicion	Kindness	Over giving
Unworthy	Worthy	Deserving
Manipulation	Care	Self-sacrificing

5. Children Need To Speak: Hear Me

"The limits of my language mean the limits of my world."

~ Ludwig Wittgenstein.

Children initially experience the world symbolically through vibration and resonance before verbal language begins to develop. The child is, in essence, proclaiming *Hear Me*.

Figure 7: Physical Location of the Need to Speak

Case 5: James

James had been diagnosed with the non-verbal learning disorder, Asperger's, on the broader Autism Spectrum. James was 7; his parents had expected that one day James would just start talking. As each year passed, that day seemed more and more distant. Experts had told James' parents about a number of effective strategies to promote speech. James' parents had tried them all - from visual supports, to imitation, to eye contact. None of these had the desired effect, that is, none of these had resulted in words coming out of James's mouth. Experts had also suggested that James' parents forget about hoping he would talk and begin to promote James' strengths in other areas of his growth and learning. Research indicates that there could be interactive and relational improvements in his life and James' could develop effective organisational skills. It was expressed that James's focus, as well as his social and emotional capabilities, could all be strengthened through these measures. James' parents had come to me with the last little bit of hope to see if there was anything that I could do that might promote language development in James.

Looking at James, he reminded me of a Botticelli angel. He was plump and wholesome; he had blonde ringlets and the most amazing blue eyes. I fell in love with James. I was so taken with his presence I forgot the central reason that he and I had met, the reason that we had come to be in the same room, was because he didn't talk. This had become the main focus in James' life, his lack of voice - rather than the many wonderful qualities emanating from his radiant little being. Even though James could not verbally communicate with the world he appeared peaceful and content. His parents said that they could not recall a time when he wasn't content; they expressed that he never got aggressive or frustrated and he was truly a peaceful child. James's parents however held the idea that their child's full potential would not or could not be realised, without speech.

When one expects verbal communication from children and this doesn't happen, one can feel at a loss or let down. This is how James's parents felt. James's parent's expectations are not unusual and they are mirrored in most civilised societies as we are geared to prefer speaking beings. The discussion on language formation, speech and making meaning continues later in this section. Jean Berko Gleason a child language expert tells us that, "We are innately predisposed to pay attention to little children and to talk to them. Let's not just assume that we are scientists sitting around watching babies unfold. We're unfolding with them."[57] If then, accordingly, we are unfolding with them as the whole of this book proclaims, then even when there is no verbal language, we are still unfolding with them. Rather than looking at what James lacks, according to expectations of others, I am intent on looking for what gifts he holds.

I did not expect James to talk, but I was interested to see what else he might communicate. "Does he seem to know things are going to happen before they do?" I asked and his parents nodded in response. "Is he highly affected by noise?" the parents nodded again. I ask these questions because there is so much else going on for James that science is only just beginning to help us understand. Recall in the *Need to Feel* I discussed the research on HSP (highly sensitive people) and people in this category process sensory data exceptionally deeply and thoroughly due to a biological difference in their nervous system. Dianna

Powell (2014) recognised in her research on autism, savant syndrome and abnormal brain function that there is the existence of extrasensory phenomena such as telepathy, remote viewing, and ESP within these people. She found that autistic children demonstrated telepathy to the greatest extent. Because of the differences in their brain function, "they see things more as they are it's like they're getting information in a pure sensory form."[58]

The general theme of the 5th Chakra energy is the physical as well as the symbolic relationship we have with language, signs and symbols. Specific themes such as: Creativity, Communication (Listening as well as speaking), Speech, Language, Voice, Authenticity, Truth, and Self-Expression as well as Symbolic - Resonance and Vibration. If we go a little deeper into the biology the associated anatomy and body systems of this 5th Chakra, which are the throat, mouth, speech issues, trachea, neck vertebrae, teeth and gums, oesophagus, parathyroid, hypothalamus, thyroid, and lymphatic system, we get more clues about what James is telling us. See the A-Z of common ailments associated to this 5th Need in Appendix 1. In the case of James, the link became evident, as the hypothalamus' primary function is homeostasis, which is to maintain the body's status quo or balance system-wide. It was James's hypothalamus that led us to a deeper understanding of his non-verbal presentation. In chronic activation of stress responses to an environment, which have been identified in developmentally delayed children, there are physiological changes that occur to help someone cope with the stress and the hypothalamic function is involved in this.[59] The hypothalamus receives and monitors information about the environment and coordinates responses through the nervous system.

Energetically we are only able to express so much energy. The child who is receiving information in a purely sensory form without needing to interpret it in the ways we have needed to before, may not as a result require the same expression of energy (that is, may not chose to utilise its energy as speech). In James's case he may not need the expression of energy to talk because he perceives (feels) and interprets (thinks about) his environment in a way that he needs for him, in a new way. The energy it takes to speak is not the most important use of energy for James' body system and so this is not activated. James was born into a new world and there is so much else going on for James to focus on rather than his lack of verbal communication, which may seem to pale to insignificance if he has access to a magical world of human superpowers. I imagine, by evoking Dianna Powell's research, that James is reading minds and energy through extrasensory phenomena such as telepathy, remote viewing, and ESP. In the next Section the *Need to See,* there is more detail about the abilities that we are seeing in children when these latent capacities and potentials such as ESP, and telepathy receive conscious cultivation in the child's life. James is unfolding, as he needs, according to a larger pattern of development than what we have known and one that perhaps does not require speech. After all James's world is not our world.

Another supporter of Autism, Faith Jegede (2012) said about her two Autistic brothers "The pursuit of normality is the ultimate sacrifice of potential." [60] Of course understanding the cause of Autism has been a contentious one on a spectrum of theories as broad as the spectrum itself. Bruno Bettelheim in Freudian fashion said that bad mothering caused Autism[61] and then recently there are many debates about vaccinations creating neurodevelopmental delays in children.[62] In 1964, Bernard Rimland's book *Infantile Autism: The Syndrome and Its Implication for a Neural Theory of Behavior* reinforced the neurodevelopmental link with Autism; a link that brought forth and was inspired by Rimland's own son who was on the Autism Spectrum.

Issues that present in children based upon the *Need to Speak* will vary among individuals, families, and cultures, although there are certain themes that could be considered the same for all. Creativity, for example, will vary for all children, and notions of creativity will also differ between individuals, families, and cultures. There are things, however, most people consider an expression of creativity. Lack of creativity may be exhibited at one end of the seesaw as a child struggling to find meaning in a creative activity (deficient energy regarding creativity), and on the other end, a child who is erratic, starting many things but never finishing them (excessive energy regarding creativity). These responses to self and life are appropriate as they arise, according to whether the child's needs are met or not. By identifying that an apathetic child is communicating a *Need to Speak* and that an erratic child is also communicating a *Need to Speak,* we are closer to being able to identify the source. Somewhere in the child's environment certain feelings and thoughts pertaining to a lack of creativity and expression are being activated.

> **Need to Speak - Common Themes**
> - *Language*
> - *Meaning Making*
> - *Language Formation-*
> - *Acquiring Speech*
> - *Truth*
> - *Telling Lies*
> - *Voice*

Language

Language is the many ways we express and communicate. It does not just relate to verbal expression, but other forms of expression, such as music, art, and importantly, body language. Children feel first and then language is added later to those feelings if it is necessary as we saw with James his communication involved extra sensory perception and as such, he didn't develop verbal language. The difficulty in the gap between feeling and spoken language lies in that fact that language is a poor indicator of feelings. Therefore, in the transition from a pure feeling state of experiencing to communicating what is felt or experienced something will be lost, as language is not a totally accurate translation of what is felt. As small children are not as articulate as many adults in verbalising the things they feel, they need attentive support to find the right words and expression.

Children have questions about the nature of the world, family histories, and things that challenge adult reasoning or verity, so many children are discouraged from questioning too much or verbally expressing their own realities when they are learning to communicate. Children should be seen and not heard still reverberates in many families and schools. It is easy to see then, that sometimes a child will shut down completely from expressing their feelings through language, as it is too difficult for them. Not because language is difficult for a child to learn, as you will see soon—they are genius in this regard—but because it is difficult due to the response of the adult who doesn't agree, cannot support, or does not want to hear the child's words. Children who are not given the space to communicate their deep felt feelings, emotions, needs, and insights to the adults in their life, on a day-to-day basis, often shut down from verbal expression.

A child who stutters is feeling hesitant about speech for some reason and we can look to see if we are putting too much pressure or importance on what children say. Stuttering involves involuntary hesitation and prolongation or repetition of sounds, and signifies a fear of the child to express itself, especially to an authority figure, so they verbally hesitate, remain uncertain, and worry that what they have to say will not be accepted.[63] Alternately, if an adult, for instance, says to a child, "What is it that makes this situation feel bad to you? I am listening to you. What you say matters to me," then they are honouring the child's expression. This type of interaction will set up good communication skills for life. (There is more detail about the relational space to offer children so they can express themselves in part three.)

Language acquisition in the child is dependant on their complex nervous system being able to integrate the sensory demands. Information supporting the language acquisition in the child has been traced to a function of the brain. Yet, when we actually look more deeply in search for the human language centres in the brain, their location in the brain is hard to find. Of course, there is much scientific evidence to support the idea that the seat of language, as well as the seat of the mind, is in the brain. This is why scientists have mapped brain regions to locate the language centre. The assumptions about language-specific areas of the brain, however, are now also being challenged.

"the number of so-called language-specific areas is multiplying on almost a daily basis. Every new functional imaging study seems to bring another language area to our attention. This all leads to the conclusion that domains like language do not live within well-defined borders, at birth or at any other point in development."[64]

Instead of the previous belief that one side of the brain dominates, both left and right brain processes are necessary to retrieve information (perceive), analyse (interpret), and work through the problem (act).[65] The information transfer from one side of the brain to the other is done in a naturally integrated manner, and whilst this is occurring, all is well, but if the chiasmic connection gets blocked, or various brain parts have difficulty recalling or retrieving information, the process stops.[66] The child's integration is aiming to work harmoniously. The idea that other parts of the complex body systems are also involved in language (such as the gut), are now being explored. The bidirectional pathways of gut and brain have already been shown to impact motivation and decision-making, and could possibly extend to language formation, which is an exciting possible research avenue.[67]

Meaning Makers

Babies learn a language, a shared communicative system that is symbolic. The sounds and vibrations a child hears and feels prenatally influence auditory and vibrational preferences after birth.[68] In fact, the mother's voice soothes the child and it releases vital bonding hormones in the child.[69] As we grow, we constantly organise and select the information our senses take in from the world, firstly through a cross-modal perception without language, and then later from the symbolic cultural and natural world through words, language, and signs. In this way, we are attempting to make sense of the world. Meaning is not transmitted to us, but we actively create it according to a complex interplay of codes or conventions of which we are normally unaware. We seem as a species to be driven by a desire to make meanings; above all, we are surely homo significant meaning-makers.[70] Daniel Chandler says that because, "we live in a world of signs, the only way that we understand anything is through signs and the codes into which they are organised." In this way, we can see that every family has symbols, codes, signs, and their own language of sorts, and this is how the child comes to know itself; through the family stories and the myth of the family, culture, and worldviews of which they are a part.

The words children use, the interest our children show in lyrics, poetry, and music, are all giving indications about what resonates with them in the way of their *Need to Speak* and self-express. Many great thinkers, including Plato, Aristotle, and St. Augustine, were interested in the relationship between the language we use, the signs, and how these relate to the individual, as well as how the individual relates with self and the world. St. Augustine, as already mentioned, was interested to dialogue with his own son, and the observations are of great interest in regard to the philosophy of language. Many thinkers are turning increasingly to experiential notions, such as metaphor and narrative, to demonstrate the degree to which we live in a semiotic engagement.

People exist and evolve in relation to their environments.[71] The expanse of our environments is being broadened almost every day with new discoveries in regard to the interconnectedness of many capacities. Neuro Linguistics Programing (NLP) is perhaps the best example of an approach of a mind-body system that assumes a systematic, patterned connection between neurological processes (neuro), language (linguistic), and learned behavioural strategies (programming).[72] Much of the broader coaching approaches are based upon this NLP principle of "change the language change the life." Ludwig Wittgenstein was instrumental in what is called the "Language Turn" in philosophy, and it is his quote that opens this part of the section on the *Need to Speak*, telling us, "The limits of my language mean the limits of my world."[73] It is true that one's language certainly reflects one's perspective.

The emergence of language could, therefore, be seen as one of the most important transitional pushes for the child seeking unity of body-mind-spirit. It is also the formation of so much more than language. It constitutes a major transitional process when the child goes from pre-verbal to becoming a speaking being, because this is the moment when naming and identification of things in the world becomes the axis on which the meaning of experience, and experience itself, is radically transformed. We all need to be conscious of, or look, to the language we use with children and our own language, which is harder to do because it has become embodied. We embody all of our experiences, and when these experiences happen, there is also a language that accompanies them. As the child goes about its day-to-day functioning, they are constantly receiving information from the natural world and from the symbolic and cultural world of words and signs. Children ingest this information (perceive) and organise it in a way of interpretation (think), which is how they make sense of the world. Children then act according to the way they understand and represent the world. Listening and paying attention to the way children speak about themselves and their world, better positions us to support children's wellbeing.

The transition to language can be softened if we can support children to stay in touch with their sensory experiences, whilst language development is taking place. Adults can do this by encouraging children to see that as well as naming things with words that the thing also can be known on other dimensions. You can have the child touch, taste, feel or smell a new thing whist also getting to know what it is called. Recalling the pacifier studies children do this naturally. If the child can feel and think in this unified way by combining their sensory experience whilst learning language from the beginnings, they maintain a unity consciousness.

Learning Language - Acquiring Speech

A child who learns language is expressing amazing innate capacities. All infants come into the world with innate linguistic skills and Steven Pinker, in his book, *The Language Instinct*, discusses how fast language learning takes place in young children. Pinker overviews all of the processes that occur in language acquisition, such as word acquisition, the production of sentences, as well as rule usage by young children. He calls the three-year-old a "grammatical genius". Pinker's language argument is briefly outlined as:

> "Language is a distinct piece of the biological makeup of our brains. Language is a complex, specialized skill, which develops in the child spontaneously, without conscious effort or formal instruction, is deployed without awareness of its underlying logic, is qualitatively the same in every individual and is distinct from more general abilities to process information or behave intelligently."[74]

Pinker says that scientists describe language as a faculty of a mental organ, or neural system, and characteristically uses computer-type models to explain the process. Language, to Pinker, is an instinct for the following reasons. There is an innate capacity for the child to learn a language and the idea of mimicry or mirroring is important in this capacity. For instance, the child learns the language of its environment. Almost all children learn to talk by instinct, but not all children learn to talk well. Reading and writing skills, however, do not seem to occur without some type of instruction. Noam Chomsky agrees with Pinker that language learning by young children happens very quickly, but Chomsky says that this cannot be explained simply in terms of imitation. It also appears to Chomsky that the structure of language is inherited in some way.

The wondrous capacities of the child, of course, might be seen in how language, and in particular, speech, happens. The acquisition of language in some special way seems to prepare the child for their world. A child surrounded by English-speaking adults, for example, will speak English, and those in a bilingual environment will become bilingual. Children who are introduced to two languages are not slowed in their development, and appear to develop both languages as if they were their native tongue. The interesting factor in bilingual or multilingualism is not so much in the acquisition of language, but rather in language retention. That is, in cases where one language is not valued or used by non-family adults or institutions, language retention is more difficult.[75] It seems that even in the case of language formation and continuation, if there is no meaning (or value) attached to the language, it will phase out.

Children are the ones to perpetuate languages, so if a particular language is spoken only by adults and not adopted by children, it will eventually die out accordingly.[76] In the same vein, just as morphic resonance, epigenetics, and quantum physics contend the implicate order is present in the child as memory from the past (family, society, culture, world), so, too, if the child does not perpetuate the beliefs, thoughts, and dominant discourses of the past, the dominant culture will also eventually die out. Our children are bringing with them capacities to create their own language and world, and their own way of healing the past by becoming aware of those things that are not needed anymore, because they do not represent the potentials within the child. We see this most particularly with new languages created by subcultures and computer coding, which are new languages for a new world.

Not all children talk as we saw in the case of James, and some talk later than families, society, or culture expects them to. Interestingly, the way we are rushed, forced, and restricted in our speech points to the fact that we are not really encouraging the most positive aspects of the *Need to Speak* in our children. Some children communicate with family every day, but have no verbal skills due to a subtly attuned nature and an intuitive, almost telepathic, knowing. Questions arise for many adults in regard to whether to allow children to find their own pace in speech versus holding them back or pushing them forward with certain therapeutic interventions. I have witnessed some children begin to verbally communicate almost all of a sudden at five years of age when they begin to interact with the other children. But there is often pressure for them to be ready and so may have speech therapy. I know it is not easy to stand up against the education system's requirements as a teacher or a parent if a child is non-verbal and in this regard this type of conflict is real for parents, as they are informed that a good command of language is necessary for the child to be accepted into school. Sometimes something else is happening in the child, as we are seeing more children than ever before that are not developing speech and verbal language as we saw with James. It is my contention that all children including those with a special needs label, are contributing to the (revisiting) and the collective shift of how we understand the self and what we call our human experience as it moves through space and time. [77] The autistic person appears to be in a direct, unmediated communication with the field of consciousness and is receiving sensory information in a way that allows for a merger of the broader consciousness, as discussed in part one. How the information processes occur will vary for everyone, but the autistic brain function appears to be picking up subtle energies in a much more sensory way (through their body as a primary transmission).

Autistic children's experiences are still predominately interpreted based upon a mind or thought based (cognitive) developmental approach rather than a whole soul (body-mind-spirit) interpretation. Parents of children labeled autistic have actually been a major force behind new approaches to working with autism by seeking for themselves, through research and learning, to better understand and be a voice for their children. This is having impacts not only for autistic children, but also in the ways we understand and approach the child more broadly.[78] The parents of special needs children have to speak up for their own beliefs in a way they have not before, or they have to learn to move away from the dominant verbal communication as a way of being, and become much more energetically attuned to their child in order to connect with them. In the case of autistic children, they are pushing the parent to their full potential too to speak their truth. After all, love, compassion and a soul motivation can move obstacles that the rational mind might see as immovable.[79]

Truth

Sometimes truth, the most basic moral and ethical capacities of being truthful, seems to go by the wayside as we look to how we educate children. Critical thinking and cognitive ability seems to take precedence over the truth and appear more important than keeping children connected. When deciding if children are ready for formal schooling, research undertaken by the Australian Institute for Family Studies (AIFS) posits that "a good start to school depends on three fundamental skills: the ability to communicate effectively; an ambition to learn; and the ability to fit in with others."[80] A longitudinal study of Australian children conducted by the AIFS psychologists declared "our children are ready for school when they know how to conform or fit in." Then, it is further expressed that the way to tell if a child fits in is by their ability to lie. The researchers explain, "Telling white lies is a common social phenomenon that helps us to fit in with our peers."[81] Children in the study participated in the peeking game, which examines how well children have mastered the art of lying.

> *"We frequently tell prosocial lies which demonstrate moral judgment and politeness, and this is an important social skill for new school children as they step into the wider world. When children begin to tell lies, it is a sign they have hit a new cognitive milestone. It shows their brains are able to manage the complex processes required to formulate a lie, and for those who can lie persuasively, that they also have the verbal skills to carry the lie through."*[82]

The balance between the cognitive ability of the child and the idea of right and wrong is somewhat skewed. Interestingly, too, even for Aristotle, it seems that as long as the goal of the lie is ultimately happiness, the lie is justified, but one's ultimate happiness is not always the result of fitting in, and perhaps, it is also derived from standing out.

Society as a whole seems more focused on our children fitting in, than it does about developing what is best for them according to them. In this regard, society might be based upon a *Noble Lie*, which according to Plato, is a story or untruth knowingly told by the influential to maintain social harmony. And not only are we often denying hearing the truth of the child, we are in fact encouraging lying. The reasons for any child to lie ought to be considered across the whole child, not just the cognitive ability, as the effect on the child of telling a lie can be destructive to the child and the functioning of the whole.

The child may well repress, deny, or project the guilt, shame, or other emotions that result from knowing that they have lied. Even though the lies in this study are expressed as prosocial—that is, the lie is justified as it is deemed and understood to be polite—the lie, however, regardless of justification, is still an action that comes from a disparity between the feeling and thoughts of the child, and is an external manifestation coming from incongruence in the child. Carolyn Myss tells us that, "Truth has its own monitoring device: that is, you can never lie to yourself about compromising a truth. Further your biology itself will show signs of the stress when you become incongruent with a truth."[83]

It is important to also note as we are focusing on strengthening the child's *Need to Speak* that it is not just imbalanced when the child lies, but the parent lying to a child is equally damaging. Even little white lies create potential imbalances that result from this unmet *Need to Speak* truthfully. In everyday parlance, there is often a differentiation made between telling little white lies, which are prosocial, and other lies; the former are positively sanctioned (as was discussed in the white lie telling study). What they don't know won't hurt them, is tautology often used to dismiss the need to tell the whole truth to children. Yet the child already feels the truth. The untruths or partial truths are just as destructive as other forms of lies. Lies might be told with words, but lies are also told by the body, by one's actions, and by being carried over genetically. We are continually sending mixed messages if our *Need to Speak* is imbalanced. Ironically, telling the truth is also largely shunned. We say to our children, "Don't ask that lady why she has no hair. It's rude!" When a child naturally expresses curiosity about a person (they see) without hair whom you think may have cancer. Or, "Don't look at that homeless man!" when a child feels empathy and wants to help someone carrying their belongings in a shopping cart. Adults may persuade the child to behave, or even coerce them to keep quiet.

Children challenge adults with their *Need to Speak* and may be discouraged from questioning too much or verbally expressing their own realities. Our children want to know the truth, and denying the truth of what is present is often the point at which children stop asking for evidence of truth with verbal questions. But the energy of the questioning and the need for confirmation of truth or falsehood does not go away. The questions unanswered or that are unable to be explored actually create confusion and inhibit the child's natural curiosity. The child is just attempting to put words or actions to the feeling of tension; tension that perhaps the adult has become immune to, or is avoiding. These types of avoidances have put many children in dangerous situations. Children should be seen and not heard still reverberates in many families and schools. It is easy to see then, that sometimes a child will shut down completely from expressing their feelings through language, as it is too difficult for them. Many children are shushed and the child's natural resonance with truth, which is a particular strength of the *Need to Speak*, is not always valued.

Telling Lies

We seem to presume that children are not as articulate as adults in expressing the things they feel because they cannot verbalise their feelings with clarity. And yet, research shows that children as young as four years of age can categorise up to three different types of deliberately false and true statements as lies and truths; further, children also believed that lies were worse than truths.[84] Children who have absorbed the energy of the family secrets will invariably express this repressed energy in some way, shape, or form. I think it is probably fair to say that given the opportunity, most people would take hearing the truth, regardless of how painful, over a continual betrayal of the truth. What they don't know won't hurt them, is an insult to the child, as children know already. As one professional told me, "Children by the age of 6 months will know every family secret." In the majority of families, secrets are communicated as much by the way in which information is revealed, as what adults refuse to talk about. Often, the child will be blamed if they bring up taboo subjects.

It is axiomatic within Western psychological models of the self that individuals need to be heard and listened to, because this enables individuals to develop their own inner voice and truth. This discourse acknowledges that the keeping of secrets, and the converse, of not expressing them in some way (through verbal or even other forms of expression) eventually becomes detrimental to one's wellbeing. It is still a hard habit to break. For Freud, the 'talking cure' was precisely the antidote to the corrosive effect of harbouring untidy secrets. Studies of adults who have maintained unreasonable secrecy have looked to its pathological impact upon the secret-keeper, such as health problems, obsessiveness, and emotional distress.[85] When looking to the effect on adolescents of keeping secrets from their parents, it was also found that what adolescents intentionally keep secret from their parents determines their wellbeing and psychosocial development in negative ways more so than what they disclose to them.[86]

Children who are free to express at an early age are more likely to continue to express what is going on for them later in life. In fact, when a child feels that they can express what they are feeling and that it will be acknowledged, they are able to cope with even very difficult situations. Life situations that are left unprocessed will lead to debilitating issues in the longer term, and not just for the individual but all of their relationships. The point to be made is that the ability for a child to express itself will also be regulated by how well the child perceives their expression will be received. How much will what I say even matter? There are many reasons adults may deflect or close down to hearing what a child wants. Mostly, this happens when adults are struggling within themselves. Sometimes we are too busy, or feel we have too much going on in our own lives, to offer the space for the child to honestly express itself. Often, parents hold back on asking children what they need, as they may feel the situation is too hard to fix or is too damaging. Studies looking at cases of divorce confirm that children want to be given a voice and be heard in regard to the decisions about their lives when there is a situation of marriage separations. Many parents do not want to trouble children and so make decisions for them rather than talking about the situation. Paradoxically, studies show that children express they could cope with the changes of divorce with more certainty if they were kept honestly informed and involved in the decisions that need to be made that involve them after such experiences.[87] If such transitions that happen in separated families can be made with an inner integrity of feelings and thoughts children can cope with even the most perceived traumatic experiences.

Voice

The voice of children is a term that indicates that the child ought to have access to verbalising and igniting their creative potentials as they grow. The notion of student voice is the idea that students can and should have a role in the decision-making and changes that affect them in schools. Student voice opportunities appear to contribute to youth development, creating meaningful experiences that meet fundamental developmental needs, especially in cases where students fail to find meaning in other school experiences. [88] The growth of agency, belonging, and competence developed in the act of encouraging children to recognise their feelings and formulate them within language and actions, has been shown to greatly enhance developmental outcomes.[89] In doing so, we come to see children actually can solve many of their perceived problems when given the opportunity. When we become aware that is the *Need to Speak* is unmet the subsequent energies of nervousness, uncertainty, yelling, and silence (mutism) can arise. When we can see this we are offered a great opportunity to transform these energies by exploring ways of relating with children that make them feel like they can express anything that is happening in their lives. Student voice is a great start.

Summary

As a child grows in age, they do not stop requiring the *Need to Speak*. They may even close down and not use verbal language during certain points in their growth. Teenagers are even known to mumble sometimes. The ability to speak about what matters and what we need is a foundational requirement, not just in childhood, but also in life. Allowing your child to speak regardless of how hard it is to hear what they say, allows them to feel they can express themselves. When we allow the *Need to Speak* it means that we may not always like what we hear, and so it is important to stay open to the expressions of the child. As caregivers, we can look to those aspects of our own life in which we have had difficulty speaking. You can ask yourself if you find it easy to express yourself, or do you feel there are many things that you are unable to verbally communicate? Do you have someone in your life that encourages you to speak about what really matters to you? Have you spoken up in the past about an injustice that you felt or experienced, and then were made to feel wrong for bringing it to attention? Do you find it easy to express yourself, or do you feel there are many things that you are unable to verbally communicate? (The various symptoms of the child resulting from the unmet *Need to Speak*, might range at one end of the spectrum as the presentation of mutism, nervousness, and stuttering, and at the other end, loud bold, and dominant behaviours.) Children (and adults) who are free to speak have a deep sense of meaning, creativity, self-expression, and great communication skills (both listening and speaking).

Tips To Cultivate The Need To Speak

At any age, in any situation, you can encourage your child's *Need to Speak* in the following ways:

- Encourage your child to say what they are feeling. You can encourage with affirmative statements, "Your voice allows you to tell others around you what you need and how you feel. It is important to express how you feel to others and not to hold back from saying what matters."

- If you are part of a big family or in a class, encourage everyone to take turns in order to listen to them and let them all express themselves. A talking stick is a wonderful addition to any dining table or classroom. If a child has trouble saying what they need, you can encourage them to write it down, draw, or use some other form of expression.

- Support your child to voice their truth. Explain, "What is true for you may be different for others. I can see how sometimes it may be hard for you to feel that you can speak your truth."

- Use welcoming words such as, "I am listening to you," as these ignite conversation. Even whilst conducting another task around the child you can still invite conversation. "I am doing dishes but I am also listening." You will sense when the child requires your full attention and you can then direct all your energy to them when they are ready.

- If your child is confused or doubtful about expressing themselves, don't speak for them, give them the space they need.

- We can encourage children that the right thing to say will always come if we relax. Relaxing sets the energy for them to draw on a supportive form of expression. You may like to ask them to visualize swirling energies of numbers, colours, ideas, sounds, and vibrations all flowing in and through them.

- Assist children to feel the part of their body, or even a part of their life, that feels blocked creatively if they are not able to talk. You can reassure them that sometimes the flow of creativity might get blocked—you can feel this as unease within your body and life.

- Comment on the things you appreciate about the child; not just one word, but a whole story of why something is so appreciated. Everybody loves to be appreciated.

- Dress up play is a magical way of expressing. Maybe you like to put on a show and entertain others. Being in character often helps a child have a safe space to express, as they can imagine someone else can do it even if they can't.

- Encourage silly talk sometimes and you can have a whole conversation in gibberish to see if you can understand each other at all!

- Have periods of silence. Many of the child's other senses are activated if you play a game in which you don't speak for a while—not as a punishment, but as a nurturance. An hour might lead to a day, in some cases, and writing notes to communicate is a fun way to activate other forms of expression other than verbal.

- Be mindful that you do not interrogate children to get them to speak. If they are not in the mood to talk, you can open the dialogue by expressing how your day was. Make this fun by recounting all the wonderful things you did. This will support them to follow the energy and share when they are ready

Needs Table 5: The Need to Speak

Potential of need as the centre point of balance

Deficient	Balanced	Excess
Indifferent	Creativity	Erratic
Withdrawn	Expression	Outgoing
Secrets	Truth	Lies
Listen to others too much	Listening	Block out what others say
Preoccupied	Hearing	Overtaking
Despondent	Communication	Demanding
Fear of speaking	Speech	Loud tone
Speaking quietly	Speech – audible	Shouting
Slow	Speech – pace	Quick
Withholding	Speech as command	Telling
No interest	Resonance	Repulsed
Shy to express	Authenticity	False truth
Mumbling	Voice	Overpowering
Clearing throat	Voice	Interrupting
Mutism	Language	Silences others
Indecisive	Creative	Gossip

6. Children Need To See: See Me

If I can dream it, I can do it."

*~Walt Disney*90

Children need to believe and imagine their best growth according to what they feel and think. The possibilities and potentials that can be imagined and dreamt about are quite astounding. The child is, in essence, proclaiming *See Me*.

Fig 8: Physical Location of the *Need to See*.

Case 6: William

William is 5, and he has recently started school. William had come home from school a few times quite distressed, because his new friends at school had told him that his imaginary friend was not real. William was brought to see me because William's mother wanted to find a way to support him to transition into school without being made fun of. The mother reported, William was mostly a happy child. He had previously been content in his own little world, but when he had started school there was a change in William. The mother described the change had come due to what other children were saying about William's imaginary friends. His mother relayed the advice she had given William, "I have told him, you cannot continue to talk about your imaginary friends anymore." She had also told William "People do not like it when you talk about things they can't see."

William's imaginary friend's name is Sam. William told me "Sam did not want to come to see you; he wanted to stay home just to be safe." This type of imaginary dialogue is common for many children with imaginary friends, and I nodded in acknowledgement, so William knew that I understood. Children literally live between the worlds (material and spiritual), and those unseen dimensions, which shape the manifest reality of our lives, are often just as strong and real for children as the seen. Children become confused when others cannot understand something that they imagine. This confusion means children often leave this inner imaginary world behind so they fit in with others or so they will not be picked on. For a long time it has been believed children with an imaginary friends need psychological help. New evidence however suggests that those who have imaginary friends are engaging in creative play. Childhood imaginary friends are linked to adult creativity.[91] Imaginary play is discussed in more detail soon as this part on the *Need to See* progresses.

William feels comfortable with me and begins to tell me spontaneously that 'days and numbers have colours. Seven is blue and Tuesday is yellow'. William's expression tells me he is very connected. Synesthesia is a neurological phenomenon in which more than one neurological pathway is activated to interpret things. If one sensory pathway or one cognitive pathway gets activated it leads to automatic, involuntary experiences in a second sensory or cognitive pathway.[92] And it also indicated to me, that William was drawing on multiple interpretations as he decided which information might serve him best. A sense of being able to see, both physically and intuitively, the bigger picture of one's existence is central to the *Need to See*. The energetic and symbolic pathways pertaining to the 6th Chakra (*Ajna*) include themes of clarity of perception, more specifically vision, imagination, dreams, psychic faculties, and archetypal and pattern recognition. When William's mother came to know that these above-mentioned associations were a natural part of our human *Need to See*, and an important part of our whole growth, she began to reflect on her own childhood. In her own childhood she said those things that only she could see as well as too much sensory information had overloaded her, especially when she saw visions.

William's mother loved hearing me say that one's imagination is a vital part of one's whole development. As William's mother became more relaxed and open to the possibility that one's imaginary friend is an important part of our lives, I reminded her of the words she had expressed earlier "people do not like it when you talk about things they cannot see." William's mother, it turns out, was actually speaking from experience and as she opened up to me, she asserted that she knew what it was like to be ridiculed for having an imaginary friend and thus had closed down many of these potentials I spoke of, in her own life. Because William's mother had been ridiculed for having an imaginary friend, it is easy to see how she would have felt that it was best for William to conceal his friend. She had to do this for herself when her parents had told her the same story about other children not understanding the friend. William's mother's parents had advised her to say goodbye to the friend. She recounted the friend was given an imaginary train ticket and sent to visit another imaginary child far away. Ingenuous as this solution of the parents seemed, it was still a solution from an *adult push* onto the child. The adult's (Williams' mothers' parents) took it upon themselves to rewrite the story about (interfere in and make the interpretation for the child) her imaginary friend, and in doing so interfered with the child's relationship to her own *Need to See* and her ability to create her own solution in this matter.

The demise of her relationship with the imaginary friend did not make sense to William's mother and this confused her as a child. The imaginary friend disappeared because the story that the child held and the story that the parents told were at odds. William's mother said to me "Just because they could not see the imaginary friend did not mean I could not." This confusion has set up a type of nervous system response in the mother, who told me she suffered from feeling on edge all the time and recalled that this started after the imaginary friend had been sent away. Children with Nervous System issues, learning challenges and problems with their eyes, ears, nose (sinus) for example, indicate an imbalance in this need. See the A-Z of common ailments associated to this 6th Need in Appendix 1.

How does one even reconcile the difference between what I see and feel and what you're telling me to see and feel? William's mother told me that as much as she wanted to support William to keep his imaginary friend, she was also concerned that he would be hurt because of it. An imaginative child requires as a first point to have modeled to them imaginative relationships and the mother was inhibiting this to a degree. Not because she didn't want to support William, but she has difficulty seeing her own unmet need. Many of us have either been forced or regulated to stop dreaming and using our intuitive capacities. Many have adopted a belief that fantasy and imagination should be left behind in the pursuit of more practical and rational approaches to our lives. Do you have a clear vision for your life, or do you feel that the things that you want to create in your life are not possible for you? Do you see yourself and others through a lens of imaginative possibilities? Can you see you are part of a much larger potential that supports you always? Do you receive clear indications for your best growth through your visions, dreams, and imaginings? Maybe you stopped feeling at some point that you could create the life you dream of, or maybe you even stopped imagining a brighter future for yourself.

Vision, for example, will differ among individuals, families, and cultures; and yet, there are certain visions we all share as humankind. When the *Need to See* is not met there will be an energetic response. On one end of the spectrum or seesaw, a child who has no vision for their life and is not able to see beyond their current conditions (deficient energy in regard to vision), and on the other end, a child may seem to live in a fantasy land (excessive energy in regard to vision). These responses to self and life are very appropriate, as they arise according to what the child needs, but is not getting. The unimaginative child is communicating the *Need to See* and a daydreaming child is also communicating the *Need to See*.

Need to See - Common Themes

- *A Soul Vision*
- *Mirroring*
- *Learning*
- *Psychic Abilities*
- *History of Schooling*
- *School Learning*
- *Alternative Learning*
- *Play and Imagination*
- *Dreams and Sleep*

A Soul Vision

The ideas about being the best one can be, always aiming for the best, seem to be associated with the idea of a divine or a superhuman capacity available to all human beings. Every child, at some point it seems, is drawn to super heroes or angels. Being able to have a vision of our greatest potential is an important one in the actualisation of such potential. If we are to see our child as a soul, that is, a part of an eternal stream of consciousness connected to all of life from the past and all that will come to be, offers children a powerful image to work with. Granted, it is not even necessary to tell children this, or even to try and find ways to show them, as this is how they are already. All you have to do is believe this for yourself as their caregiver, because if you believe it, the child will feel it. Holding a feeling of sacredness in regard to your child is supportive of the reality of who they are, and yet, as we move through our day-to-day experiences, we rarely remember this truth. Such an affirmative image of the child is an accurate reflection of the child's true nature, and yet the whole soul concept has been difficult to reconcile and animate in our lives and the lives of our children.

As we grow, a less than grand vision often replaces the imaginings of all the possible dreams we have for our lives and ourselves. Donald Winnicott, mentioned earlier, conceptualises the self as consisting of a *True Self* and a *False Self*. *True Self* is that self that experiences life as, and of, aliveness. This aliveness is unifying in the sense that it is not just about the mind, but includes the body's life-sustaining functions, such as the heart's action and breathing.[93] The *False Self* is a constructed self that is in opposition to the *True Self*. Winnicott's conceptual picture of the self, posits that the *False Self* develops from wanting in a manner that supports what others want and need. As you know by now, I would reframe this to say that the *False Self* develops as a result of the separation of the unified feeling, thought, and action of the child. The feelings I have must be denied, repressed, or done away with if I am to exist for another. This way of relating then becomes central to the self, and in contrast to the *True Self*, because we seem to have the propensity to want to please and, of course, belong.

A *False Self* it seems is a better option than no self, or at least a better option than feeling always a separated or fragmented self. As we move through life and seek unity of body-mind-spirit, we are looking out to the world in a way to grasp those things that resonate and mirror back our felt sense of connection and unity. If we cannot see this reflected back, it seems natural then, that we would need to hold onto something that makes us feel unified, even if it's a substitute. We need to find some reflection, even if it is a false or unhealthy one. The child, in its natural push for unity, will grasp what holds meaning for them. As expressed throughout, you can see now that children's behaviours, issues, and symptoms often become the thing they hold on to. The problems start to become central to the life of the child. When an adult wants to assist a child, they can offer them opportunities to rework the representations and interpretations, children have and, in effect, the visions they hold about themselves. There is a foundational need in all of us to be seen as a soul, and from this point, any assistance offered to the child allows for the origin of any unmet need to be identified more quickly.

As mentioned earlier another of the most significant transitional opportunities for maintaining unity of the soul occurs when a child sees its own reflection for the first time. This idea is understood as *Mirror Theory*, which is marked as the point when the child sees and recognises itself in the mirror.[94] In Object Relations Theory the child transitions from the idea that it is all-powerful, to the idea that it is not so. The child transitions, in a moment, from the feelings, thoughts, and way of being in the world that assumes greatness and a divine unity; the child is mostly working in a harmonious and integrated way. When we begin to observe ourselves as separate, we begin to interpret the inner and outer world from this point of separation. This perception of separation is quite traumatic. When the child sees itself for the first time in a mirror, they see a separation between what is felt and what is seen. Observations made of children that enter 'the mirror stage' report that the child at first seems perplexed by the image that they see reflected back to them.[95]

Perhaps the child may wonder, "Is that who I am? I have felt that I was more than just what I see in this image. I am bigger and more expansive than what I see." Adults then encourage the separation by saying things like, "That is you! Look at you!" and the like. While looking in the mirror at their own image, the child begins to construct a relationship to itself and others that is based upon its image, not its essence. We become objectified to ourselves. *The False* Self or ego emerges and the confusion is hard to reconcile. This transition can be softened if we can support children to stay in touch with their sensory experiences, whilst the recognition of the image is taking place. I often consider the difference for our children's sense of self and belief in their *True Self*, or their ability to see themselves as a soul, if the first time a child saw their image in a mirror, they were met with, "that is just a reflection of you. The real you is your soul; you cannot always see your soul, but you can always feel who you are. Although you seem separate from your image, you are not separate from anything; it is just an illusion." Of course, we might not use those words, but if we could, for instance, repeat to the child as we look at them in the mirror, "What you see in the mirror is just a part of you.

The other parts are inside and come in the form of the feelings you feel." This may be a significant enough measure to allow the thought or idea of unity to be maintained. I believe this transition is pivotal to how we come to see ourselves from this point on. [96]

The child is reportedly mostly perplexed because they may wonder, "How do I find what I felt to be me before I saw the illusion of me? What in the world will give me that feeling again?" This reassurance of unity as a soul rarely occurs, and so the journey, back to unity begins. And as we grow, the search intensifies. Typically, in the child's search for meaning, we see them seeking a reflection, a representation of their unique brilliance in the outer world. What they see reflected back is just a projection of their own parents, society, and what their culture deems best, grafted onto them. This is not always conscious, and yet as expressed previously, what is expected of the child from others (consciously or unconsciously) becomes the principal guide in the child's forming ideas of self. The rise of the selfie is perhaps the transitional need of the new generation to find themselves beyond the projected image. This is perhaps also why 'the mirror principal' as a transformative practice, begun by Louise Hay in 1984, is such a powerful self-help technique. Mirror work entails looking at oneself in a mirror and repeating positive affirmations. [97] Without images and reflections that incorporate the most affirmative vision, one of the soul (body-mind-spirit), a child will continue to go about life looking for the meaning of their existence in the outside world. They may look to dominant institutions such as the media, peer groups, family, or educational authorities to mirror back their unique brilliance, but often what is reflected back is far from soul affirming.

From this point of the *False Self*, the child ceases to perceive their experiences from the essence of who they are, from their True Self, their soul, and begins to observe and then further speak about themselves as an individual and separate being. Thus, children begin to view themselves as copies of something or someone else rather than unique creations with a unique destiny. *The Society of the Spectacle*, proposed by Bebord and discussed in the *Need to Love*, highlights how these bonds and ideas about being our greatest self are tied to an image rather than the reality of who we are. Plato's legacy reverberates again, and his Forms of Good Truth and Beauty seem to be tied today to material and often confusing notions for our children, which obscure the chance of them seeing themselves as souls.

Mirroring

How the adult (parent, mother) assists the child in these times of realisation of separation becomes paramount in securing the child's wellbeing and unity. This is always for Winnicott, the mother, and as you have seen, the bond that is formed from the earliest moments in the womb means the mother is the child's everything. If the mother wants to support her child to navigate the transitions as a unified whole, or at least return to unity as easily as one can, the mother needs to demonstrate to the child that she has faith in the child's abilities. In fact, the mother needs to feel confident in the child's capabilities if she wants the child to feel confident in his/her own capabilities. Mirroring, as has been mentioned on numerous occasions throughout the book, is a central theme in the way a child absorbs its environment and is best summarised in the following way: The mother, in order to support the child and allow the child autonomy and independence, has to distance herself gradually and smoothly. She also has to allow the child to come to know that it is a separate entity from her in the gentlest of ways, so the child does not take it personally. This can be achieved if the mother simply acknowledges the child's inherent greatness. Or, as Winnicott says, this happens well when the mother accepts the infant's illusion of omnipotence, as well as her ability to provide gradual disillusionment.[98]

When the primary caregiver (usually mother, at least initially) can keep an affirmative relationship with the child and see the child as a soul, the child can gradually come into being in the world in a way that finds a balance point between knowing it's a soul, but also knowing it's a human being. However, if there is an imbalance in the mother due to her own unmet needs, she may hold on to the child as a means to satisfy them, and whilst doing so, continue to meet the child's needs, but excessively. If the mother believes that she is the only one who can accomplish the meeting of the child's needs, even well after the child can do things for themselves, the outcome will be a sense of frustration in the child's sense of omnipotence. The child wants to feel all their greatness as a soul, but they are not able to activate this if someone is doing everything for them all the time. If the mother discourages the infant to forge an attachment with others or withholds affection and fails to meet the child's needs, the child will equally respond to life from a profound sense of frustration. This tendency for human frustration may be eased, not by continuing to blame the mother for not knowing what the child really needs, but by seeing the child as a capable and competent soul, even when they're not fully able in a biological sense.

In psychoanalysis, the focus on attending to the importance of instinctual experiences and the individual's reactions to frustration, there is also an innate capacity to overcome the frustration of not feeling unified and transitional phenomena holds the key.

> *"Psychoanalysts still tend to think of health in terms of the state of ego defenses. We say it is healthy when the defenses are not rigid, etc. But we seldom reach the point at which we can start to describe what life is like apart from illness or absence of illness. That is to say, we have yet to tackle the question of what life itself is about. Our psychotic patients force us to give attention to this sort of basic problem. We now see that it is not instinctual satisfaction that makes a baby begin to be, to feel that life is real, to find life worth living. In fact, instinctual gratifications start off as part functions and they become seductions unless based on a well-established capacity in the individual person for total experience, and for experience in the area of transitional phenomena. It is the self that must precede the self's use of instinct; the rider must ride the horse, not be run away with."*[99]

Consequently, the child needs to develop a sense of self that is grounded in its own competencies and to express what it feels it needs. The degree to which this process unfolds toward the child's best flourishing can be assisted by caregivers as they become mindful of certain imbalances in the child. If accomplished in a good enough way, adults can safeguard the child from anything that might not support the child's omnipotence or, practically speaking, the unity of feeling, thinking, and acting, or at the very least, notice when this has occurred. Allowing the child to see its greatness as a soul enables them to see a higher purpose of their existence and important patterns of energy that supports its dreams, imagination, and vision. [100]

Learning

We need to ask, is it really an illusion that the child is omnipotent, as it has been suggested above? After all, we now know that they are, indeed, one with the greater energetic force that creates and sustains life. Of course, this has been a challenging acceptance, and yet, we see this thinking latent in the process of seeking unity that is innate. Why is it so difficult, then, to allow children to unfold according to their own plan? Perhaps because we believe we need to teach and that children need to be taught to learn. Children are learning all the time. However, all children learn differently. Some children appear to not like learning at all, but that is just an appearance. We are all born with a natural capacity to learn. Language learning, learning patterns, morphic resonance, the field, and inherited memory, all display how much the child is absorbing and learning without any conscious awareness at all. How we know what children know, as well as how they learn and what is going on for them has been greatly assisted by research in embodiment – that is the reality that because humans have bodies that are, "multiple overlapping and time-locked sensory systems that enable the developing system (child) to educate itself—without defined external tasks or teachers—just by perceiving and acting in the world."[101]

When we look more deeply to these types of studies that consider babies' abilities; we see that they are well equipped to solve problems, and they do this mostly through exploration (play) via an adaptive (as opposed to a maladaptive) innate ability to achieve goals.[102] Although babies are observed to explore, move, and act in highly variable and playful ways that are not goal-oriented and seemingly random, in fact, it is through whimsical activity that babies are discovering both new problems and new solutions.[103]

> *"Young mammals, including children, spend a lot of time in behaviour with no apparent goal. They move, they jiggle, they run around, they bounce things and throw them, and generally abuse them in ways that seem, to mature minds, to have no good use. However, this behaviour, commonly called play, is essential to building inventive forms of intelligence that are open to new solutions."*[104]

We are all born with the ability to perceive beyond our senses. The multimodal capacities of the child allow even the youngest of infants to perceive beyond the senses. The information that is encoded out there in the field of energy and supporting the child's growth and advancement, as well as the functions happening in the child's biological body at a cellular level, really do position the child as a remarkable being. The unifying perception of infants as clarified by Eva Simms earlier, suggests that the gestural presence, the non-verbal spontaneous actions, offers a valid basis for reinterpreting the discoveries of developmental research, and in particular, those adult-centric or deficient models of psychological and cognitive development.[105] Recall in order to demonstrate the unity of the child, Simms looked at pacifier studies conducted by Meltzoff and Borton that showed the degree to which infants actually perceive across different sensory modalities, without the need for prior learned correlations and do so instinctually.

Psychic Abilities

Children possess the capacity to intuit subtle energies, and are doing this all the time as they embody the world, and come to understand themselves through each of the

Chakra energies. How a child interprets this energy and then practically applies this knowledge in service of their optimal growth has not, until now, been fully understood within the Western technological rationalist paradigm. This, however, is assumed as a natural way of being in the world, particularly in India and Japan. Sri Sri Ravi Shankar started the *Art of Living Process* in 1981. This intuitive mind process helps children to tap into the intuitive abilities of the mind, which is demonstrated by them seeing colors, reading text, and identifying pictures with eyes closed.[106] These deep faculties are sometimes referred to as 3rd eye perception.

These potentials are present in every child as latent potentials that often receive no conscious cultivation in the child's life. The sensory perception mentioned in the first part in the section titled, *Child Genius*, extend to telepathy (knowing what someone's thoughts are), knowing or seeing in one's mind's eye what is going to happen before it happens (clairvoyance), knowing or sensing feelings from other people, animals, plants, and environments (clairsentience), knowing or hearing things aural that others cannot hear (clairaudience), and receiving information from objects (without knowing their history) often get repressed as growth happens.. The *child's push* to express and utilise these capacities is often denied. To make these wonderful faculties flower they require proper attention, which is not often available to the child. An adult that encourages these inclinations will often be one who values these or had wanted them valued in their own childhood. For many parents, the focus on their children's learning is not about these types of potentials, but just coping with the demands of schooling. Parents become overwhelmed in regard to how children are progressing, a progression, that is tied to how well children are learning and fitting into the developmental frameworks of educational institutions. The predominance of children being expected to learn particular things in a certain way so that a school report can relegate a score, places a lot of pressure on both children and adults. Because of this we forget that learning is such a natural state of being. And we also, to a degree, just continue to educate from a limiting past, largely because that is just the way it has always been. With new knowledge, however, we are pushed to explore other options in regard to our children's learning, and open to much potential that we have no measure for yet but there are still some conditioned beliefs to overcome in this regard.

History of Schooling

In the United States in the 1800s, Horace Mann, who was credited as the *Father of the Common School Movement*, argued that, "universal public education was the best way" to turn the nation's uncontrollable children into disciplined, judicious, republican citizens. [107] With the advent of industrialisation, schooling was deemed to be the best way to instil skills and to eradicate ignorance, as was highlighted in the *Need to Act*.[108] This line of education is mainly concerned with teaching the three R's and critical thinking. Critical thinking, in a broad sense, means teaching students the rules of logic, or how to assess evidence, and this method is woven throughout the Western tradition of education, from the Greeks to the Scholastics to the present day.[109] The critical thinking movement has emphasised reasoning skills, and found that the curriculum and purpose of education, generally, is to foster critical thinking.[110]

The common school movement and early childhood education was researched for its validity in the 1960s by Moore and Moore A review of over 8000 studies was conducted focusing on early childhood education and the physical and mental development of children. In their published work, *Better Late Than Early: A New Approach to Your Child's Education*, they presented evidence that childhood problems labeled as juvenile delinquency, near-sightedness, and behavioural problems were the result of increasingly earlier enrolment of the student. They also explored school readiness issues, coordination, ability to focus, and emotional stability. The authors note that the increased enrolment of students in special education classes was due to children not yet being *emotionally* ready for the degree of learning that was being asked. Emotional bonds and attachments are necessary in supporting the child's feelings of safety and security, which need to be made at home with parents in the early years, according to the findings. Starting formal education before age 8-10 years is harmful, and the authors suggest this damage could not be replaced or corrected in an institutional setting.[111]

When is the best time to make these transitions to formal education? The belief that a child must be educated early, and that earlier is better in order to fill them up with rational knowledge or to absorb the right teachings, has been present since Aristotle. Aristotle believed that the individual's morality, emotions, and intellect were all set and determined personal characteristics or inclinations, and education was the only way to develop them. Aristotle saw individual character and personal responsibility as driving the individual toward a virtuous life. Virtue, therefore, is a disposition to behave in the right way.

Recall here that for Aristotle, the child needs to be taught how to behave in the right way and this right way is taught at school or other educational institutions.

School Learning

Schools have learning discourses, which primarily focus on the cognitive and rational aspects of the child's learning, so that a standardised report can measure a grade. Children who get poor grades, according to these standards, are labeled as having difficulty learning. But no child is a poor learner. Vital signs about what children really need to be supported to learn often go unnoticed in many classrooms. For instance, a child who gets up to use the toilet frequently, or daydreams by continually looking out the window, or wriggles in its seat, is often labeled a poor learner. Maria Montessori recognised that as soon as a child finds something that interests them, their ability to concentrate becomes clear. Unless a child can see a bigger picture and vision behind learning certain things, in certain ways, they will always resist it. However, children are coerced to focus on learning tasks, which results in an imbalance. Because learning is an embodied and holistic process, if a child is distracted, confused, unsettled, or nervous whilst trying to learn a new skill, or they have a lot of emotional tension occurring in their life, they will have difficulty integrating new information.

Children, who are forced to learn, can present with ADD and learning and attention issues, because the child's nervous system becomes overloaded. Children who are allowed to take a break when they are stuck on something, return refreshed, because to take the pressure off and give space, allows them to integrate and be ready to *get* what they could not understand before. A Child's learning challenges are never the real issues; they are simply an indication that brings to attention that the child has an important need that has gone unnoticed or unmet. The degree to which the child's needs are met, and how those in the role of caregiver respond to the child's expression of their needs, is instrumental not just to how a child learns, but the overall wellbeing of the child. Children learn at their own pace in their own way, but often they are rushed into learning things before they are ready.

Alternative Approaches to Learning

There have always been some thinkers who have recognised the child as a competent individual capable of active engagement with the world and significant in its own right at each stage of development. In this vein, many alternative systems of education have arisen from the work of Erik Erikson, Maria Montessori, and Rudolf Steiner, who paved innovative ways toward educating the many aspects of the child's whole self. These thinkers may not have explicitly spoken about the child as complete in body-mind-spirit, but they have all recognised the need of educating the whole child, and referred to the soul of the child in different ways. In her writings for educators, Montessori said, "Our care of the child should be governed, not by the desire 'to make him learn things, but by the endeavour always to keep burning within him that light which is called the intelligence."[112]

Montessori saw the first six years as critical for the child's development. Her concern was for the holistic and spiritual development of the child, because she believed the young child has a different relationship to the environment compared to adults, and that the child literally "incarnates" the world around him. "The things he sees are not just remembered; they form part of his soul." Montessori expressed that children will seek growth and development because it is consistent with their nature, and the direction of a child's life is contained within its own soul.[113] Montessori believed that the force of life itself guided the child and that because of this the child would be directed by its own push. To unfold in this way of the soul, the child needs a focused relationship with his parents and environment to form his individual self. Montessori observed that parents can and often do fail to do what is essential at this time, "because of the habit we have of thinking the child has no mental life."[114] However, Montessori said that simply by offering the child immediate and prolonged contact with the mother, the transition into the world would be smooth and inviting rather than traumatic.

Montessori believed that a child passes through periods when abilities are easily incorporated into his/her schema, and referred to it as "a passing impulse or potency." These sensitive periods are critical to the child's self-development. During these times the child unconsciously knows when it is time to learn a specific skill, and the child's intensity toward a skill reflects his need for that particular acquisition. However, when the sensitive period passes, acquiring the skill will be more difficult.[115] A sensitive period not recognised often results in a troubled child, and accordingly, Montessori viewed these "tantrums of the sensitive periods as external manifestations of an unsatisfied need."[116] Montessori's educational philosophy reveals a focus on understanding the needs, development, and potentialities of the child, and these were paramount to the child's ability to learn. Concerned about the perception and social status of children, Montessori wrote that:

> *A child is condemned by adults to places of exile until he reaches an age when he can live in an adult world without causing others distress. It is only then that a child is admitted to society. Prior to this he has to obey adults like a person deprived of civil rights.*[117]

Education, therefore, must suit the developing soul of the child. By respecting a child's developmental pace, as well as his or her needs and abilities, the child is given choice. Montessori thought that when the rights and needs of children are accorded deeper respect, we might be able to move away from educating children in ways that suit us. Montessori did not posit a particular needs theory for children or for childhood education, but rather principles for raising the child to meet the needs as directed by the child. Montessori's principles have been seen as pre-empting concepts and thinking that are still considered cutting edge today; principles that place a child's wellbeing front and centre regarding her or his experience, especially in regard to the idea of whole child learning. As more teachers are looking to whole child pedagogies and parents are looking for more holistic approaches we are seeing resurgence in this type of thinking.

Marian De Souza has advocated the implications for the child of having access to an education that starts from a basis of harmony between the cognitive, affective, and spiritual dimensions of learning. These aspects, De Souza argues, ought to be complimentary "as they promote meaning and connectedness and effect transformative learning." [118] Jack Miller proposes holistic education, which is in line with the holistic approach to psychology; that is, that human functioning cannot be fully understood solely in terms of their parts. Jack Miller states that:

> *"Holistic education focuses on the relationship between the whole and the part and suggests that teaching and learning approaches need to be rooted in a larger vision. If techniques are isolated and unrelated they can become dysfunctional. The holistic vision includes a sense of the whole person who is connected to his or her surrounding content and environment."*[119]

Less than holistic approaches toward education are more along the lines of a type of *transmission* learning, as opposed to the *transformative* learning inherent in holistic education, according to Miller. For many, the spiritual dimension of education is now being recognised as central to the whole, and attempts are made within the pedagogy to nurture it.

The varying ideas that have been held overtime in regard to the education of the child could also be traced back to the variance between Plato and Aristotle's ideas on the topic of education and the soul. Recalling that for Plato, education was one of letting the child unfold; and for Aristotle, it was to teach and put information into the child. Any child, however, who is exposed to positive scripts about who they are and how they fit within the world, do well in many other areas of life.[120] If Montessori had known about the Chakras, I am pretty sure she would have appreciated them, after all, they allow for the understanding of the natural patterns of energy that occur with each child at each and every point of their growth. The child's needs always arise as a result of an intricate dance between the child's biological and spiritual needs.

Play and Imagination

Visualising, imagining, and pretending are all pivotal to the child's *Need to See*. Learning, pattern recognition, and focus are all improved by imaginary play or pretend play, as it is sometimes called.[121] Play improves a child's social and emotional skills, their language skills, as well as their cognitive skills. Teachers are aware of the necessity of play and how it informs learning. Parents know how much their children learn when they are role-playing, dressing-up, or imagining a world beneath the sea. Research on children's early learning and development highlights the importance of play, and supporting children in their play actually enhances and contributes to the child learning, rather than it takes away from it.[122] The gestural and embodiment studies say this is because we are integrated whole, and we are looking to harmonise disparity. And yet, the dominance of a certain type of learning is hindering the child's full-bodied learning, which is vital for the integrity of self. The evidence presented in part one, regarding solid-state physics, argued that the human being is embodied energy and that each energy centre must be attended to simultaneously. Neglecting one at the cost of another can result in an imbalance. Equilibrium is maintained when all needs are met. Imagination and learning are vitally connected, as we see with the abilities of psychic wonder in many children.

Both of the cognitive greats Jean Piaget and Lev Vygotsky linked play with cognitive development and championed the many cognitive benefits of play. In a large review of play, Smilansky & Shefatya cited verbalization, vocabulary, language comprehension, attention span, imagination, concentration, impulse control, curiosity, problem-solving strategies, cooperation, empathy, and group participation, as all improved by play.[123] The benefits, however, have not been easy to measure because the paradigm that sees the brain as the centre of learning and also the seat of consciousness, views the child's intelligence and learning as the brain's by-product. The *Need to See* includes the organ of the brain. However, the vast neural networks of the brain-body relationship, as opened up by the Pert Model, offers evidence that the unified self is both body and mind. When there is a problem with learning, children become confused, frustrated, and less focused. When brain integration is lost in this way, ceasing the task, and then trying the job again when in a less stressed and a more relaxed state, appears the best thing to do.[124]

Even the way we measure intelligence has shifted focus away from the brain alone, and Howard Gardner's model of Multiple Intelligences (MI)[125] defines intelligence as a set of abilities used to solve problems and obtain goals.[126] Gardner sees MI as existing as potentials inherent in each person, yet varying genetically regarding individual competencies and potential for development.[127] Each domain of intelligence is seen as a system in itself, distinct from a generalised intelligence.[128] Some have suggested that Rudolph Steiner's pedagogy is permeated with such intelligence.[129] Steiner advocated for the developmental stages, however, only while respecting each child's individual abilities and rate of progress as they emerge. A central idea of this book is that children know when they are ready to bring forth potential, and are goal-directed by their innate *soul push*. To recall Arnold Gesell, the child is only ready to advance when its nervous system is ready.[130]

The influence of the organ of the heart in the wellbeing of individuals, as discussed in the *Need to Love*, links the heart and the brain as vital to the child's functions of learning.

Perhaps giving logic to the old saying, his heart is not in it; the correlation between children with congenital heart disease and neurodevelopmental issues is significant. These include learning disabilities, behavioural abnormalities, inattention, and hyperactivity. Imbalances of this *Need to See* and the energy centre of body-mind have been noted as fear of the imagination, dreams, irrational intuitive insights, learning difficulty, sleep issues, and lack of vision for the future.[131] Imaging studies have revealed a high prevalence of structural brain abnormalities.[132]

To recap; quantum physics, epigenetics, and morphic resonance all concur that we learn by adopting habits from the past. The inherited collective memory from the past members of the species (parents and grandparents most particularly, but can extend out to cultures and nations too) sits in a type of transformative suspension. We will adopt patterns of learning and other knowledge that replicates those already within the family. Another simple way of understanding this is through the phenomenon called the 'Hundredth Monkey' syndrome, whereby a new behaviour or idea spreads from one group to all related groups, and if a critical number of members acquire the behaviour, the new group starts replicating the behaviour and having the same idea, regardless of geographical proximity.[133] Amazingly, this insight or phenomenon was discovered before 1975, prior to the Internet.

Dreams and Sleep

When a child has trouble sleeping, wakes frequently, or has trouble settling to sleep, there may be some resistance to feeling the comfort, peace, and solutions that sleep brings. The emotional factors that cause sleeping issues are generally based on fear. A child who is afraid and cannot verbally express their fears will have trouble sleeping. In clinic, I see many children present with sleeping problems; a signal that the child is experiencing a situation of unusual unrest. This will have to be resolved if the child is to feel safe to express their feelings, emotions. Sleep problems are not something to be trained away, but rather vital indications about the unrest in the child's environment.

Freud most popularly told us that dreams offer the imagination an opportunity to rewrite the unprocessed energy of the unresolved experiences of the day. Also, sleep allows for learning to be integrated. Interestingly, sleep disturbances particularly at bedtime, are frequently reported by both parents and children with ADHD.[134] In one study, both parents and children reported on the quality of sleep in children with diagnosed ADHD. Children with ADHD reported their own sleep to be more disturbed than the control group did on the sleep self-report, particularly on items relating to bedtime struggles.[135] Children also need support to take responsibility for whatever aspects of life that they can appropriate to the life-stage.

Children who are severely traumatised have been reported to have a significantly greater number of dreams than those who have not suffered trauma, and their dreams included a higher number of threatening dream events. These results were obtained after researchers asked the question,

> *"Do children who live in an environment in which their physical and psychological wellbeing is constantly threatened have a highly activated dream production and threat simulation system (TSS), and do children living in a safe environment that is relatively free of such threat cues have a weakly activated system?"*[136]

The answer was yes to both of these questions. The child's waking experiences need to be processed and integrated into their schema in a way that they can construct their own meaning of the world. Bad dreams portray a way of a reworking and unifying feelings and thoughts and result from a need to try and solve a problem, to focus and integrate new information, or even to become accountable for their learning. The child's traumatic environment or stressors and worries become replicated in the dream so that the child may attempt to make sense of it.

A connection between the dream and mirror behaviours has been made in a study that demonstrated that students who had frequent dream-enacting behaviours (the culmination of nightmares) also scored high on a measure of mirror behaviours (the propensity to imitate another person's emotions or actions). The conclusion was that "individuals who frequently display mirror behaviours are also prone to nightmares". [137] Mirror behaviours as discussed in the section on the *Need to Love*, have been defined as the ability to empathise with other people's emotions and/or imitate the actions or speech of others. Children who empathise with the worldviews of others might also take on the other's worldviews, and in a comparative way, have their unmet needs expressed in dreams. The emotional contagion is real in families and the social world. Looking beneath the behavior of the child to research studies on mirror neurons, which concur with morphic resonance, we can see people align their behaviour with others in social and family interaction. [138] This research also tells us that there is "strong evidence for a human mirror system in the central nervous system which appears to originate from the motor system."[139] Visualising ones highest potential then, which is often not encouraged in the child, as we see from the research on mirror neurons, is paramount in how we come to see ourselves – because, the representations offered to children are those that they have a tendency to replicate or mirror from others. Research evidence of mirror mechanisms in humans and their anatomical localisations in the body, is incredibly exciting in light of the *Foundational Needs Model*, as the details of the anatomical localisation are already found within Chakra theory.[140]

Summary

As a child grows in age, they do not stop requiring the *Need to See,* they just demand a different type of vision and imagination, just as we all do when we are not sure how things are going to come together or work out. Children (and adults) who cultivate the *Need to See* have a deep sense of meaning and can focus and integrate new information, and so become accountable for their own learning. The need to see also supports one's clarity, intention, and intuition. If we can dream it we can do it, as Walt Disney tells us, which, could be equally reversed to say, If we do it, it is because we have imagined it into existence. Exploring this in light of the *soul push* and recalling James Hillman's quote in the first part chapter two, *The Child as a Soul,* "It is impossible to see the angel unless you first have a notion of it," our children need to see themselves as souls in all their brilliance if they are to become it.

Tips To Cultivate The Need To See

At any age, in any situation, you can encourage your child to feel loved in the following ways:

- Encourage your child to visualise their highest potential by offering representations of their innate brilliance. Offer stories and narratives that speak to *greatness*, stories of heroes and saints open children to all their possible magnificence.

- When teaching or trying to instill information into a child try to assist them to focus on smaller, more manageable tasks. These are easier to process and integrate than a big too hard task, which can be overwhelming.

- The child who daydreams or continually looks out the window can indicate that the child needs help to integrate information and stimuli. You can assist the child with meditation or mindfulness practices.

- Mediation in classrooms has been shown to be helpful in integrating fragmented comprehension, and improves attention span in children

- The child who wriggles in its seat is indicating they feel disinterested and disconnected. You can assist by being mindful of what the child is interested in and what matters to them.

- Active learning and integration of embodied processes within classroom tasks supports whole body integration.

- Find novel ways of integrating child specific meaning into the child's formal learning task. Refer to the total needs and the tips contained in each section on the Needs to give you prompts.

- Encourage the child to imagine the end result of a task they are working on, as one's imagination elicits the same physiological response as really doing something.

- If a child is having trouble sleeping, make space before bedtime for the child to express their worries. It is often only after settling from a busy day that things come to mind. A child who is afraid and cannot verbally express their fears will have trouble sleeping.

- Allow children to set the course, or even a class, once in a while. Ask them to work on designing and imagining the optimal classroom or learning environment. Their ideas will be invaluable.

Needs Table 6: The Need to See

Potential of need as the centre point of balance

Deficient	Balanced	Excess
Illusion	Visualisation	Over fantasising
Lack of imagination	Imagination	Over imaginative
Poor recall	Memory	Over retention
Lack of focus	Focus	Rigid thinking
ADD	Concentration	ADHD
Not recalling dreams	Dreams	Nightmares
Inadequate	Self-evaluation	Inflated opinion
Close-minded	Pattern recognition	Obsessions
Learning difficulties	Learning (rote)	Focus on intellectual
Don't learn from past	Learning (life)	See life as hindrance
Can't see big picture	Insight	Problematic thinking
Muddled thinking	Clarity	Misperception
Disorganised	Organised	Over attention to detail
Lack of vision	Visionary	Impracticable

7. Children Need To Know: Know Me

Twinkle, twinkle, little star,

How I wonder what you are!

Up above the world so high,

Like a diamond in the sky[141].

Even from an early age, children *Need to Know* about the deeper values guiding them, the purpose of their lives, and why they do the things they do. The child is, in essence, proclaiming --*Know Me, so I may know thyself.*

Figure 9: Physical Location of the *Need to Know*.

Case 7: Mimi

Mimi was a very inquisitive child. She asked questions about everything. Her parents were unsure of how much to encourage some of her almost crazy notions, things that she comes up with every single day. Some of Mimi's questions seemed odd to Mimi's parents. For example, they had not indoctrinated Mimi in any religious concepts and yet at 8 she was asking all type of questions about God. Questions like, "if you don't believe in God then whom would you pray to mummy, if you wanted to say a prayer?" And "Do you think that the God other children talk about would be the same as my God?" Of course, the depth of inquiry from Mimi, given no framework of religion would seem peculiar. I reflected briefly on meeting Mimi about my own desire to know about the soul at the same age. My frame was Roman Catholicism and the God I would need to pray to, would be a certain type of God. Of course, as a practitioner, I am acutely aware of projecting my own past upon those that come to see me, and yet as we now know, we revisit our past purposefully. If we as adults have explored our past from the most expansive interpretations, we are then able to bring much more clarity to the child's experiences, even when these experiences challenge our beliefs about what might be occurring for the child.

Mimi's questions were not all of a religious nature and sometimes they came in the form of declarations not questions at all. Some of these declarations scared Mimi's parents and they had made the appointment to see me to try and work out where these questions were coming from. Mimi's questions, I expressed to the parents, were tied to her *Need to Know* and I said we had no current model that helps us to consider that such questions are part of the child's natural and purposeful *push* for unity. In my model questions concerning one's purpose in life, searching for a deeper understanding of oneself and the wider world, a feeling of being connected to the greater cosmos in ways that is often not acknowledged or hard to express, are all part of the energy of this *Need to Know*. The pathways of energetic and symbolic dialogue in the child's life pertaining to the 7th Chakra energy (*Svastka*) are self-knowledge and feeling connected to the greater cosmos. This Chakra is often referred to as the spiritual centre and is associated with themes of peak experience, imminence, self-knowledge, higher powers, divine nature, or highest purpose according to one's belief system.

Mimi, as well as being inquisitive, also had a physical issue with her skin; it looked to me like vitiligo. The associated anatomy and body systems of this 7th Chakra have been identified as the muscular system, skeletal system, and skin. Children with skin issues, muscular problems (growing pains) and issues with the skeletal system (particularly posture and stance) indicate an imbalance in this need. See the A-Z of common ailments associated to this 7th Need in Appendix 1. I asked Mimi's parents about the skin discolouration on Mimi's right hand. I could not see it any other place, although it was winter, and Mimi's body was covered except for her hands and face. The parents said that she was born with the discolouration on that hand alone and blood tests as well as an ANA test confirmed Vitiligo.[142] Mimi was proud of her hand, in fact she believed that because of the discolouration, she possessed special abilities. She expressed, "it's my magic hand that can do things the other hand cannot, and not everyone has a magic hand." Although Mimi's parents looked rather uncertain about Mimi's declaration of special powers, I nodded as this made a lot of sense to me.

I could convey to Mimi's parents that the skin is the largest sensory organ. In fact, the skin feels and reads all the things in the environment in a purposeful way. The skin itself along with hair, have been referred to as the body's antennae.[143] Skin has been known to have spiritual features since ancient times. "Spiritual and religious significances of skin are revealed through how much of the skin has been and continues to be covered with what types of coverings, scalp and beard hair cutting, shaving and styling, skin, nail, and hair coloring and decorating, tattooing, and intentional scarring of skin." [144] The symbolic and real connection of the skin to one's spiritual experiences is just beginning to be understood by medical science. In fact, studies undertaken to measure the "Psychoneuroimmunology of the skin is elucidating how the mind can influence the skin and skin disorders."[145]

Mimi's parents were more concerned about Mimi's grandiose ideas about her special ability and her insistence of talking about God, than the correlating science. Mimi's mother expressed quietly to me whilst Mimi was preoccupied with her sister colouring in at the table in my office, that the encouragement of Mimi's grandiose ideas from me were not helpful. She continued that they had come to see me to stop such grand ideas. I could feel myself being reprimanded for holding such a view about Mimi's greatness and recalled how I had made an obvious nod in agreement with Mimi's expression, which may have upset the mother. Again, childhood memories resurfaced for me. Throughout my own growth I had arrived at a point where I was confident to express that Mimi's greatness, was not just reserved for Mimi; in my experience this was a feature of every child. Of course, not every child will express the same potential and yet, I have seen almost every child express some type of potential often not recognised or even denied by caregivers. I reassured the parents in a soft tone to match theirs, that it was important to ascertain what these expressions actually meant for Mimi and her best growth, not what we as adults have decided her expressions mean. Both parents nodded in agreement.

I went on to say that children come into the world with a unified consciousness (the integration of body-mind-spirit) and life begins as a wondrous dance between the integrated body-mind-spirit, in which the child and the world are one. Over time, as has been expressed as a central theme in the book, this unity is challenged. It is, therefore, a deep need of the child at all ages to know who they are at the fundamental basis as a unified soul. Children are constantly looking to know how they are connected to the wider world, where they come from, and where they will go. When the answers to such question do not satisfy the child, they will *push* for an interpretation that does. As Mimi looked around my office, she asked questions about some of the objects on my desk. "Is that doll for helping women to get ready to have a baby" she asked about the Ashanti doll sitting atop my desk which 'represents fertility and good luck and is even used by young girls as a way to prepare for motherhood.'[146] Yes, I said, that is exactly what the doll is a symbol for. As Mimi looked at me, I noticed her mouth curl upward ever so slightly. It was a lot like a smirk. I had even before I met Mimi, observed children receive vital information, with great accuracy, as they held objects, even pinpointing certain historical events. Mimi could do the same. I decided to play a game with Mimi. I handed her a variety of objects and asked her to tell me a story about them.

What progressed was a show of skill in knowing the history as well as the symbolic meaning of many objects on my desk. The most interesting aspect of this encounter with Mimi and her magical power was that she wanted to hold each of the objects in her right hand. It appeared indeed that the hand represented some special power. Interestingly, also I had noticed that Mimi had not held the Ashanti doll earlier, and yet she still gave information about it. The magic hand story was the meaning Mimi called upon to grasp a way of expressing the things she felt, those things she knew that not many others could affirm as purposeful. I told Mimi that she had a special way of reading information and that her hand was important in that, but her whole body could do the same thing. I expressed that this ability was important for her and for her life. This ability would help her to know many things about herself and others that would in turn be a gift for the whole of humanity.

Of course, I did not fix Mimi's need to question as her parents had hoped, what did shift however, was the frame that Mimi's parents now had to comprehend their daughter's curious nature. And how science could now confirm such processes are necessary for our human growth and evolution. A heightened sensitivity to others and the planet seen in children at this time in history appears to be just part of a larger purposeful transformation in our human consciousness. This shift in consciousness both individually and collectively, sees us opening to a broader awareness of all material phenomena and a 'comprehension of meanings that expands beyond the immediacy of everyday life toward higher and deeper experience.'[147] The access the child has with the field of consciousness supports its unified growth. Mimi's questions about God are actually reflective of a knowing that resides within each of us that there is a field of energy supporting our best growth and highest potential. The word that has been used to express this energy throughout time and across culture has been named God. As I have examined elsewhere, the child's spirituality is not confined to religious practice or belief. When the child is a unified whole, they have direct access to the spiritual dimensions out there as a vital part of their inner experiences.

Themes that present in children based upon the *Need to Know* will vary and will also differ among individuals, families, and cultures, although there are certain themes that could be considered the same for all. Take, highest potential for example, if not recognised and met in the child's life, there will be an energetic response; on one end of the spectrum, a child not feeling that they can accomplish anything (unrealised potential, apathetic, deficient energy) and on the other end, a child may continually want to be the winner (excessive energy in regard to highest potential). These responses to self and life are appropriate as they arise according to what the child needs, but is not getting. An apathetic child is communicating a lack of acting on its highest potential, and the child who has to continually be the best is also communicating a *Need to Know* about its highest potential. By identifying that it is the unmet *Need to Know* that lies at the origin of the child's behaviours, we are closer to being able to identify the source. Somewhere in the child's environment, certain feelings and thoughts pertaining to a lack of highest potentials are being activated. The needs table at the end of this section shows a variety of excess and deficient responses in the child if the *Need to Know* is not met.

> **Need to Know – Common Themes**
> - *Know Thyself*
> - *We Come from the Stars*
> - *Childhood Spirituality*
> - *Embodying Spirit*
> - *Highest Potential*
> - *Concepts of God*
> - *Technology*

Know Thyself

To *know thyself* is an appropriate philosophical and spiritual position to align with the *Need to Know*. As adult's, we teach children about many things. We believe that the more knowledge a child acquires from outside by way of teachings, the better equipped they will be to have the best chance in life. We often fail to teach children the most important type of knowledge, that is, to *know thyself*. I understand, too, that adults who were assumed not to know for themselves when they were children, may find it hard to hand over authority to a child; after all, we have been waiting a long time to grow up and claim this for ourselves. As caregivers, when we can allow children to lead, or at least be willing to explore what they might be telling us about their own knowledge we are better situated to meet their needs.

If the child's environment at home, school, and with peer groups is a place to question and discuss one's feelings, one's thoughts, one's direction in life, one's connection to a greater source of knowledge, and in essence, what we call spiritual values, then children learn to feel and think for themselves as a matter of course. Allowing children the space to think through their own problems and interpret their feelings with our support, teaches them that there may be many answers to a single situation. I have a habit of saying that children know more than we realise. Children need to be given the space to arrive at solutions for themselves about life and their own challenges. This is essential to their *Need to Know*. This way of relating teaches children that they have access to their own answers, and also that there may be many answers to a single situation. Research concurs that children who are granted the freedom to possess knowledge are more open-minded, as they have been encouraged to take part in broad-minded discussions at all points in their growth, and because significant adults asked for their opinions, they came to believe that their knowledge was important. Philosopher Gareth Matthews, advocates for the child as an active agent in his or her own philosophical questioning of life and self. Matthews also claims that the many theories of childhood, such as cognitive development, children's rights and needs, as well as theories concerning the place of children in society, should constantly be reviewed because they do not account for this type of self-knowledge.[148]

We Come From the Stars

When I was studying philosophy, I had a teacher who said that he had a friend who had worked in a laboratory on the genome project. My professor said his friend had asked him "Do you know that we are all made of stardust?" Of course, it could be postulated that the professor was sharing this story as philosophical teaching point to help one expand the way one thought about oneself as finite beings. Or perhaps to ruffle a few logical thinkers in the class, or maybe even to get us interested in the 'big bang' theory. However, there was something about the way my professor told the story that felt true to me. It was like he spoke directly to a truth I knew in my soul and I just felt there was something to this. Something in me knew that even down to the cellular level, we are connected to a field of energy which is the same field of energy that births stars. Then, many years later, I actually came across scientific proof that we are indeed made of stardust.

This proof was gifted by husband and wife pair of astrophysicists wrote a book called, *Living with the Stars: How the Human Body is Connected to the Life Cycles of the Earth, the Planets, and the Stars.*[149] In an article about the book, one of the author's commented:

> *Very little of our physical bodies lasts for more than a few years. Of course, that's at odds with how we perceive ourselves when we look into the mirror. But we're not fixed at all. We're more like a pattern or a process. And it was the transience of the body and the flow of energy and matter needed to counter that impermanence that led us to explore our interconnectedness with the universe.*[150]

Do children already know this? Yes, of course, they do.

The child's whole self is integrating all types of awareness and knowledge through their physical being from the field out there, and all of the functions of the bodily organs are affected by the individual's relationship to both his/her internal and external world. [151] If our children were encouraged to know they come from the stars, then they would never doubt themselves as the magnificent beings they are. Of course, not many of us have been encouraged to know ourselves in this way.

When we think back to where we have come from, from our individual and collective pasts, we can perhaps see that we have truly been limited in many ways. And we can see that we also still continue to limit children based upon limiting beliefs. Freud's case of Little Hans was interpreted from the level of awareness of the man who did the interpreting at the time he did. This brings to a close the reason why I have insisted on using this outmoded case of Hans to compare then to now. If Hans had been offered a broader, larger quantum representation of why his fear was presenting, compared to the one that he held before the phobia, such a new story might release the holding pattern of the energy of the unknown within the child. Every child experiencing a phobia could be said to be vacillating between the idea that, "At any time I could be disregarded or separated from my unified self, when all I wish for is to be known as a unified self – as a soul," and simultaneously, having to cope with their body's physiological response to the trauma of this separation.

As has been mentioned, Freud considered that the psychic or mental life was not active in the child. The residue of such thought is still present in the models of child psychology, as we are still mostly stuck to a limited way of perceiving the child, even now. Hans did not trust, and was not persuaded by the truth-claims of his parents who represented to him the adult world. This disbelief was not because he had no idea, but because he saw through the illusion. Children can judge and discern right from wrong, truth from falsehood, very early on. Their complex body system is more advanced and astute than we give credit. At this point, just so that we may all have some resolution in the matter of Hans, I conclude his story. Let it be known that we can rest assured knowing that Freud eventually, thankfully, cured the child of his phobia. Perhaps Hans imagined that Freud would know how to cure him as well; after all, the professor was an expert and would know the answers to his problems, and the ones his parents could not answer. On Freud's first meeting with the child (all other prior communications were made between the father and Freud), Freud alerted Hans to his role and place in the Oedipal drama in the way a small child might understand. In the playing out of this script, almost as if in a final dramatic scene, Freud tells Hans:

> "*Long before he was in the world I had known that a little Hans would come who would be so fond of his mother that he would be bound to feel afraid because of it; and I had told his father this.*[152]'

Reflecting on this, Hans says to his father after they had left the meeting with Freud, "I didn't know that the Professor talked to God."

Elsewhere I have claimed, that implicit in Hans' observation and communication to his father after his meeting with Freud, was that the child had a tacit acceptance that Freud enjoyed divine powers of precognition, powers that alerted him to the coming of Hans and his problems.[153] Whereas here I add that Hans, when given a reflection of the relationship that he held with God—one that saw him as a soul—he was reconnected and unified in a way that was not possible before. In this brief moment, as simple as that, Hans came to know who he was.

Childhood Spirituality

My exploration into Freudian theory led me on to research more deeply, the spiritual life of the child, because I came to see how many of our psychologies since Freud still follow dualistic and separated models of human growth. On top of this separation of self, I came to see that all human development theories plot the biological and cognitive development of the individual as a journey from the bottom up. Of course, we recognise that the child, smaller in size is more dependent to begin with; and becomes bigger and more independent. Like all growth in the natural world, nothing is born fully developed and, thus, a series of progressions lead to the fully formed organism. This type of growth has been favoured with the vertical development models; the ladder type measures that show the visible growth of the child. The consideration of the unseen, immeasurable, and un-manifest forces that are guiding and informing the self are a little more difficult to measure, but as I have argued throughout nonetheless, pivotal to our human growth.

The idea of studying the child's spirituality hit somewhat of a tipping point in the earliest few years of the 21st century. The spiritual aspect of the self, which had so long been reduced to the disembodied aspect of the mind, emerged as an important theme within academic thought, especially in relation to the child.[154] Work undertaken with children in vast disciplines, such as anthropology, sociology, psychology, and education, was beginning to focus increasingly upon the phenomena of spirituality and the role of spirituality in promoting wellbeing. It is still an important field of enquiry. Marian De Souza, as mentioned earlier, argues for a harmony between the cognitive, affective, and spiritual dimensions of learning.[155] Many others have looked to how spirituality can be nurtured in the child. Hay and Nye, who have conducted extensive research on childhood spirituality, say that what they call 'Relational Consciousness' is central to children's spirituality, and further that spirituality is universal or generic to all people.[156]

Ken Wilber's Integral Theory recognises the importance of states of consciousness and refers to spiritual capacities and this type of invisible growth as horizontal growth. Integral Theory accounts for both inner and outer worlds, as well as the horizontal and vertical aspects of the development of the self within the broader structures that frame the self and self-understanding. Wilber's is a detailed philosophy and goes a long way to a true recognition of a human whole development model. Without going into depth here in regard to Wilber's thinking I just want to raise the following aspects as it pertains to the spiritual development of the child. In his book, *Integral Psychology*, Wilber includes a chapter entitled, 'Is there a Childhood Spirituality?' Wilber maintains that infancy and childhood definitely have spirituality; but only the lowest stages of spirituality, which by most definitions, according to Wilber, do not appear to be spiritual at all.[157] These lower stages are based on Wilber's hierarchical progression of spiritual development that is reminiscent of all developmental models;. a stage to grow into rather than a state of being.

Integral and transpersonal theorists view the self (regardless of culture) as developing on all human dimensions (body-mind-spirit) into a fully embodied life.[158] The potential and purpose of children, then, still becomes measured in regard to the adult. James Fowler also suggested in his work, *Stages of Faith* (1981) in that the staged spiritual development occurs across the life span.[159] Due to a dominance of hierarchical developmental models within Western institutions, it has gone unrecognised that the child has a unified connection. When we begin to view the child as emerging as a whole, simultaneously, at all points of growth, and that the integrity of the body-mind-spirit can and ought to be maintained, we may see an integrity of the whole self become apparent like never before. In essence, we may become observers of a true integral being from the beginnings.

Embodying Spirit

One of the most significant themes concerning children's spirituality is the relationship the child has with their feeling nature and the felt sense of their own body, often called body awareness, or body wisdom.[160] This connection places the child's physicality as essential in the conceptualisations and discussions of spirituality in the life of the child. In the same way that the body is not separate from the mind or the spirit, the child's body wisdom is an integral part of the whole child, and integral to the meaning that the child attaches to its experiences.

I saw the vital importance of recognising the body-mind-spirit interaction and connection that occur simultaneously in the child, so as to better understand the child, and its needs for wellbeing during each and every growth period. The idea of embodied spirituality more generally accounts for the body-mind relationship in spirituality, and considers that spirituality is an integral and active aspect that is informing a person's overall development.[161] According to Hyde, et al, "physicality—conscious bodily perception—as an ontological way of knowing is a natural predisposition of humankind"[162] Because children (and young children in particular) do not always have mastery of the verbal skills needed to give expression to their thoughts, they tend to be far more in tune with their physicality. I contend the denial of the spiritual aspect of the child at each of their otherwise staged growth, is the reason that we do not understand the child's foundational needs to secure their wellbeing and reach their potentials.

Spirituality offers a core support or ultimate concern as to how we might comprehend the lived experience of the child, and this aspect of the self is a part of the whole, not a portion to be added on at a later point in time.[163] As I have promoted throughout the book, the use of the word spirit is not an out of body or otherworldly idea at all, it is tied to the actions of the child. Each time the child acts; it is a demonstration of their spirituality in action. As has been mentioned already many thinkers have posited that if our understandings of consciousness do not account for the divine aspect of our human experience (from the beginnings), then we will never truly be able to sustain wellbeing. We are spiritual beings having a human experience, according to Teilhard de Chardin.

As we are becoming more aware of the subtle energies that permeate both the individual and the cosmos, the aspect of spirituality has to be incorporated into the models of child growth, not as an add on, because as we have seen the child acts as a whole from the earliest interactions. The child *Needs to Know* who they are at a deep, fundamental level as a spiritual being. This *soul push* demands that we all value the childhood spiritual potentials, so they do not have to go underground or be by-passed.

Highest Potential

Imagine, as I have asked already, if you grew up knowing you are a soul with a divine purpose that is unique to you? What would one then view as his or her highest potential, given that this means everyone is born with inherent greatness already?

Remember for Abraham Maslow, one's highest potential – our highest human need, was for self-actualisation or realised individual potential. Maslow emphasised that self-actualisations is a process of growing and developing in order to achieve individual potential. Maslow's hierarchy suggests that human motivation deals first with fulfilling basic needs such as basic physical requirements, including the need for food, water, sleep, and warmth. Once these needs have been met, a person can move on to other, more advanced needs. This hierarchy is shown as a pyramid with the lowest levels consisting of the most basic needs and at the top of the pyramid, needs that are more complex. As the pyramid ascends the needs become progressively more psychological and social.

There are five levels to Maslow's Hierarchy of Needs. Maslow attributed four levels to what he calls lower-order needs or deficiency needs, while the top level is considered growth needs. The deficiency needs must be met before higher-order needs can influence behaviour.[164] From a soul perspective, one's potential is not something we grow into. As we saw also with Wilber's spiritual development, he deemed it not possible for children to be self-actualised or integral, as this is only possible when one grows. As the study mentioned in the *Need to Act*, highlighted that whilst fulfillment of Maslow's needs was strongly correlated with happiness and wellbeing, people from cultures all over the world reported that self-actualisation and social needs were more important to them, even when and if, many of the most basic needs were unfulfilled.

As I have repeated throughout, models of growth that see the child climb up the ladder to reach their potentials are defunct and as such are not a true representation of the human holistic growth process. The idea that is we can remain as a whole through each and every transition in life, which naturally sees us seesawing as we attempt to maintain balance. In effect then, a child's highest potentials means that they are bringing the totality of their wholeness to each moment. Children are activating their highest potentials when they feel, think and act in alignment. From a soul alignment the child has access to the *all* the energies supporting its highest growth in an unadulterated form. Then we can begin to consider -- If I can be the best I can be today, the rest will take care of itself. The implication of this statement means that to see our children as the best they can be in each moment, the range of representations that we offer children needs to be broadened to honour their potential and capacities as magnificent beings, inclusive of the aspects of body-mind-spirit. When children's needs are cultivated in each Chakra centre within *each Foundational Need*, we see the emergence of new potentials in the child. The energetic paradigm allows us to take the leap and see spirituality as spirit in action, shaping our biological bodily experience, with every action we take.

Concepts of God

Spirituality, like all vital needs is best instituted by modelling conscious and attuned behaviour. Even if children are a part of a cultural religion, their spirituality can be embodied in a way that tolerates other cultures and styles of worship for the fundamental unity that they share. Many children, however, have negative associations with religion that can affect their wellbeing. In a study titled *God is Watching You*,[165] the researchers were interested to see if religion increased pro-social behaviour when children engaged in a game. Children were found to give more money to strangers when God concepts were implicitly activated than when not, and this also occurred when children felt a presence of supernatural watchers. The authors concluded that the implications for this research showed that theories that posit religion or God concepts facilitated children's actions. Such findings support the idea of such benevolent energy in the emergence of large-scale societies of co-operators, is vital.[166]

Yet, in another study, when kindergarten children were asked about concepts of self, others, and God (in questionnaires specifically targeted to the quality of the teacher-child and mother-child relationship), there was no concept of a punishing God in any of the responses. These findings were contrary to what the researchers expected. A harmony and closeness in the teacher-child relationship, however, predicted that children's working models of self and others explained children possessing a loving God concept.[167] Hay and Nye have observed over time in discussions with children about themselves, others, nature, and God, that children forged distinct connections and references to a spiritual nature, mostly in terms of a God, but also a grandeur in nature, as well as an energy or force that maintained the child's best interests at heart.[168] Significant links between religion, spirituality, and health are being found with new measures of discovery. Recent advances in the delineation of religion and spirituality with concepts and measures, theoretically and functionally connected to health, allow more insight into the connection between spirituality and broader health. Presently, these relate only to correlations between physical and mental health (e.g. closeness to God, religious orientation and motivation, religious support, and religious struggle).[169]

How the child comes to know itself in the world has been highlighted by this deep exploration into the spiritual aspects of our children's lives. In essence, I contend that it is centred on our human *Need to Know*, that we are connected to a higher power, God, or the universe in ways that appear evident to children from the beginnings. The study of children has faced the same issues that faced early feminism; that is, when new knowledge or new ways of interpreting phenomena is presented, it inevitably challenges dominant paradigms and discourses. And so we need to all push for better ways of understanding the child in its totality.

Many feminist researchers have made important changes in the way children are studied, and also the way researchers regard them.[170] Anthropological research that centres on children's perceptions of illness and dying, places as central the idea of child's meaning concerning those things that matter:

> *The first premise is that human beings act toward things on the basis of the meanings that the things have for them. The second premise is that the meaning of such things is derived from, or arises out of, the social interaction that one has with one's fellows.*[171]

In a similar manner to Kübler-Ross, Bluebond-Langer opened the discussion about the child's view on death and dying, demonstrating the depth and knowing of children. Many small children ask questions about God, life, and death, which often make adults uncomfortable. The approaches that see death as a transition into a new consciousness are supportive of the child's *Need to Know*. Reflecting on my own sister's passing when I was a small child, I know I was somewhat comforted by the idea that she lived on somewhere, somehow.

This type of wonder is critical to our human *Need to Know*. John O'Donohue, author of the book *Anam Cara*, reminds us that,

> "It is uncanny how social reality can deaden and numb us so that the mystical wonder of our lives goes totally unnoticed. We are here. We are wildly and dangerously free. The more lonely side of being here is our separation in the world. When you live in a body you are separate from every other object and person. Many of our attempts to pray, to love, and to create are secret attempts at transfiguring that separation in order to build bridges outward so that others can reach us and we can reach them. At death, this physical separation is broken. The soul is released from its particular and exclusive location in this body. The soul then comes in to a free and fluent universe of spiritual belonging."[172]

When the best time for a child to be given certain information about such sensitive topics such as death and dying is a question I am asked a lot. Perhaps, it is more important to discern, or at least be mindful of, when a child is trying to understand something, that we do not deny or reject certain things or topics, but explore them with the child. The instances of depression and suicide, so prevalent in children today could indicate the degree to which children are tragically separated, not just from their unified selves as souls, but also from all other life. The law of inter-dependence, as mentioned in reference to the Dalai Lama in the *Need to Love*, sees the notion of viewing our connection to all as the highest of human relating, and that we are never too young to know this. After all, we come from the universe. Our *Need to Know* is a magical, imminent, wondrous thing, and when it is blocked or halted, we suffer many issues pertaining to a *lost* soul, or at the very least, a dark night of the soul.

Technology

Being connected to the source of all knowing has truly allowed human beings to advance in ways that are quite phenomenal. Our connection to social networks and webs of information, in the last 20 years in particular, have opened up many fluid ways of giving and receiving information for the evolution of humanity. A steady stream of diverse cosmologies (worldviews) and epistemologies (knowledge systems) from all parts of the globe sees us having access between worlds like never before. I possess a book that belonged to my mother since her childhood called, *A Tale of Two Cities,* and when I see this book in my library, I often wonder at how this same book would have brought an entirely different world alive for her. Today, many children have access to a much broader world of knowledge and information about many cities. The World Wide Web was only established in 1995, and one generation later, we are faced with the startling reality that today, a child of age eight has potential access to more information than most 80-year-olds have been exposed to in their lifetime. Of course, the lived experience and wisdom gained in 80 years of life would not be present for the eight-year-old.

Nevertheless, in one generation (20 years) we have seen the transference of information taught to children by experts, to a shift that sees children themselves having direct access to information about anything they wish, simply by typing a keyword into the now symbolic all-knowing search engine. We are poised at the edge of a period where we currently have one foot in the old world and the other in the new world. Technological advances are not going away, and many adults are ill-equipped to deal with the many outside influences in which children are in touch. In trying to moderate, control, and protect children, it appears that some parents and educators feel that they can or should eliminate these influences altogether. Without taking our children out of society and those perceived environments that do not serve their growth, it is perhaps more important to support children in managing the many situations, events, and experiences they encounter. All children react differently to change and new experiences, and yet, the child's overall capacity to transition through change is quite remarkable. The technology and media aspect of children's lives is just another environment that the child is learning to manage and integrate in the service of a unified soul. This adaption toward new technologies, just like the child creating new languages demonstrate clearly that children truly do surpass the past ways of being as they activate their *Need to Know*.

Summary

As a child grows in age, they do not stop requiring the *Need to Know;* they just demand a different type of approach to questioning and beliefs, just as we all do when something does not sit well with what we know to be true for us. Opening to expansive worldviews, religious differences, and being able to explore many possibilities, supports the child's *Need to Know*. Supporting children to open up to broader knowledge systems and beliefs expands their internal horizons and helps the child to know how they are connected to a source of wonderful information, available to them anytime. The various symptoms of the child resulting from the unmet *Need to Know,* at one end of the spectrum may present as apathy, lack of purpose, and self-doubt in the child, or at the other end, overextending the meaning of everything, and obsessive or rigid behaviours. All of the child's seven needs are vitally important to be cultivated, however, the *Need to Know* allows the child to have a felt sense of who they are within a larger purpose and within divinity. Children with a strong *Need to Know* can approach unfamiliar environments and new experiences with an inner balance.

Tips To Cultivate The Need To Know

At any age in any situation, you can encourage your child's *Need to Know* the following ways:

- Open discussions with your children to explore the notions that everything and everyone is your teacher. "What did you learn about yourself today?" conversations at the dinner table are a wonderful ritual.
- Encourage discussions on religious diversity and the wonderful variety and offerings that come from someone else's perspective.
- Inspire your child with stories about worldviews of interdependence, and a knowing that they are one with life.
- You might like to undertake a focused meditation with children that support the following phrases:

You learn from everything around you; If you close your eyes, you can try to imagine yourself soaking up the information of the whole universe, just like reading a book; and, Knowledge from the past, as well as the future is available to you, as well as knowledge about distant lands and galaxies too. These themes open the child's 7th Chakra energies, igniting the child's *Need to Know*.

- Restore confidence in children who feel they don't know anything by taking a moment to help them imagine themselves being the greatest that they can be.

- Support children if they have trouble making a decision to pay attention to their feelings, while also asking the cosmos to help. This opening of thought will allow the child to attract many wonderful ideas and a knowing beyond their mind.

- Encourage your child to know that there is an infinite supply of information available to them and that the most important information for them will be remembered.

- Affirm to the child the important part they play in the *whole* (family, society, and culture, extending out to the whole world), "You are a part of the whole, and anything that you do has an effect on everything and everyone else. The world would not be the same without your brilliance."

Needs Table 7: The Need to Know

Potential of need as the centre point of balance

Deficient	Balanced	Excess
Dependent on others	Self-knowledge	Grandiose
Lack of meaning	Meaning	Obsessive
Lack of purpose	Purpose	Over extend
Unrealised potential	Potential	Self-importance
Apathy	Belief systems	Rigid
Separation	Unity	Addiction
Fragmentation	Wholeness	Attachment
Lack of faith	Divinity	Spiritual addictions
Self-doubt	Higher power	Blaming God
Dissociation	Connection	Disdainful

PART III
SUPPORTING THE SOUL

Chapter Five
Being In The Question

The important thing is not to stop questioning.
Curiosity has its own reason for existing.

~ *Albert Einstein.*[1]

The *Foundational Needs Model* (FNM) takes us a long way toward the aim of an improved philosophy of the child because it allows us to identify how the child's unmet needs present in a variety of ways. With this knowledge we are better equipped to support the child especially when life situations create certain fragmentations to return to a state of balance and wholeness. The FNM also helps us to identify our own limitations and unmet needs as adults. When we as adults become more aware of the unhealthy patterns of relating that have restricted us, we may all move forward with more unity and realise our unique human potential. The FNM offers a very useful map to understand the child and its needs, however the child itself will always offer us the truest reflection of what they need. By relating with children in a way that not only supports the FNM, but further matches the inherent unity of the soul (I Feel, I Think, I Act), we are moving toward improved relationships with our children.

In order to really know what our children need; however, we must ask them and we must also be aware of those things that cannot be communicated verbally. In essence we need to treat children with the highest positive regard if we are to improve our relationships with them as well as their relationship to themselves. By both creating and holding a supportive space for children to express what matters to them, children can in fact discover for themselves not just what they need, but how they might communicate it. As you are now aware, the most valuable skill to teach our children is that their feelings are directing them toward their best possible outcomes. To encourage the alignment of children's feelings and thoughts means we also have to support children to trust their feelings, even when sometimes there is no way of knowing what the feelings mean. This chapter describes the process of *Being in the Question,* which aids adults to become familiar with and then to begin to activate this type of support. *Being in the Question,* is a 3-step process that assists adults to meet children at their level of need without projecting their own limiting patterns, beliefs, or behaviours onto the child.

Adults, however, as we have seen established throughout, can only relate to children from the degree of emotional maturity that they possess and in this regard we all have aspects of an unresolved past. As we are collectively becoming more aware of the aim for unity in self, we can relate to children with more enhanced sensitivities and a subtle attunement. This in turn allows children a greater degree of agency. This chapter then, offers both a theoretical as well as practical framework that I developed for relating with children. *Being in the Question* is an approach that can be used with confidence in any environment or setting where adults work with children. *Being in the Question* offers an interactive relational space whereby the child is positioned as the facilitator of its own feelings and thoughts, and adults are the interpreters of the child's expression. It is a three-part relational approach for adults and children that can be applied in any situation in which adults interact with children and children interact with each other.

BEING IN THE QUESTION

- *I Feel*

  The first part of the process is attunement. In this first step we begin by attuning with the child's feelings, which requires we attempt to hold the space to feel ourselves what they might be feeling. This requires a level of self-awareness in regard to our own emotional life.

- *I Think*

  The second part is wonder. This step gives children a relational space to begin to question the possible reasons, to think about, their feelings, without adult projection (thinking for themselves assists the child to arrive at a thought that resonates with their feelings).

- *I Act*

  The third part is responsiveness. This step allows the adult to support the child to act - or take action in way that supports those feelings and thoughts in harmony.

To relate in this way the adult, parent, or caregiver, has to consistently be in the question of the meaning of the child's experience. Not to presume or guess, and to use a questioning role in attempting to understand the child's needs. In short, the main reason we see children struggle to voice their needs is because in the actual adult-child relational space, children do not always feel safe to express, as their feelings on many matters are different to what they are told they should be.

Children are always expressing a language of need through their issues, symptoms, and behaviours, which has been referred to throughout as the *child push*. In seeking to identify and discuss when the needs are met, and in effect, mastered in the child, the resulting action will set the child on what is termed adaptive pathways. There is, however, some skill required on behalf of the adult to open a space for such communication with the child, and a requirement for a release of control – that comes as the *adult push*.

We may examine the following question,

"How can we position ourselves as adult caregivers, teachers, and parents, to see from the child's perspective so as to better serve them?"

The difficulty of arriving at a true child's perspective can be challenging. We can nevertheless begin with the most important assumption -- that is, the child is the best guide to his/her life because the child has within itself a vast supply of information that assists them to navigate the best way forward for themselves, according to themselves.

PROMPTS TO REMEMBER

- Children need to be given the space to feel. From this space they can begin to pay attention to the language of their bodies and their emotional life, which offers knowledge about their needs and wellbeing (both metaphorical and very real knowledge).

- Children need help to process their feelings, thoughts, and actions, as well as help to understand the *language* of their bodies.

- Children need reassurance that their signals of need, such as their feelings, issues, symptoms, emotional outbursts, and body responses are always supporting their best growth; even if this is counter to what they are told or are led to believe by others.

Holding the Space – Attunement (*I Feel*)

In order to transform the limiting patterns and beliefs that are not supportive of our children highest growth it is necessary that we learn to hold space for our children. In order to hold the space for our children and others we first must make the space. I know how difficult this can be, because as we manage the many demands we have as parents, teachers, and caregivers of children, we are managing a variety of other significant aspects of life. Making space requires time; more than this, however, it requires an intention to be present and a commitment to attune with your child. The consequence of adults becoming more attentive is recognised as what is broadly termed mindfulness.[2]

The mindful approach requires that adults engage in moment-to-moment awareness, hold compassion and unconditional acceptance of the child, as well as maintain emotional awareness and self-regulation of themselves.[3] Being mindful is a big part of the process of deeply connecting with children. However, it does not guarantee to make it easy, unless there has already been some inner inquiry undertaken on the part of the adult.

If an adult has not learned how to be attuned to their own feelings and thoughts, they will have difficulty with the concept of *knowing thyself,* and so will struggle when their children mirror their unknown selves back to them, and show them things they may not like seeing. The sections on each *Foundational Need* in part two of the FNM, gave examples of this point with reference to each of the seven needs. To recap the idea: if we have repressed, denied, or projected our own lack of fulfillment, grief, or disappointment, then our children will trigger this in us. Even the most willing adults will not always find the child's expressions, behaviours, and challenges pleasant or easy. Making the unknown known, in this regard, comes with a set of challenges—even for the most open-minded.

If we as adults can consider our personal and unconscious repetitive cycles and patterns as fields of influence on our children, we are pushed in our own attempts to transform ourselves. I know this is true for me. Believe me however; just because I advocate for an improved way of viewing and relating to children, does not mean I have been the perfect mother or that it has come easy to me to allow my children to direct their own way forward. In fact, many times I seemed to be groping in the dark. I often joke that I have just become quite good at seeing in the dark; after all, we each have our own shadow to embrace as part of our soul unification. This means that as adults we must come from a stance and in essence ask ourselves, "How is what I am doing today, or even what I have done in the past, having an impact on my child now?" Not to place blame or feel guilty about our past but to push beyond our limited past when we come to interpret children's needs.

In order to understand what we can do to support children as they shape the future, we need to explore our own past and make peace with our childhoods. Only then can we allow children to be free to follow their own direction, without the felt constraints from us. When adults can soften and open to the *child push* they open to what the child is expressing about the things that occur for them. Thus, come to see the importance of the child's expressions based on their bodily responses, actions, and behaviours. Often it is not quite what adults imagine and yet in children's behaviours, challenges as well as their curiosity, we see them pushing to seek meaning as a unified whole. Finding the answers that feel right for them, those things that resonate and have meaning to the soul, allows the child to move forward in the best way for them.

The better we know our needs as parents and caregivers of children—the better equipped we are to assist children to meet their needs, and essentially, to know themselves. Then when we see responses expressed by the child in the form of a demanding question, a defiance, screaming loudly, hitting or biting another child, or whining and moaning when asked to do something we can see they actually have a deeper meaning.

- When a child is anxious, they are proclaiming *Soothe Me*, because I am still learning to soothe myself.

- When a child has a tantrum, they are proclaiming *Free Me* from the emotional confusion.

- When a child is rebellious, they are proclaiming *Allow Me*, to do things my way sometimes.

- When a child is angry, they are proclaiming *Love Me*, when I seem the most unlovable is when I need it the most.

- When a child does not want to talk, they are proclaiming *Hear Me* and listen to all those things I do not, or cannot say.

- When a child has difficulty learning, they are proclaiming *See Me*, and please see what I see.

- When a child is hypersensitive, they are proclaiming *Know Me*, and my deep connection to all, so that I may *know myself*.

When we see behaviours we don't like, we can ask ourselves a question like, "I wonder what my child is *feeling* to respond to life that way?"

Then when you can take pause, and even take a breath, you can ask yourself a question, rather than always projecting onto the child, you can also explore what the child might be feeling at the same time. For example, "What would I have to be feeling to respond to life like that?" Enquiring into a child's responses by asking oneself the question, "What would I have to be feeling to do that?" allows one to consider what a child might be experiencing. As you do this you begin to align and attune with your child. To come from such a relational stance requires a mindful approach. In such a relational environment, we are positioned to allow the child to open so we can then ascertain the purpose of the response, behaviour, or issues they are facing. In a dialogue that allows for an open-ended answer and also expresses to the child how you yourself might feel in such a situation (without, of course, making it about you), the focus becomes about the feelings, thoughts, and emotions beneath the child's action, not the behaviour itself.

If adults can remain in the question when children experience certain things without reacting to the triggers that a child may bring forth, it allows the adult caregiver space to monitor their own internal responses, those narratives and stories and their associated feelings and thoughts that are embedded in the unconscious and arise in interactions with the child. If there is no space to discern where the child's responses might be coming from, they will mostly remain stuck in a loop. The child's unease, distress, unhappiness, depression, efforts for attention, and misbehaviour, as well as physical manifestations such as stomach aches and bedwetting, can be recognised by the caregiver as an unmet need and attend to it appropriately so the patterning can be realised. Epigenetics tells us that we adopt patterns of relating that replicate those already within the family and are sitting in a type of transformative suspension. By being responsive to the child as well as one's own self, the underlying unmet need can begin to be recognised.

When you attune with the child in this way you may then get an inner prompt or awareness in the form of an answer, such as, "If I am unsure or anxious about a new situation, I will ask a lot of questions to feel safe."

Examples of other questions you might ask:

- "If I was told what to do by someone all the time, I might act defiantly too,"
- "If I got to a point of wanting to scream myself, it would be because I had literally had enough of something"
- "If I felt like biting or hitting someone, I would have to be feeling very frustrated."
- "If I am in pain, I might whine and moan."

I am sure by now you get the point. The thing is, sometimes we have to actually evoke the very behaviours that we see in our child in ourselves. We can role-play in our mind, in an attempt to attune with the feeling underneath the child's behaviours. Of course, personally, I have never intended to scream (but it has happened), and I may never have bitten anyone, and I hope I have never moaned out loud when I was in pain, but I have to be able to feel, in a reflective way, what these expressions might mean to me, and I can often recall a time when they may have seemed like good options. This has been a necessary practice for me in order to get closer to understanding my own children first, and then to understand all the children I assist. Like many adults, I have inhibited such instinctual responses due to moral and social codes of conduct, and conditioning which has basically denied these natural, albeit not always acceptable, responses.

You may take a pause and feel into the situation and ask – so as to become attuned with your child, something along the lines of,

"I know sometimes I feel like screaming when I feel like I have had enough of everything." "Sometimes I even feel like I'm going to explode." "Can you tell me what you are feeling?" "Can you tell me what made you feel like biting that child?" "Can you show me if you are hurting or in pain anywhere?"

The responses of the child to such questions will allow you to explore the unmet need fuelling the resulting behaviour. If insight or an answer does not come easily to you, you can take some deep breaths and feel into the situation. Sometimes I meditate on it, and sometimes I pray for guidance. In essence, we as adults have to reconnect to our own feelings and thoughts before we can begin to meet the needs of the child in this way.

When the child is given the space to feel the dynamics and explore the feelings that have led them to scream, bite, or moan, for example, and come to see why they have acted in a certain way, they can talk about these feelings more easily. This allows them to explore the salient unmet need that lies beneath the surface of any presenting challenge Of course, the belief that assumes the child is capable and competent is foundational to this approach, and again, we, as adults, need to re-align ourselves so we may get closer to knowing how children perceive the environment around them.

The general argument throughout this book has been that the child is signifying all of the time what they really need. How the child acts in life and their expressions and responses to life are all important indications as to what they really need. Through the child's symptoms, behaviours, and issues (otherwise termed imbalances), both children and caregivers are supplied with extremely important information. But too often this information is not used in the most skillful way. The reason to disregard or overlook important signals is not always due to a lack of care, however, but more a lack of awareness about the child's needs.

Being in the Question – Wonder (*I Think*)

Being in the Question is a term then that captures the mindfulness and wonder of relating with children that allows adults to see, hear, and feel the child on the child's own terms. As has been expressed earlier in part one, this state of being is about the adult taking an unusual position (from a Western cosmology) of naiveté and respect for the child's wisdom by allowing the interaction with children to be framed by the question, "Please show me what is happening for you?" We are not projecting what we think is occurring, or even what we think ought to be occurring; we are asking what is actually happening for them in any given situation. Because it has always seemed so important to me to validate children's experiences, it also seemed that the most commonsense thing to do was to encourage the child's own sense of curiosity. Rather than struggling with the many questions or concerns they have, allow them to solve their own issues.

It was in fact my own sons' wonder and puzzlement that reignited my wonder and puzzlement from childhood in so many ways, and as I attuned with their innate curiosity, I reconnected with my own. As a consequence, I found the greatest joy in mothering. It was a question one of my sons asked when he had just begun to have a command of language, around age two, that taught me how to relate with him from his perspective. He asked me one evening while I was driving, "Why is the moon following us, mummy?" to which I had no reply. I mean, I knew that the moon was not following us in a logical sense, but I didn't feel that he needed to hear that. Pausing for a moment, I asked him the same question back. "Why do *you* think the moon is following us?" My son proceeded to give me his perspective, and he didn't give just one reason, but a few. He said, "The moon loves us and follows us because it is dark," and then he said, "Because it wants to help us see better," and also, "It wants to go where we are going." If I had expressed to my son that the moon only appeared to be following us, I would never have heard how things felt to him. And I would not have had the flash of insight that if I am truly to understand my child, I need to allow him to express how things occur for him, rather than putting my ideas onto him or telling him anything. It struck me at that moment that children do not always ask questions to get an answer, but to express their own meaning in the hope others may know them and be understood in their essence more deeply.

It can take us a while to come to the realisation that our children may not even accept the answers that we offer, or take the advice we give them. In my own mothering, I felt there must be a better use of my energy than trying to control and contain my children. It is not that I let them get away without taking responsibility, but I was watchful to listen to them, rather than tell them. The push of the soul to grow and expand in its entire brilliance means invariably a new question will always arise. Curiosity is a natural part of the soul seeking its purpose and unity, and this push does not leave the child; the push will not stop until an answer satisfies their curious nature. Of course, the child's curiosity might get masked, inhibited, or even become an obsessive behaviour; it may get transformed into a certain way of relating, but it is always present, sitting just beneath. Children encouraged to know that they will naturally question things as a consequence of their magnificence, and because of this, they can rest assured that even if no one has an answer that feels right to them now, they must not stop trusting their feelings, as the answer will come eventually, somewhere, somehow.

As adults, once we come to realise that it is futile to use our *adult push* against the *child push* and we see if we truly want harmony, we have to become good at working with the *soul push*. It can actually become simple for all involved if we just allow children to answer the questions, they have for themselves. After all, given that we now can see that we as adults cannot put the meaning on our children's experiences, and that they will make meaning for themselves regardless, it seems to short circuit a lot of pain. If questions that arise for children are encouraged and affirmed as being purposeful to their soul, they will welcome even the most complex of inquiries. Being in the Question not only assists the child to discover the meaning of any experience or puzzlement they may be having without assumptions or projections, but it also allows them to become the mediator of their experiences and to trust their own capacities. In effect, this way of relating meets many of the child's *Foundational Needs*. When children know that whatever they are feeling will be welcomed, they begin to relax within themselves and this opens the space for growth to occur in its own time.

Given the space to feel, children spontaneously begin to question the possible reasons, to think about, their feelings, without adult projection (thinking for themselves assists the child to arrive at a thought that resonates with their feelings). Children who feel at home with their feelings and thoughts do not need to run or hide from themselves *(Need to be Safe and Secure)*. If a child finds it difficult to face their feelings, you can assist them by modeling a warm, open space to communicate and express what they are feeling *(Need to Feel)*. From this space, the child can then move toward showing you or figuring out for themselves, what they need and what feels best for them *(Need to Act)*. Feeling loved and heard *(Need to Love and Need to Speak)* allows the expression of the child to surface with ease, and allows caregivers to be mindful not to answer or put words onto the child's experience. Children need to see and have demonstrated for them that it is okay to question the way things are, to have different visions or ideas, or even to feel that they can make a mistake or change their view about something *(Need to See)*. In fact, even a so-called mistake is a fantastic opportunity to see beyond limiting patterns. The child needs to know that you are just as interested in supporting them as you are to look at and reconsider your own past, and that they are, in fact, teaching you in their *Need to Know*.

In considering the following questions, we may get a register of how well we are cultivating the *Foundational Needs* in our own lives, so we can support the children in our lives to do the same.

- Do you know how to *soothe* your child?
- Are you comfortable letting your child be *free* to explore their full emotional spectrum?
- Do you *allow* your child to follow its own direction?
- Can you show unconditional *love* if your child does something to hurt you?

- Do you make space to listen and *hear* your child's expressions?

- Are you open to the visions your children *see* for themselves?

- Can you receive information from your children about what they *know*?

If we answer no to any of these, that's okay, as from this point on, we will just know that we have some potentials to realise. We can make a decision to move through our feelings of blame or guilt if they arise in response to the way we may have sometimes cared for children in the past. But now that we know better, we can begin to do better. By drawing on our innate potential, we can ask more questions about what else we can do as we undertake such a critical role as a parent and caregiver. These questions, you will notice, do not offer a way to shape the child; they are awareness prompts of reflection. These questions will hopefully encourage you to pause, even if it is initially just for as long as it takes to read them. When you do, please let them settle within you. Educators of children can also reflect on the questions noted above, as they pertain to groups of children in their care. Therapeutically, these questions offer an affirmative stance for the child.

Questioning leads to better understanding of the child, and also to the child feeling valued. However, in truth, many adults struggle with directing the attention to the child's needs, as they are not entirely aware of the degree to which they are caught up in their own needs, or do not realise that the child is reflecting valuable information to a curious parent. When we hold the idea that we know best there is no room for anyone to question anything. It is like a wall comes up or a door gets closed in front of us.

Perhaps we fear the questions our children ask or the answers they give, or we are busy with other, more important concerns, or we may even be afraid of our children's criticism. If this is the case, then we need to remember that we can become aware of our own emotional response to the child's experiences as the first point of relating. It can seem problematic to change the way we meet the needs of our children and to open a dialogue willing to accept the reality that we may not know how to meet their needs, and that we are in need of some assistance. Such a way of relating with children requires vulnerability and openness not often freely demonstrated by parents toward their children.

Entering the Conversation – Responsiveness (I Act)

For adults, an interactive perspective such as *Being in the Question* might proceed in the following way; by asking the child, "Please show me what is occurring for you?" This request assumes that the adult is interested in the child and their experience, and sends a clear message, spoken or unspoken, that, "I am here for you." You can even verbalise this statement out loud, but you must be prepared to hold the energy of this statement in your actions. This is an act of responsiveness. Once you express a statement such as 'I am here for you' you need to demonstrate that you mean what you say and are actually interested and keen to see what you can do to help—not to solve or fix something, but to listen with compassion. By holding the space in this way with children, you are giving them the energetic space to explore and question the meaning of things, which is rather different from intellectualising or trying to figure out what is happening from a cognitive sense.

This way of arriving at answers to certain problems is very natural for children. Children are full of wonder, and if you have spent more than five minutes with a child, you may have noticed this yourself! Gareth Matthews conveys to his college students that doing philosophy is natural and that, as children, they were already doing it. Matthews' book, *Philosophy and the Young Child*, is full of examples of the inherent philosophic nature of children. Matthews' points out that the puzzlements of children are, in fact, the beginnings of philosophy. He notes that Aristotle told us that philosophy begins with wonder. The following passage from the book succinctly relays Matthews' thought:

> *"Aristotle also suggests that the wonder that initiates philosophy is akin to puzzlement. And Wittgenstein says, 'a Philosophical problem has the form: I don't know my way about'. Sometimes philosophical puzzlement is dissolved. One learns to find one's way about; perhaps one reasons one's way out of difficulty. But sometimes the puzzlement is not dissolved, at least not for a long time."* [4]

Children ask a lot of questions, and it has been my experience that children do not always require answers to such questions. They do, however, need space to *Be in the Question* for themselves as to the meaning of their puzzlement. Tobin Hart recognises that children may be uncertain of how to make sense of certain experiences (especially if they do not have the cultural model to assist) and yet, he says, "However it weaves itself into a lifetime the wonder remains within us as a touchstone."[5] Children, Hart adds, need help to integrate some of their vision into everyday life.

As demonstrated throughout, by becoming aware of how they feel and what they think, children can manage their own energy with more power in service to themselves and the world. Therefore, put quite simply, when children understand and can express when there is harmony or disharmony between those things they feel and the thoughts they hold, (and these are often subtle or not always felt by everyone in the same way), then they can attend to it. By allowing space for the child to tune into the meaning of the feeling or bodily response for them, it means we also help them to appreciate their unique sensitivities. Children become good at appreciating that the way they feel and think determines how and why they act in certain ways. They can see how their feelings and thoughts have an impact on their emotional lives and their biological systems which lead to all the physical presentations we see in the child's behaviours. With the FNM, the child and adult are able to see the meaning of why the child has acted in a certain way or why they have a particular problem in their lives.

Responsiveness from the adult allows the child to act out or take action in way that supports those feelings and thoughts in harmony. The puzzlement that we are not comfortable with in our own lives as adults, will not be easily reconciled if we do not work in a new way with our children's puzzlement. It is up to us to pause now to consider what it is the child might be missing due to the attempts of adults to try to solve their puzzlement for them rather than allowing them to unfold and question the meaning of their lives from the highest possible perspective for themselves. To do this means we have to get comfortable with feeling uncomfortable, because often the issues and assaults on our children's own natural growth and unfolding are not visible or obvious. I have seen many parents who felt that they had a very open relationship with their child, be taken by surprise by what surfaced, things that the child had not told the parent, for various reasons. The degree to which children are inhibited or forced onto a certain path is not always apparent, and yet, it is vital that we have ways of recognising this is what is happening. When unrecognised, children painfully fragment and disconnect from particular aspects of their wholeness due to the expectations of others, even in the most seemingly (to adults) simple of situations. Being mindful of the child's needs as they grow means we will be more aware of any imbalance if and when it surfaces. We can regularly ask the following for ourselves.

What do my children really need? What happens when my children do not get what they need? What ought I, as a caregiver do to support my child at each age to ensure that wellbeing is a foundational platform in their life? How do I support the development of children in a way that capitalises on their full potential?

By adopting the process of attunement, wonder, and responsiveness, we have a way of relating that mirrors the function of the soul. To attune (feel), to wonder (think without adding projection) and to respond (act from these integrated processes) supports the child to know themselves in ways that we have not been able to support before. The answers to the questions just posed, come from philosophy itself. By simply reframing the conceptualisation of the child as a soul, it allows us to re-centre the child as an entity with an authoritative voice— a being that has relative autonomy and interests—a distinct entity that cannot be discerned through adult formulations. A lack of an operational definition of the child has meant we have missed much of what children really need. When we see children possess nascent, but fully functioning capacities, we can move away from simply transmitting information, we can now begin to allow children to feel and think for themselves, which is a transformative type of living and learning. When we can meet the child from the FNM, as well as *Being in the Question* with them, we are open to a new philosophy of and for the child, to emerge—a *Childosophy*.

The wisdom of the child can be supported by handing back to children a way to understand and interpret their experiences, from a unity that is the foundation of who they are. Not by getting somewhere, but by being united as they travel through all their experiences. When the child possesses internal integrity of body-mind-spirit, they act in a way that is in accord with their highest potentials. Wellbeing is the result of the composite, whole self, working in harmony. Abiding in a state of wellbeing or unity of soul allows the child to draw upon their own inner resources, which are manifold and always guiding them in their best direction forward. Potential is not a measure, a mark, a grade, or even a wonderful achievement. All these things are laudable, and yet, without the inner feelings and thoughts accompanying the meaning of the child's external achievements, the child's real soul potential is often denied.

Experience shows that when children draw on interpretations from ideas of a unified self, they naturally make decisions about what is right and wrong, how they should care for others, and how to be most loving in the world. Children make decisions centred on the idea of activating their best potential, which is innate to the soul. Teaching children compassion, for instance, becomes unwarranted when children are supported to know how everything relates to everything else, as compassion is the natural by-product of such a knowing. When this interrelatedness is modelled and imbibed by those around the child, they are pushed to move toward them, as the soul knows these things very well. When children are simply aware that they are interdependent souls that are in communion with others and all of life, it opens them up in a whole new way of being and enables them to wonder about the possibilities of their existence. I often marvel in wonder about the potential for our children if only they had access to such expansive knowledge about who they really are.

What then? I see in my mind's eye a group of children being exposed to a philosophy teacher (just as I was in the story I recounted in the *Need to See)* who tells them a story that inspires them to consider the possibility contained in the question, "Do you know that we are all made of stardust?

Conclusion

"I find that all my thoughts circle around God like the planets around the sun, and are as irresistibly attracted by Him. I would feel it to be the grossest sin if I were to oppose any resistance to this force."

~ Carl Jung,[6]

The push of my soul has been circling around the two themes of children and the soul, it seems for my entire life. You have seen how my understanding of this *push* has changed shape as I have grown. As a little girl growing up in a religious family, the notions of soul and God were framed within a particular story and with a certain language. As I have matured, the stories that I hold about myself and my world have expanded. My language has expanded too. I often prefer representative language and metaphor as I find that many things I feel have no set words. Interestingly, as Carl Jung expresses so beautifully above, all of my feelings and thoughts really, in essence, circle around God. My interpretation of God has changed shape as I have grown, and yet, the original feeling remains. To me, as you have seen, God is the life sustaining, benevolent force that is invested in my best growth, one that I am not separate from. As a little girl, had I known that it was natural sometimes to have no words for certain feelings, perhaps I would not have felt so alone. Had I known, too, that questioning my life and my self was important and pivotal at every age, I might have been confident enough to ask more questions. Had I also known that my questions could actually only be answered by me, I might not have sought others' approval so much. Maybe, had I known that my questions and my self-development were connected to the self-development of all human beings, and in particular children, would things be different? Who knows? But I do know that my wonder will remain, nevertheless, like planets around the sun.

The various definitions of the *push* that I referred to in the beginning of this book have been demonstrated throughout; firstly, in the *child push* as children push adults in their attempt to stay integrated as a whole soul; secondly, in the manner in which the *adult push* is forced upon children, as children are shaped, motivated, and directed by adults; thirdly, the ultimate push, in the *soul push* to maintain unity in order to manifest its destiny. I have demonstrated how these pushes, in their variations, all point to the same energy. The *soul push* however as you have seen has not always been an easy one to understand and integrate for humanity outside of religious frameworks. And most certainly, its importance has often been disregarded, because the things about the *soul push* is, the only one who can truly know the true meaning of one's soul push, is one's self.

Midwife of the Soul

If we as adults can come to *know thyself* we offer a mirror to our children, one that reflects the soul. As Socrates and Plato after him espoused we could not really teach another, but we could draw forth what was already within a person, and that in doing so; people could discover their own wisdom. Socrates said philosophers are midwifes of the soul and the greatest position to meet another from in order to help them bring forth their own wisdom was to *know thyself*. I love the idea of being a midwife to the little one's souls, as allowing children to bring forth the potential of their soul is my life's work. This work requires that I continually work on myself as well so that I do not project my unconscious, unhealed past on to the next generations. The importance then of a model of the soul, which allows adults and children to trust and value their *soul push*, means they are working with life, rather than against it. The significance of the theory of the soul, as well as the FNM as a map for the soul, positioned in this book, is that if we are truly to know what children need, we ought to know ourselves first. Then from a position of self-knowledge and authority over one own life, one can attune with what it is that children need. By knowing ourselves as adults, we will come to self inquire about own motivations first. Are those things we feel and think aligned? What might I need when my feelings and thoughts are not aligned? What do I feel pushed toward and why? Where is the *push* coming from?

The insights that I have gained over time, by being with these particular questions, as you have seen in the book have come in many ways. My childhood wonder, as well as the wonder of every child I have worked with, especially my own children, has allowed for much growth. And for various reasons, some of the insights I obtained in response to my questions could be shared with others. Many things I saw and heard were often beyond any explanation. I have been blessed to witness children that spoke of past lives in great detail and were struggling to comprehend how they were here now. I have seen children express their parent's deeply guarded secrets, and watched as parents became irritated with the child for uttering the unspoken truth. I have seen children have nightmares that appear to have no origin with the child at all, but can be linked to something that occurred for a distant family member, and even in some cases at some other point in the continuum of the child's soul. I have seen children receive vital information, with great accuracy, as they hold objects, even pinpointing certain historical events. I have seen children spontaneously emerge with a language that the parents have never heard. I have seen children with phobias that, like in the case of Hans, are an existential longing to know that they are a soul. I have witnessed children describe other planets and speak of how they feel displaced and long to go home. In these experiences, I just knew, somehow, that they were accurate and true; these things I felt and saw in children resonated deeply with me.

I have also seen the gift for families of children who are developmentally delayed or on the autism spectrum experience astounding growth in consciousness, presence, and love, all as a result of accepting their child just as they are. Many deep rewards are offered to parents who are interested to know how things are occurring for their child, aside from what they are led to think or told to believe. Mostly, I see children with common issues pertaining to fragmentation of feeling and thought. A self-harming behaviour might be traced to an experience of the child from five years of age where they felt abandoned and unloved at the commencement of school. A child feeling powerless, which originates from being bullied by others in a social setting. A child with a learning difficulty with an original imbalance linked to the mother's beliefs about capabilities or learning a particular subject. Once the origin of imbalance is acknowledged, the pattern of fragmentation can be released. These holding patterns have been protecting the child, so they did not have to feel the pain of unexpressed feelings that could not be understood. The awareness of the origin of the feelings has deep meaning and makes much sense to the child. The resonance of things that are true and make sense to us is very healing.

The question for me then became, how do we incorporate the child's ways so those who are not children or have forgotten what it is like to be a child, can understand what children need? Through intensive study and clinical experience, I came to realise that I was part of a larger emergence and the unfolding of humanity. Today, thankfully many of these same unexplained experiences that I observed in children can now be clarified in greater detail thanks to progress in scientific research, and what has been termed a rise in human consciousness. In the academy especially, the last fifteen years has seen a period of heightened interest in studying the child. It seemed to me through an explicit focus on the importance of spirituality in childhood aside from purely religious studies, a shift in the ways we understand the child had begun. The childhood movement itself actually echoes the same concerns, efforts, and resistances that the feminist movements experienced when women sought equal recognition to men. Perhaps as Montessori recognised "The study of the child may have an infinitely wider influence, extending to all human questions. In the mind of the child, we may find the key to progress."[7]

This endeavour for *The Push for a Child Philosophy* is not just about our children; it is about our humanity and the forgotten, repressed, and often-wounded aspects of our total human experience. At this point the collective, as well as the individual child, are asserting their need for recognition. Not as objects of adult projection, or as future adults themselves, but as wondrous souls. At the same time, fortunately, it appears that women who have not felt it was possible to fully embrace the role of being a mother without forgoing the equal rights that their mothers fought so hard for, can rest assured that there is great value in mothering. Of course, you have to feel this for yourself.

As I expressed in the first part of the book, it was when I became a mother that I began to realise my untapped potentials, and it was also the point in my life where the themes of the soul and childhood collided. The growth that I have experienced from my role as a mother has no measurable boundary, and at the same time, it is the most soul-nourishing and fulfilling role I have had to date. I am not a grandmother yet, so this may change. Within the connection to my children, I have had continually mirrored back to me all of my unrealised potentials and all the unhealed wounds from my collective past. Mothering has answered many of my questions, and it has also ignited many more. Intuitively, well before the science confirmed it, I felt that there was a deeper meaning beneath my own children's experiences, and that these were somehow related to something much bigger than a single, separate existence. Many great thinkers, educators, philosophers, and parents in the past did not have the support of modern science, but still knew much about the importance of the soul and its role in our lives. They all explored, in various ways, how we as adults ought to work with the *child push*. This resonance also gave a deeper meaning to my own childhood experiences, and all of the deep felt feelings that I had tried to hold together in some semblance, ever since I was a little girl.

The *soul push* is now supported by new scientific findings that tell us that non-physical fields of energy and unseen energetics are shaping our human experiences. Morphic resonance and epigenetics highlight that the child acts as a direct mirror for the total of the past, and that the child also contributes to the collective memory affecting the future. If we can be the best version we can be, then our children will not have to carry our unhealed past any further. As epigenetics reminds us the origin of the feelings, thoughts and emotions are actually carried in the cells of our descendants and shape their lives. The biological expression of the past generations lives within our children. Of course, this can seem overwhelming to consider because then the many reasons that our children do what they do becomes harder to discern. However, it is within this dynamic that we are offered an opportunity to transform consciousness in a wonderful way. When both adults and children are supported to have their needs meet simultaneously, there is a much better chance of activating the support we all need for the day-to-day issues and challenges that we face.

If we are to allow the child full authority over their inner lives it requires adults learn how to be present with our children. It is important to note that by in *Being in the Question* we get closer to understanding from a place of wonder, what is occurring for our children, from their perspective. Nevertheless, to begin to open to the child's experience in a true sense, we need to become aware of how far from our own unity of feelings, thoughts, and actions we have strayed over our own lifespan and be prepared to transform ourselves. My reconnection to my own wholeness began as a mother as it does for many women. Having a transformation in this way often opens to a broader perspective of what the feelings of particular experiences in the past mean in the now.

In chapter two, I discussed birthing my first child I mentioned that at this time I had the strangest feeling that

I had given birth before. I had let go of trying to understand this feeling then, but it had never left me. My own exploration of life and the research I have conducted allows me to find a resolution with this memory. It may at some future point in time be open for review, but at this point in time, I feel wholeness in regard to that experience. Following all I have discussed in the book; it is easier to see that somehow inherited memory may have merged with my present moment experience of the actual birth and this resonated deeply with me. Where this memory had come from could, however, still be interpreted in varying ways. Answering a question such as, why had I experienced that feeling during the birthing of my first son and what did it mean for me and my best growth? can only be interpreted from the model, worldview, or perspective that I hold. As I hope is clear by now, my interest has been to offer the most expansive model available in the service of the little ones.

From the theory presented throughout, you are now aware that my own memory, as mentioned above, could be interpreted in various ways. Perhaps, this memory could have been a memory from my mother; after all, she had birthed seven children, and epigenetics supports this account. Or it could be the inherited collective memory from all women who had birthed children before me, and morphic resonance supports this account. Or it could have been from a point in time on the continuum of my soul's experiences held as a memory from a past incarnation, and reincarnation and quantum physics supports this account. Or it could have been a memory from my own birth experience. I was born with the umbilical cord around my neck and when I was birthed after much distress, I was blue and had to be resuscitated.

This would have been a traumatic time for my mother and me, as the research on birth trauma highlights it is. Because our first experiences are deeply embedded and embodied, it seems natural that for much of my own experience, I have literally had to push through adverse conditions to return to unity. However, I did feel a deeper purpose in these experiences, which has allowed me to a degree to push for others too.

Of course, as with each person's experience, there will be possible variable scenarios to any singular or particular feeling. My experience is mentioned, to highlight the wonder that arises when our understanding of children can be broadened and to begin to interpret why they feel the way they feel, within a tangible way to begin to incorporate the ideas of the past, as well as the child's inherent soul brilliance, in a new way. The tendency to want an answer for what is going on for our children that is set and determined, without considering what it means to them, is because we are not often able to hold more than one possibility in suspension. The most accurate answer must resonate with one's soul. If the answers or the thinking about our feelings do not match, as you are at this point well aware, the soul will continue to push for unity.

When adults become consciously aware of the subtle and very tangible dynamics of the child's energetic landscape, they are better equipped to support the child. When adults are aware of their own patterns of behaviour from the past and know more about the collective human patterning in the way of the *Foundational Needs* that we all share, within families, societies and cultures, we can open to a world in which children will not have to keep repeating and returning to themes we have not mastered yet. They will be free to move toward their own soul's purpose with much more clarity. Perhaps, from this point on, we may now ask with a new energy; What might children really need if we assume they have everything already within them for their perfect self-awareness and growth?

The Anatomy of the Soul

The theory of the child as a soul presented in this book, along with the FNM positions us to appreciate the child's wisdom like never before. In actual fact, we can rest assured that we can confidently move forward knowing that new science matches what many great philosophers and mystics have long known; that human beings are not separate and isolated but are in fact unified and whole. How the child's physical, emotional, mental, and spiritual needs interact and inform each other can now be understood. What is going on beneath the surface of the child's behaviours has been a curiosity for many of us, and will continue to be an area of significant growth. By delving into the microscopic world of the genes, cells, and molecules that make up the human biological body system, we can now understand more fully what metaphysicians of all eras have been saying—every thought we think effects the physiology of our human body, right down to the microcellular processes. We know from Pert's research that if you are experiencing pleasure, for example, that neuropeptides or chemicals associated with pleasure will be found in your body. Alternatively, sad chemicals are found in your body when you feel sad. This reveals the degree to which the things that children feel and think actually have a tangible impact on how they behave. This process is not just happening now from the present moment experiences of the child's life but is also interacting with the totality of the child's environment from the past. As the child attempts to unify feelings and thoughts in the present moment, it is integrating a vast amount of information for itself and its entire lineage within its own nervous system. The child has the potential to transform the past and is actually pushing to do so, for its best growth and potential.

My intuitive view from my early interactions with children, later confirmed by clinical practice and research, was that whatever was presenting in the child had a metaphysical origin and a very real purpose for existing. The energetics, by way of feelings, thoughts, and emotions, and stressors (trauma) arise as a result of an unmet need in the child's body system. It is, of course, not possible to see the internal molecular process that is occurring when the child's feelings and thoughts are not aligned, and yet, we can see the external imbalance. The child's behaviours, symptoms, and physical issues have their basis in the feelings and thoughts that the child holds about certain things in their environment. The actions of the child on the outside mirror the microcosmic process of perceiving, interpreting, and distributing on the inside at the cellular level.

Within this book, you have been shown the way the child is being pushed toward its own unity. The components of the themes of the Chakras as they align with the human nervous system allow us to re-interpret how the issues and common challenges of children all circulate around particular unmet *Foundational Needs*. By identifying the source of the issue, we come to see the symptom has served a purpose as a necessary process that has had to occur as a push to remain unified. The more we come to see our children as experiencing subtle energy in all of their interactions, the more we realise that feelings, thoughts, emotions, spirit, and the physical body are interrelated. The action of any one aspect of our component self ultimately affects each of the others. The dynamic interplay occurring between body-mind-spirit from the beginning ought to be promoted and cultivated. The FNM offers critical inclusion to the current brain-based and behaviour-based models with its anatomical locations (based upon 5000 years of wisdom) and opens the most wonderful research possibilities. The future of research is exciting and perhaps one day the FNM will be used as a neuroanatomical basis for identifying the types of stress the mother feels and the corresponding childhood issues presenting from particular types of maternal stress and trauma, as I have found. Pert's Model, allows for a reconsideration of brain-predominated understandings of stress.

When we continue to ignore the various expressions of our children (as merely bad behaviour, for example), and do not explore the associated themes of why they respond the way they do, we are, albeit unconsciously, teaching them dysfunctional ways of dealing with their concerns. Physical bodies are designed to be open and to activate the multifaceted dimension of the child's consciousness. It is for this reason, too, that I have argued that all of the *Foundational Needs* should be cultivated simultaneously, as opposed to using a graduated system of development over time. Just as every organ and body part is present at birth, so are the energies that work together to unify the soul. When we cultivate every aspect of the child simultaneously, it leads to a strengthening of the self in a way that fortifies the body-mind-spirit at each and every stage.

Getting Serious

Understanding the meaning of why our children are responding to life in the way they do can be answered by broadening our horizons to see the child as a soul. The call to us as adults is to consider the child as always responding appropriately to their environment (even if we cannot see what they are responding to) and this has never been more urgent. One of the biggest hurdles for adults is actually overcoming the limited and long-standing beliefs they hold about the child. Of course, there will always be a new and improved opinion, as well as a plethora of how-to guides for parents and adults. Paradoxically, as this book has highlighted, in contrast to many other parenting approaches, if the parent meets the child from a position of self-knowledge, they can consciously be centered as they pay attention to the child's expression of need. In doing so, adults come to realise that the child is showing them in every moment where they are situated in terms of wellbeing, and what they may need to do for themselves to reach their potential. This impact becomes amplified when we have a model to assist us to purposefully reconsider any loops of patterning within children that might be healed.

For children to *know thyself* they need to be surrounded by adults who *know thyself*. It is also evident to me that as we prepare for the push, many adults must cultivate a more assured respect for their own capacities and potentials as parents, and this has to transform within us now. Parents and caregivers are being pushed to trust their own deep, intuitive feelings and to follow their push to seek ways that help them to expand. Expansion has to come in the way we interpret our children's challenges and behaviours, instead of the all too often quickly diagnosed approaches.

Because there has not been a lot of support for intuitive practices, for doing what feels right to us instead of what is decided by others, we can believe there is not a great deal we can do. I see many parents and caregivers that have become despondent in this regard, as the touted advice regarding raising children often keeps both adult and child quite limited. However, there is much we can all do for the little ones, and they require our push.

If you are a parent, you are the best parent for your children. You know your children better than anyone else. In fact, you know them so well that sometimes you may even forget where they start and you finish. I believe the ideal of such interdependence is essential for the bigger picture of humanity. As we now know, we regress to review our own pasts as our children grow, we can do so more consciously, and thus support children in ways they actually need, so they may begin to be free. A parent who is not totally sure of the motivation for having a child will struggle to find the motivation to nurture and sustain one. If you are a teacher or educator of children, the children in your class are there for a reason; you are perfect for each other. A teacher who has not embraced their role will impart this lack onto the children with whom they interact.

Even those caregivers who have pushed past many of the conditioned responses when relating with children, and embraced their role, may still struggle sometimes to understand the motivations of the child deeply. This approach then, will serve you well, and you will come to recognise more easily when the feelings and thoughts that you hold about your children are becoming manifest in them. We need to stop assessing and analysing children based upon their willingness to be compliant and cooperative within staged models of development, where they are always seen to be not quite ready. The FNM does not offer the next latest solution to problems with children. In fact, this approach does not even see problems as problems per se. The FNM addresses the vital energy underlying the common themes (the so called problems) that occur in the daily life of the child, and then offers manageable tips and unique insights for adults and children to work on together. Notice too, that even though there are no overt prescriptions in the FNM, as no two children are the same, there are still definitely common needs that we all share as human beings.

I have been interested in showing that every child is a complex fusion of all of its life experiences. Each child is the most evolved of the family line as a continuum of consciousness, as well as a culmination of an entire family lineage. The idea that there might be one-size fits all approach available for your child is a rather futile one. As the caregiver, when you attune, wonder, and respond to your child, you also come to *know thyself* through this same process. When you open to exploring the needs of your child as they arise, you realise much about yourself, too. We cannot teach our children what we have not mastered. With an improved view of the child and their needs, as presented here, we can shift out of the mind-set of having to coach children to be positive and happy as the final goal (so to fit in with adult projections) and move toward allowing the child to activate its own child centred self-awareness to *know thyself*.

Working with the Foundational Needs Model

We have seen examples and research in this book that demonstrates the degree to which children who have an unmet need in any aspect of their life, will subsequently have a presenting physical, emotional, or mental imbalance. The FNM accounts for the origin of these many imbalances as they relate to the child. The *Needs Table* at the end of each *Need* section offers a deeper interpretation of how imbalances manifest in both excessive and deficient ways in the child. These tables are in no way the complete picture of what is occurring for your child, but they do go a long way in assisting you to recognise the patterns occurring in the lives of the children in your care, so you can more easily identify the child's required need. From this position, when children experience imbalance, you are ready and set to help them reunite. You can add your own awareness to the tables, which I know will become a rich resource. The sooner we realise why the child is responding the way they are and what they are indicating to us about their needs, even in the most subtle imbalance, the sooner these disparities become rebalanced. The risk of the child adapting more serious concerns is also abated.

I am not suggesting, however, that you become excessive in your surveillance of children. It is advocated that once you identify the need of the child, you can relax into a deep knowing that you are present and available for them, and watchful of their expression of need before it becomes a more serious concern. In this present moment mode of relating with the child as they indicate subtle imbalances, you will notice that the long-range outcomes of where a child should be by a certain time, or which projected pathways they should take to arrive at job X or situation Y, become less relevant. You will notice, too, that external measures and attainments, as well as the many other ideas you receive about what children should or should not be doing, will not take you away from the deep bond and attunement that you have with your child. If you attend to the unity of the whole self as the child grows, then the rest really does take care of itself.

The paradoxical reality of the child's life is this—the child is capable, competent, and brilliant already, and yet, especially, and particularly in its earliest years, the child is extremely vulnerable. Plato says that the child needs the proper soil for the soul's growth. We are coming to see some twenty-three hundred years later, that the soil we offer in the way of our thoughts, beliefs, and emotions, as well as the conditioned ways we train or teach children, may, in fact, be limiting their capacities. We now know the child's absorption of the environment is happening well before the child is conceived. Knowing more about the *Foundational Needs* of children in body-mind-spirit as they pertain to the Chakras, opens up a whole way of cultivating and knowing ourselves as adults, as well as assisting children to become mediators of their own lives, and to know themselves for the wondrous beings they are.

The benefits for the child of learning about the different aspects of their souls, body-mind-spirit, and how they all work together based on the child's feelings, thoughts, and actions, is that they can begin to comprehend how their experiences affect them. Additionally, they are enabled to see how powerful and capable they really are. Children gain much insight when they know how their anatomy is altered by how they feel and think, and also by their environment. Alternatively, the child can learn how to cultivate certain energies in themselves that will bring out their latent capacities, and to focus on any area of their lives in which they wish to experience more harmony or unity. We have not seen what is possible when we begin to apply such an affirmative and self-aware model for our children. We are looking to a world that our children's children inhabit, and which is entirely different from our own. As Jung remarked regarding working with the energy of Kundalini -- it is a world of eternity. What was once a rare occurrence of energy cultivation is now a reality for our children.

When we position children's concerns according to the seven *Foundational Needs*, it is possible to discern that the child's thoughts, perceptions, feelings, emotions, behaviours, and intentions are a fusion of the energetic information they are both receiving and transmitting. This information, as has been expressed throughout this book, is working in accord with the child to bring forth the best in them. The child's highest potential will also vary for each child, as it has to do with its own soul. The push of the child to seek unity is its search for meaning, geared toward their best possible growth or highest potential— and this is a powerful force indeed. When we reflect back on a view of the child from Aristotle's lens, we see the end goal of its existence is to attain happiness or "the good life", which many people still aim for, even well after they reach adulthood. Plato's aim was to seek the highest good (God), and we could know this aim by remaining connected as whole souls. Children are motivated toward their highest good naturally. Wellbeing is the wonderful side effect of having integrity of the self that is in alignment with the energy field promoting the best possible growth and highest potentials.

Looking Ahead

The FNM and the theory of the soul affirm that children hold within themselves the answers to their own dilemmas, as well as the map to their futures. The resolution, therefore, to the child's unmet needs does not reside outside the child, but within them; at least in the sense that the child needs assistance to navigate their needs, and have them met by an important other before they can do this for themselves. When we can come to see that the child's life experiences are a series of transitions that require the integrity of body-mind-spirit, we can be more aware of the unity, or lack thereof. We have no requisite to be concerned about a child not doing or being this or that at a particular stage, nor about what they will become. The idea that one's greatest potential is something to grow into misses the point of cultivating the vital needs of our children as they are growing and transitioning through even the earliest of experiences. Regardless of the worldview, model, or expectation that a child grows up with, it does not stop the child from acting out against those things that are not supportive of its soul. The child's unifying nature is always evident beneath those struggles and challenges.

The *soul push* to maintain unity as a path, transcends ideas of children being parented and educated to be positive, because sometimes the *soul push* to unify does not feel very positive at all. Children's protests against their environment (family or education system) can be seen as a signal to the (astute) adult that there is an unmet need in the child's life. That is, they indicate that the child is attempting to return to its inherent unity so that it may be a whole soul. Difficult transitions, therefore, offer wonderful insight to caregivers, by way of an opportunity to help the child rework the representations (interpretations) they hold about themselves, and those that are offered to the child that are not in accord with their best selves. When a child comes to know and trust its soul (body-mind-spirit) as a reflection of a divine reality, their greatest self (either the child's concept of God or a greater force), then all transitions that the child goes through will be from a state of inner integrity. If there is an imbalance, there is a perennial opportunity for re-integration of the aspects of the self that are undergoing change. There will be requirements and necessities at these points to which to attend, and these are what I continue to call needs. The wounds of childhood can leave deep and lasting consequences if not healed, and thus we see that the self is always in formation, and we will always have to go back if we have left something behind. Most of the wounds from childhood are the result of a lack of understanding about the reasons that one's feelings and thoughts are at odds. Adult relationships with children that are based on attunement, wonder, and responsiveness, are in effect paying attention to the child's signals of need. Simultaneously supporting the needs of children at all stages of growth will support the child in a myriad of ways, in preference to the lopsided outcomes of the past.

There are always going to be many important questions that arise when we consider how we might help children to usher a new way forward. In this endeavour, it is important to show children how to understand themselves, rather than finding someone else to tell them how they feel or what they should think. Without helping our children to understand their *Foundational Needs* and how to meet these for themselves, it matters not what we do for them, even with the best intentions. The point to be underlined is that if we don't allow children to draw on their own inner resources, to truly *know thyself*, our children will be fragmented and continue to struggle fruitlessly throughout their adult lives. There is a collective *push* for us all to become more aware of our human motivations and attend to what children really need. And as we are now becoming more aware than ever, we can see that if it doesn't start with us, the next generation will have to push even harder before they can know their true nature. We all get a choice in the ways that we nurture, teach, and heal the little ones in our lives. If we are attuned to children from our own unified soul, then we can pause for a moment to consider; might there be something that I can first transform in myself, or from the past, so that I can meet the child as the brilliance they are? I believe when we are ready, we will experience the prompts that are right for us because once you begin to work with your *soul push*, you are evoking a powerful force. And even if you do not have all of the answers you need right now, you can rest assured that the answers will emerge, in the perfect time, somewhere, somehow. After all, this is the very nature of the soul, *pushing* us to be the best we can be.

Acknowledgements

So many people have joined me on the journey that made this book possible. The origins of this book go back a long way and stem from both my clinical practice as well as my academic journey.

For all the teachers who supported me along the journey, I bow to you. Dr Karen Lane and Dr Ian Weeks are stand out mentors who cultivated my scholarship, embraced my soul musings beyond the academy, and encouraged my *push* in a deep and meaningful way. Thank you.

To some I have not met, Carl Jung, James Hillman, Carolyn Myss, Anodea Judith, Candace Pert, and Bruce Lipton for paving the way with your work and informing my own *soul push*. To Stuart Sovatsky, much gratitude to you for your work and for giving me the opportunity to present my work at a World Congress 10 years ago.

I am eternally grateful for those who have read and reread aspects of my work over time and made suggestions for how I might bring the depth of research contained in this book out in a digestible from. Special thanks go to Cath Nitschke and Tracey Blundy for offering your honest feedback in a caring way - thank you for embodying loving kindness in friendship.

Thanks to those that offered editorial support Cambridge Scholarly Press, Jo Spring, and lastly but by no means least, to Melissa Watkins - for you dedication to me and to Kate Erlenbusch, of *Word Love*, who worked with me on the final stage and became one of the book's midwives. Gratitude to Melanie Bedford for working the art for the front cover and all the art you created for me over a span of 10 years now. Your art captures the essence of Childosophy and I am so grateful to you. Thanks to Jodie Beckley for your graphic skill in altering the art for this book.

I thank my clients for helping me grow and to some in particular for allowing me to share your stories in this book. Much love and gratitude to all of the children who have taught me about myself – not only my own sons but also each child whose parents have trusted me.

To all the women who have seen the value in my teachings and trained with me to be Childosophy Children's Wellbeing Practitioners, knowing there was something that resonated with them and for trusting me even before my research was complete. Special gratitude to Michelle Hand, Maria Freytag and Lesley Thomas thank you for your continued commitment to me.

To all my family and friends for your encouragement and support always especially my sister and soul companion Julieanne -- you support me every day to live in accord with my *soul push*. Thank you, Dr Jess McColl, for your guidance and friendship over many years. I am forever grateful to Danielle Fraser and Rhonda Nelis for your lifelong friendship -- and thank you Chris Carroll -- You three always have my back. Thank you all particularly most recently for being there for my sons, when I could not.

Eternal gratitude to my sons, Dillon Haire and Austin Haire, for showing me the wonder of motherhood and the gift of possible transformation for generations to come. Thank you for loving my whole self and being my most protective shields as I have weathered some storms.

To my invisible and otherworldly guides, St Thérèse of Lisieux, Sri Aurobindo, The Mother, and Dolores Cannon, for showing me the way back -- I look forward to the next time we meet. To the medical staff at the Geelong Hospital, ICU, this book would not have been written without your miraculous holding space.

To my ancestors and my descendants and to their children's children – I love you. I thank you. I wrote this book for you.

Glossary

Being in the Question: A term, as well as a relational approach, that signifies the mindfulness and wonder of relating with children that allows adults to see, hear, and feel the child on the child's own terms.

Chakras: Centers within our physical body that link our energetic body to the external world; these centers are vortices of pure energy. The Chakras energetically connect all aspects body-mind-spirit and these aspects work in harmony.

Child: A soul that is a unified and composite body-mind-spirit; connected to a source of energy supporting its best growth and an active participator in its own destiny.

Child as a mirror: Child reflects the behaviours of other people; the feelings, emotions, beliefs, thoughts, and actions as well as the speech and language of those who are present and those who are no longer present but come from one's family, social and cultural lineage.

Embodied spirituality: Accounts for the body-mind relationship in spirituality that considers spirituality as an integral and active aspect that is informing a person's overall development.

Embody: To express and give a tangible form (to an idea, quality, or feeling).

Emotion: An instinctual response; a habitual reaction to a feeling. The emotions, in my experience, often indicate a false interpretation, which has already been transmitted energetically to the child based upon how things have been interpreted in the past. Emotions are automatic and as such are often *not* the most accurate interpretation of what is occurring now.

Epigenetics: The precedent to one's gene expression: epi = before. Epigenetics tells us that our genes (our biology), is altered by experience, and these changes can be passed on to future generations.

Feelings: That which we perceive in our environment, which come firstly through the sensory body. These are our perceptions and the energies that we sense before we have made an interpretation about them.

Field theory: Pertains to a field as an energetic force, invested in our highest growth according to our unique destiny or the *push*.

Foundational Needs Model (FNM): A whole child needs model that supports human needs from the beginnings. The Foundational Needs closely align with the seven principal Chakras. Each of the Foundational Needs allows for an interpretation of a physical location in the child's anatomy, the corresponding thought patterns, and psychological aspects, as well as the often-inhibited potentials as they manifest through the child's behaviours and issues.

God: A field of energy invested in our highest growth according to our unique destiny. The human being – soul is pushed toward a unity and self-realisation or enlightenment. This is what it means to be aligned with part of a greater ideal: *God*.

Mirror Theory: In Neuroscience; mirror neurons help one recognise and imitate the seen and hidden actions of others and are involved with empathy. The mirror neurons are also connected to motor neurons, the sensory responses and neuroscience is trying to locate the anatomical locations.

Mirror behaviours: Behaviours that mirror and empathise with other people's emotions and/or imitate actions or speech of others.

Morphic Resonance: Rupert Sheldrake's theory that posits all living organisms have a prototypical energetic field that supports growth and evolution.

Schema: One's internal story, about oneself, which develops over time

Soul Physic: The soul is complete and does not have to get anywhere. It does need to stay unified to manifest its destiny and thus the physic is about cultivating the souls needs simultaneously at each age.

Soul Process: A tripartite process; I Feel, I Think, and I Act, occurring in the self as further correlated to the child's body-mind-spirit.

Soul Theory: Aspects of body-mind-spirit work in harmony as a whole to reach highest potential in accord with divine purpose.

Transitional growth: An approach to growth that recognises each transition children make requires them continually reach for a state of unity and balance. If these experiences are managed well and approached consciously it allows the child *to feel* they can move forward without having anything denied, restricted or prohibited. This secured type of growth means the child manages all transitions well.

Appendix 1

A to Z of Children's Ailments

Numbers are the Foundational Needs Correlations

A
Absorption, gut, 3
Aches, (see part of body)
Adrenal, 3
Allergies, (see part of body)
Aggression, 4
Anger 4, 3 & 7
Anxiety, general 1 & 4
Anxiety, around people, 1
Appetite, lack of, 1
Appetite, excess, 3
Apathy, 3
Asthma, 1 & 4
Attachment issues, 1
Aversion to school, 1

B
Balance, loss of, 1 & 3
Bedwetting, 2
Bites, 7 (see part of body)
Birth Trauma, 1
Body odour, 3
Boils, 4
Bladder Issues, 2
Blood problems, 4
Bowel, 3

Brain, 6
Bruises, 4
Bronchial/whooping cough, 5

C

Cancer (see part of body)
Chills, 2, 4
Circulation, 4
Conjunctivitis, 6
Congestion, 4
Constipation, 2
Coughing, 5
Cramps, (see part of the body)
Cysts, 4 also see location

D

Deafness, 5
Depression, 3
Destructive behaviour, 3 & 6
Diabetes, 4
Diarrhoea, 2
Digestive disorders, 3
Dizziness, 7

E

Ears - ringing, 6
Ear ache, 6
Eczema, 1 & 4
Emotional outbursts, 2
Eyes, 6
Itchy, red, tired, watery, 6
Eating problems,

Binging, purging 3

F
Failure to Thrive 1 & 4
Fatigue, 2
Feet problems, 1
Feet, swollen, 4
Fears, Of dark, animals, people, places, 1
Focus, 6
Food Intolerance, 1
Foot odour, 1
Foot, leg pain, 1
Flatulence, 3
Flighty (running away), 1
Fighty (resistance), 3

G
Gagging, 5
Gas, 3
Glandular Fever, 5
Gall bladder, 6
Genitals, 2

H
Hair, 7
Hands, 4
Hay fever, 4 & 5
Headaches, 6 & 7
Head banging, 6
Head lice, 3 & 6

Heart, 4
Hiccups, 3
Hives, 3

I
Immune System, 1
Impetigo (school sores), 4
Incontinence, 2
Indigestion, 3
Infection, 4
Insect bites, 3
Irritability, 4
Itchiness, 7

J
Jaundice, 3
Jaw problems, 5
Joints, 1

K
Kidney disorders, 3
Knee problems, 2

L
Language, 5
Non verbal, 5
Difficulty with, 5
Lice, 3
Loneliness, 6
Learning challenges, 6
Lying, 5
Lymphatic issues, 5

M
Motion sickness, 3
Mouth ulcers/thrush, 5
Measles, 2
Maternal Deprivation, 1
Memory retention poor, 6
Mal absorption issues, 3
Muscular, 7

N
Nail biting, 5
Nausea, 2
Nervousness, 5 & 6
Neurodevelopmental issues, 6
Nightmares, 6
Nose, sinus, 6
Nose bleeds, 6
Nutrient deficiency, 1

O
Object attachment, 1 & 4
Oedema/swelling, 2
Overweight, 4

P
Pancreas, 3
Parasites(worms, ringworm), 3
Phobias, 1 & 4
Physical pain (See body location)
Pneumonia, 4
Posture, 7

Psychic abilities, 6
Psoriasis, 7

Q

R
Rash, 3 & 7
Reflux, 3 & 5
Reproductive system, 2
Respiratory infections, 4
Rocking, 1 & 7

S
Sensory processing issues, 6
Seizure, 6
Separation Anxiety, 1
Settling to sleep, 6
Shoulder or arm pain, 4
Sibling Rivalry, 4
Sinus Problems, 6
Skin rash, 7
Skin sensitivities, 7
Sleep patterns 6
Sore muscles and joints, 7
Sore throat, 5
Speech, 5, delayed, slow or hurried
Speech difficulties, 5
Spine, 7
Stomach Ache, 3
Stuttering, 5

T
Tapeworm, 3
Teething and gums, 5
Thumb sucking, 1 & 5
Teeth grinding, 5
Thrush, 2
Toileting, 2
Tonsillitis, 5
Trauma, 1 & 2
Tantrums, 2

U
Upper respiratory, 4
Urinary system, 2
Ulcers, 1 & 3

V
Virus, 1
Vomiting, 3
Vertigo, 7

W
Warts 4, (see part of body)

Worms, 3

Wheezing, 4

Wind, 3

Appendix 2:

Foundational Needs at a Glance

THE NEED	Symptom *Your child may feel.*	Symptom *Your child may have a physical issue with*	Solution	Help your child to Affirm
The Need to be Safe and Secure	Afraid of change. A fear when separated from you. Insecure.	Legs, bones, feet, rectum Immune system	Assist your child to feel safe by your reassuring actions to them. Don't push them away. Teach them about their body and help them set clear boundaries in regard to physical touch. Teach them to ground through practices such as being in nature and meditation.	It is safe for me to be here I trust my bodies wisdom
The Need to Neel	Impulsive. Lack of emotional control, Fussy, Uncertain, obsessive,	Reproductive system, urinary system, bladder, endocrine	It is normal for children experience a wide range of emotions. Help them to accept all of their feelings. Model healthy approaches to emotions. Be mindful of the emotional energy of the home and other environments.	I accept my feelings I move easily and effortlessly

The Need to Act	Powerless, shame, withdrawn, indecisive, over active	Stomach and digestive system, adrenal glands	Allow children to follow their own intuition. Ask you child what they feel they should do? Give your child opportunities to follow their own lead sometimes	I honour the power within me- I am enough
The Need to Love	Unloved, sadness, sorrow, hurt, anger, irritable	Heart, circulation, respiration (asthma) breathing	Presence of being, turn off distractions and give quality time. Connect with child in a way they feel loved. Spend time in devotion and loving service.	I am worthy of love I am loved and loving
The Need to Speak	Nervous Uncertain of expression Yelling – Silence	Throat, mouth Voice (speech issues) teeth and gums, lymphatic system	Make space to listen to your child. Even if what they express is not what you want to hear. Use positive vibration words. Encourage room for expression. i.e. "Tell me how you feel about that"?	I can express myself I am heard
The Need to See	Distracted, confused shy, Lack of focus, Unsettled sleep or dreams	Brain (Learning challenges- Focus) Eyes, ears, nose (sinus) Nervous system	Assist your child's imagination, (make a vision board of their passions). Set daily or weekly intentions. Allow your child to imagine themselves as their greatest self	I see all things in clarity- I can manifest my vision

The Need to Know	Hypersensitive to the environment and people. Frustrated, Lack of connection	SKIN (issues) Muscular (Growing pains) Skeletal (bones, posture and stance)	Assist your child to see the higher purpose in the situation, bring self-awareness by helping the child see the deeper patterns in their experiences and why they keep creating certain situations.	Divinity resides within me: I know my unique brilliance

Index

A

A to Z of Children's Ailments, 6, 405

Abraham Maslow, 227, 339

Acquiring Speech, 271, 276

ADHD, 111, 150, 232, 317

Agency, 212, 220

Albert Einstein, 353

All You Need Is Love, 244

Alternative Learning, 296

Anam Cara, 344

Anatomy, 384

Anger, 405

Anna Freud, 86

Anna Karenina, 183

Anodea Judith, 397

Anxiety, 143, 153, 405

Aristotelian, 75

Aristotle, 71, 72, 74, 75, 77, 82, 94, 117, 179, 189, 274, 281, 308, 313, 370, 392

Arnold Gesell, 117, 133, 315

Artificial Intelligence, 39

Attachment, 143, 144, 194, 246, 405

Attachment Theory, 143, 144, 194

Attunement, 143, 357

Autism, 266, 269

Autonomy, 212, 218

Aversion, 405

B

Balance, 405

Bedwetting, 405

Biology, 79

Birth, 79, 405

Birth Trauma, 405

Body, 161, 162, 332, 405, 425

Brain, 406, 414

Breathing, 168

Bruce Lipton, 90, 397

Bullying, 244, 255

C

Cancer, 406

Candace Pert, 125, 397

Carl Jung, 54, 56, 121, 250, 375, 397

Carol Gilligan, 245

Carolyn Myss, 282, 397

Case 1: Sally, 5, 138

Case 2: Tommy, 5, 172

Case 3: Jeremy, 5, 208

Case 4: Ella, 5, 240

Case 5: James, 5, 266

Case 6: William, 5, 292

Case 7: Mimi, 5, 324

Chakras, 24, 25, 28, 96, 105, 119, 120, 121, 122, 123, 124, 125, 126, 127, 128, 131, 133, 234, 313, 385, 391, 401, 402

Child Genius, 306

Childhood, 35, 98, 148, 293, 330, 335, 336, 425

Childosophy, 102, 373, 398, 425

Concepts of God, 330, 341

Control, 187, 222

D

Dalai Lama, 79, 80, 81, 82, 251, 344

David Bohm, 88

Depression, 406

Development, 245

Diki Tsering, 80

Discipline and Punishment, 212, 214

DNA, 89, 90

Don Glassey, 128

Donald Winnicott, 108, 297

Dreams, 296, 316

Dreams and Sleep, 296, 316

DSMIV, 122

E

Electroencephalography (EEG), 100

Electrophysiological, 258

Embodying Spirit, 330, 337

Embryonic Beginnings, 123

Emotional, 158, 177, 178, 187, 308, 406

Emotional Control and Self-Regulation, 177

Emotions, 177, 178, 179, 186, 402

Empathy, 244, 256, 257

Epigenetics, 89, 90, 361, 402

Equilibrium, 314

Eva Simms, 95, 305

F

False Self, 101, 297, 298, 299, 301

Family, 194, 280

Father, 307

Fears, 161, 407

Feelings, 177, 181, 183, 402

Formation, 271

Foundational Needs Model, 6, 124, 231, 319, 353, 389, 402, 425

Freedom, 212, 228

Freudian, 153, 269, 335

G

Genius, 94

Georg Hegel, 248

God, 59, 66, 72, 75, 81, 82, 85, 100, 128, 246, 260, 324, 326, 329, 334, 335, 341, 342, 343, 375, 392, 394, 402

Gopi Krishna, 121

Grandparents, 4

Gratitude, 244, 260, 261, 397

Guy Debord, 249

H

Hard Times, 216

Heart Coherence, 244, 259

Hierarchy of Needs, 227, 340

Highest Potential, 330, 339

Holding, 222, 297, 357

Holding the Space, 357

Horace Mann, 307

Howard Gardner, 315

I

Imagination, 314

Implicate Order, 88

India, 81, 87, 127, 146, 230, 306

Integral Psychology, 336

Integral Theory, 336

J

Jack Miller, 312

James Fowler, 337

Jeremy Bentham, 217

John O'Donohue, 207, 344

K

Ken Wilber, 336

Know Thyself, 56, 330

Krishnamurti, 230

Kundalini, 121, 122, 123, 128, 131, 162, 392

Kundalini Spiritual Emergence, 122

L

Language, 268, 271, 273, 275, 276, 277, 304, 408

Learning, 126, 276, 296, 304, 309, 310, 314, 408, 414

Learning Language, 276

Lee Sannella, 121

Lev Vygotsky, 196, 314

Louise Hay, 300

Luce Irigaray, 244

M

Maria Montessori, 15, 96, 164, 309, 310

Marian De Souza, 312, 336

Martin Seligman, 189, 190

Maternal Deprivation, 143, 148, 409

Meaning Making, 271

Memory, 409

Michael Foucault, 217

Microbes, 234

Midwife of the Soul, 376

Mirror Theory, 298, 402

Mirroring, 244, 257, 296, 301

Model of Wholeness, 23

Morphic Resonance, 93, 403

Mother, 128, 399

Mothering, 380

N

Need to Act, 25, 37, 112, 113, 124, 158, 160, 165, 191, 193, 198, 207, 210, 211, 212, 213, 221, 223, 227, 229, 232, 233, 235, 236, 307, 340, 367, 414

Need to Be Safe and Secure, 25, 94, 113, 132, 137, 140, 141, 153, 163, 166, 183, 202, 246

Need to Feel, 25, 94, 108, 147, 158, 159, 163, 171, 172, 174, 175, 176, 177, 178, 185, 187, 195, 202, 203, 252, 255, 259, 267, 367

Need to Know, 26, 132, 246, 323, 324, 329, 330, 331, 342, 343, 344, 346, 347, 348, 367, 415

Need to Love, 26, 145, 160, 239, 243, 244, 247, 253, 255, 260, 261, 301, 315, 318, 344, 367, 414

Need to See, 26, 109, 163, 258, 269, 291, 293, 294, 295, 296, 314, 315, 316, 319, 367, 374, 414

Need to Speak, 26, 109, 199, 265, 270, 271, 274, 275, 278, 282, 283, 286, 287, 367, 414

Nel Noddings, 245

Nervous, 294, 414

Nervous System, 294

Neuro, 275

Neurocardiology, 259

Neuroscience, 96, 257, 402

Niels Bohr, 88

Noam Chomsky, 277

O

Object Relations Theory, 298

Obsessive Compulsive Disorder (OCD), 195

of Schooling, 296, 307

P

Parental, 197

Parenting, 2, 214

Parents, 2, 50, 91, 192, 193, 200, 280, 306, 314, 387, 425

Personality, 227

Phobia, 153

Physical Body, 143, 161, 170, 171

Physical Body Awareness, 143, 161

Piaget, 133, 245, 314

Plato, 67, 71, 72, 73, 75, 76, 77, 78, 82, 85, 186, 274, 281, 301, 313, 376, 391, 392

Play, 177, 195, 196, 197, 296, 314

Play and Imagination, 296, 314

Pleasure and Pain, 177, 193

Potential, 170, 373

Power, 112, 212, 228

Psychic Abilities, 296, 305

Q

Quantum, 87, 88

R

Ravi Shankar, 306

Recognition, 244, 248

Reincarnation, 79

Resilience, 221

Robert Coles, 86, 246

Robert Emmons, 260

Robert Frost, 171, 195

Rudolph Steiner, 315

Rupert Sheldrake, 93, 258, 403

S

Schema, 403

School, 296, 307, 309

Search for Meaning, 44, 45

Self-Motivation, 212, 224

Self-Regulation, 187

Separation, 143, 155, 170, 410

Separation Anxiety, 155, 410

Sexuality, 177, 200, 201

Sibling Rivalry, 244, 253, 410

Sigmund Freud, 86, 153

Sleep, 317, 410

Socrates, 57, 376

Soul, 5, 12, 41, 59, 68, 70, 71, 72, 73, 99, 117, 129, 296, 319, 384, 403

Soul Physic, 129, 403

Speech, 268, 410

Spirituality, 330, 335, 336, 338, 341

Sri Aurobindo, 60, 181, 399

Sri Sri, 306

Steven Pinker, 276

Stomach Aches, 212, 232

Stress, 143, 150

Stuart Sovatsky, 122, 123, 251, 397

Sutras, 24, 120, 128, 425

T

Tale of Two Cities, 345

Teachers, 4, 314

Teaching, 161, 373

Technology, 330, 345

Telling Lies, 271, 283

The Beatles, 239, 240

The Chariot, 71

The History of Childhood, 49
The Moral Life of Children, 246
The Myth of Er, 78
The News, de Botton, 248
The Political Life of Children, 246
The Republic, 73, 78
The Spiritual Life of Children, 86
The Tao of Physics, Fritjof Capra, 87
Theory, 36, 68, 194, 227, 245, 270, 336, 403
Tibetan Buddhist, 78, 79
Toilet Training, 212, 222
Trauma, 143, 150, 411
True Self, 297, 299, 301
Truth, 7, 73, 268, 271, 280, 282, 301

U

Upanishads, 24, 120, 128

V

Victor Frankel, 45, 227
Violet Oaklander, 106, 199
Voice, 245, 268, 271, 286, 414

W

Walt Disney, 291, 319

Wellbeing, 227, 373, 392, 398, 425

Werner Heisenberg, 87

Will, 212, 227, 228

Will to Meaning, 227

Will to Power, 228

William Braud, 103

Y

Yoga, 24, 120, 128, 162, 181, 425

Notes

¹ Erikson, E. (1968). *Identity, youth, and crisis*. New York: W. W. Norton

² The book moves on from, and yet includes, the research from my doctoral thesis *Philosophy of Childhood: The Foundational Childhood Needs and Wellbeing* (2013). You can access a vast and broad reading list (including the thesis) and many resources on the topics covered in this book at childosophy.com.

¹ Maya Angelou *Mom & Me & Mom*, 2013 *ebook*

LET'S BEGIN

⁴ Montessori, M. and Costelloe, M. (1972). *The Secret of Childhood*. New York: Ballantine Books.

³ The term "helicopter parent" was first used in Dr. Haim Ginott's 1969 book *Parents & Teenagers* and is used variably with the terms 'tiger parenting', 'lawnmower parenting,' 'cosseting parent,' or 'bulldoze parenting.' In general reference those parents who hover over their children and do not allow them the space to develop and do things for themselves.

⁴ Dvivedi, M (1980) *The Yoga Sutras of Patanjali*, Delhi: Sri Satguru Publications

⁵ Figure 1. As well as all figures in the book that position the *Foundational Need* as it corresponds with each Chakra, have been graphically altered by Jodie Beckley from art of Melanie Bedford for Childosophy.

⁶ The Chakra themes adapted to the Foundational Needs Model were originally chosen from the work of Judith, A., *Eastern Body,*

Western Mind, (1996, 2004) Berkeley, Calif., Celestial Arts. And the Anatomy and body system correlations are from Myss, C., *Anatomy of the Spirit*, (1996) and *Why People Don't Heal and How They Can*, (2004) New York, Gramercy Books. There are a variety of other sources that I have used and referred to over the years that announce the same energy themes of the Chakras, however, Judith's and Myss's appear the most identifiable and almost universal as far as Western interpretations are concerned. Many suggest there is more than 7 Chakras and, of course, there are varying and different interpretations of the human energy body as well. My reference to the 7 Chakras is established as the 7 needs as foundational wisdom and information required for the next step in our evolution.

CHAPTER ONE

[1] *Speech by President Nelson Mandela at the launch of the Nelson Mandela Children's Fund on* 8th May 1995 at Mahlamba Ndlopfu Pretoria South Africa.

[2] Andrew Stables, (2008). *Childhood and the philosophy of education.* London: Continuum International Pub, p. 44. A full discussion of the concepts of the child as proposed by Stables can be found in Thérèse M, (2013) *A Philosophy of Childhood: The Foundational Needs and Wellbeing,* Deakin University.

[3] Frankl, V. (1963). *Man's search for meaning.* Boston: Beacon Press.

[4] De Mause, L. (1974). *The History of Childhood.* New York:Psychohistory Press.

[5] *The History of Childhood*, DeMause, 1974, p. 17

[6] See *The History of Childhood,* DeMause, 1974 where DeMause offers a chronological graph that places the dominant childrearing mode beginning in 300 BC as *Infanticidal*, then *Abandoning*, up until the late

middle ages' *Ambivalent* up until 1700, and then *Intrusive, Socialising,* and in the 1970s, as *Helping.*

[7] Elias, N., *The Civilising of Parents*, (1998) In Mennell and Goudsblom eds., *The Norbert Elias Reader* (1998) Oxford, Blackwell Stables, A., *Childhood and the Philosophy of Education* (2008) London, Continuum International Pub.

[8] DeMause, 1974, *The History of Childhood* p. 63

[9] *C. G. Jung, 1953 – 1991, Collected Works. 17, par. 154 Princeton University.*

[10] Plato, *Theaetetus*, 150 b-c

CHAPTER TWO

[11] James Hillman, (1997), *A Souls Code in Search of Character and Calling*, Grand Central Publishing

[12] *Story of a Soul: The Autobiography of St. Therese of Lisieux*, translated from the original manuscripts by John Clarke, O.C.D. Third edition (1996)

[13] Aurobindo, Sri, *The Life Divine* (1977, 2005) Pondicherry, Sri Aurobindo Ashram

[14] For a wonderful interpretation from Osho on mothering, see <http://oshotimes.blog.osho.com/2011/05/the-delicate-art-of-motherhood-osho/>

[15] Basu, et al, *'Can the incidence of obstetric anal sphincter injury be reduced? The STOMP experience'* (2016), European Journal of Obstetrics and Gynaecology and Reproductive Biology. Published online April 29, 2016.

[16] The child's perspective has often been overlooked due to a lack of power; that is, the adult power over the child. Leena Alanen placed this argument in light of a new sociology for childhood. (See Alanen,

L., *Rethinking Childhood, Acta Sociologica, 31*, 53-67 (1988) There is more discussion on the adult-child power dynamic in part two, *the Need to Act.*

[17] Belenky, M., *Women's ways of Knowing* (New York, Basic Books, 1986), gives a detailed perspective on the woman and the issues that have faced her over time for the parallel issues that are now facing the child. A point in note is also that women still largely raise children; of course, both male and female are involved in this role, but it is still predominately women raising children, and in other caregiving roles such as teaching, the percentage of women is much higher than males. www.data.worldbank.org.

[18] In Buddhist, Hindu, and even the early Western philosophies prior to scientific knowledge there is the notion of 'two worlds'. The differentiation of material and spiritual realities here is made to facilitate a clearer elucidation of the ideas of consciousness more broadly. It must be stated from the outset, however, that the distinction is drawn for clarity of mind and that many thinkers, especially in the Eastern philosophical traditions, see no 'real' difference between human or divine consciousness in its subtlest form.

[19] Plato *Phaedrus*, 246a-254e

[20] A full discussion of these concepts can be found in Thérèse M, 2013 *A Philosophy of Childhood: The Foundational Needs and Wellbeing*, Deakin University.

[21] This general account is found, in *Physics* II 3 and *Metaphysic*s V 2. cf. Falcon, Andrea, "Aristotle on Causality", *The Stanford Encyclopedia of Philosophy* (Winter 2012 Edition), Edward N. Zalta (ed.),

[22] *Nicomachean Ethics* --NE 1.7, 1098a, 3–4

[23] *The Republic VII*, 518 B sq

[24] *The Republic VI* 491

25 *Nicomachean Ethics* NE 5.1.

26 Law, S. *The War for Children's Minds* (2006) London, Routledge, p 123

27 Matthews, G., *Philosophy and the Young Child* (1980) Cambridge, Mass., Harvard University Press, p.2 and Matthews, G. (1994). *The philosophy of childhood.* Cambridge, Mass.: Harvard University Press.

28 Plato, *The Republic,* Book 10, 608-D

29 Metempsychosis is the word used for transmigration of the soul by philosophers. It has a Greek origin. See *Nietzsche and the Doctrine of Metempsychosis,* in J. Urpeth & J. Lippitt, *Nietzsche and the Divine,* Manchester, Clinamen, 2000.

30 Plato, *The Republic* Book X section 3

31 Gananath Obeyesekere, *Imagining Karma: Ethical Transformation in Amerindian, Buddhist, and Greek Rebirth,* University of California Press, 2002, page 15

32 Adams, C. J., Classifications of Religions, Geographical Encyclopedia Britannica, 2007 Accessed, July 15, 2010

33 Stevenson, I., *Reincarnation and Biology: A Contribution to the Etiology of Birthmarks and Birth Defects* (1997) Praeger Publishers see also Stevenson, I. (2000) The Phenomenon of Claimed Memories of Previous Lives: Possible Interpretations and Importance, *Medical Hypotheses,* 54 (4): 652–659, Apr. 2000

34 Stevenson, 2000, *The Phenomenon of Claimed Memories of Previous Lives: Possible Interpretations and Importance* Abstract Apr; 54(4): 652-9)

35 Kalachakra Tantra, Philosophy For a wonderful book on this topic see *Kalachakra Tantra: Rite of Initiation* by His Holiness the Dalai Lama, Wisdom Publications, 3rd edition (October 1999)

36 Tsering, D. (2000) *The Dalai Lama, My Son: A Mothers Story* Viking Adult.

³⁷ *The Dalai Lama My Son* p. 76. 77.

³⁸ Tsering, D. (2000) Also later, she was told the dragon was Dhondup and the others were showing him the way to his rebirth. (pp. 77)

³⁹Kaviratna, Avinash C., Sharma, P., The Chakara Samhiti (1913) Vol 5, Sri Satguru Publications

⁴⁰ The Charaka Samhita offers the theoretical network of Ayurveda, "Charaka Samhita and the Susruta Samhita, both being recensions of two ancient traditions of the Hindu medicine" (See E. Schultheisz (1981) *History of Physiology*, Pergamon Press, page 60-61)

⁴¹ There is part of the works mentioned above that are dedicated to "identifying and classifying seeds, roots, flowers, fruits, stems, aromatic leaves, barks of different trees, plants juices, mountain herbs, animal products ranging from their milk to their excretory waste after the animals eat certain diet or grasses, different types of honey, stones, salts and others." The Chakara Samhiti, Vols 2,3,4 (See Kaviratna, A vinash C., Sharma, P. (1913) The Chakara Samhiti, V ols 5, Sri Satguru Publications

CHAPTER THREE

[1] Genetic heredity espouses the notion that 50 per cent of one's traits are passed from each parent (the parent themselves accounting for 25 percent from each parent and the remainder of the 50 per cent from one's grandparents (12.5 percent from each of the 4 grandparents). Cooper, GM., *The Cell: A Molecular Approach*, 2nd edition, Sunderland (MA): Sinauer Associates, (2000) *Heredity, Genes, and DNA* Available from:
https://www.ncbi.nlm.nih.gov/books/NBK9944/

[2] Coles, R. (1990). *The spiritual life of children*. Boston: Houghton Mifflin.

[3] Fritjof Capra, interviewed by Renee Weber in the book *The*

Holographic Paradigm, pp. 217–218 see also Fritjof Capra, *The Tao of Physic* (1975) Berkeley, Shambhala

[4] This energetic field has been variously termed, *The Field* by Lynn McTaggert, (2008), *The Divine Matrix* by Gregg Bradden (2007), *The Akashic Field* by Ervin Lazlo (2007), and biologist Rupert Sheldrake refers to it in his books Sheldrake, R., *A New Science of Life*, (1981) Los Angeles, J.P. Tarcher, Sheldrake, R. *The Presence of the Past*, (1988) New York, Times Books as the *Morphic Field* (2005). There is more discussion of morphic fields as we progress.

[5] Bohm, D., *Wholeness and The Implicate Order* (1981) Routledge

[6] Phillip Hunter (2008)). 'What genes remember'. Prospect magazine., Iss. 146, May.

[7] Bruce Lipton, (2005). *The Biology of Belief.* Santa Rosa, CA: Mountain of Love/Elit Books. See Verny and Kelly, 2006, p. 156, cited in Lipton, 2005

[8] Lipton, (2005). *The Biology of Belief.* p. 155

[9] Sheldrake, R., *A New Science of Life*, (1981) Los Angeles, J.P. Tarcher, Sheldrake, R. *The Presence of the Past*, (1988) New York, Times Books.

[10] Mark Wolynn, *It Didn't Start with You: How Inherited Family Trauma Shapes Who We Are and How to End the Cycle* (2016) Viking

[11] Smith, L. and Gasser, M., *The Development of Embodied Cognition: Six Lessons from Babies, Artificial Life*, 11 (1-2), pp. 13-29

[12] Simms, E., *The Child in the World: Embodiment, Time and Language in Early Childhood* (2008) Great reference for child embodiment.

[13] Meltzoff, A. and Borton, R., *'Intermodal Matching by Human Neonates* (1979) Nature, 282, 403-404. p. 404

[14] Ignatius of Loyola, *In Founding of the Jesuits*, in Foss, M. (1969) *The Founding of the Jesuits (1540)* New York, Weybright and Talley

[15] Michael Apted *7 Up*, ed. Bennett Singer, London, Heinemann. The latest installment of the series was aired in 2013 and is available on netflix.com

[16] Wills, G. *Saint Augustine's Childhood, Confessions Book I* (2001) London, Continuum, p. 94

[17] McTaggart, L., *The Field* (2008) New York, NY, Harper

[18] Hawkins, D., *Transcending the Levels of Consciousness* (2006) W. Sedona, AZ., Veritas Publishing

[19] Braud, W. and Anderson, R. *Transpersonal Research Methods for the Social Sciences* (1998) Thousand Oaks, Calif., Sage Publications 1998, p.216

[20] Braud uses the example of Albert Einstein to make a similar point. Braud recounts Einstein noted that in his creative moments of research "the words or the language, as they were written or spoken, do not seem to play any role, rather, the elements in his thoughts were visual and of some muscular type." Einstein (1954, pp. 34) cited in Braud (1998, pp. 219)

[21] David Hawkins has kinesiologically calibrated a map of human consciousness through 20 years of primary research with the Institute of Advanced Spiritual Research. Hawkins has defined a range of values corresponding to well-organised attitudes and emotions (localised by specific attractor energy fields, much as electromagnetic fields gather iron fillings). The level of consciousness of any human being varies he says, and the ways that various levels of human consciousness express themselves are profound and far-reaching; their effects are both gross and subtle. Hawkins, D., *Power vs. Force* (2002) Carlsbad, Calif., Hay House. Hawkins, D., *Transcending the Levels of Consciousness* (2006) W. Sedona, AZ ., Veritas Publishing

[22] Oaklander *Hidden Treasure: A Map to the Child's Inner Self* (2006) London, Karnac

[23] Oaklander, (2006)

[24] Oaklander, (2006)

[25] Simms, E., *The Child in the World, Embodiment, Time and Language* (2008) Detroit, Mich., Wayne State University Press, p 95

[26] In my work as a Childosophy practitioner, I use a chart as a conceptual map that expresses in a visual form how the mind, body, and spirit (needs) correlates to each of the seven main chakras. By referring to this map while using a muscle test to measure the energetic imbalance in the body system, I can discern where the energy is stuck (fixed or concentrated) in a person. The technique commonly used by kinesiologists to measure the body's response is called a muscle test, or muscle monitoring. This technique is a useful diagnostic tool for any individual at any stage of their growth. By using the muscle test, a process to measure the child's body-mind responses to information s/he receives. A practitioner can offer feedback to the child about the status of the composite self. The muscle test is a functional body reply that does not discriminate against a preferred means of knowledge and offers information on all levels of one's being. See Diamond, J., *Your Body Doesn't Lie*, (1997) Enfield, Eden Grove. See Rosen, M. and Brenner, S., *Rosen Method Bodywork* (2003) Berkeley, Calif., North Atlantic Books

CHAPTER FOUR

[1] Gesell, A., *Maturation and the Patterning of Behaviour* (1933) in Murchinson, C. eds., *A Handbook of Child Psychology* (1934) 2nd ed., Worchester, Clark University

[2] Dvivedi, M (1980) *The Yoga Sutras of Patanjali*, Delhi: Sri Satguru Publications.

[3] The Chakras control the flow of *prana* and distribute it over energy channels called *Nadis*. The three major *Nadis* are called the *Sushumna*,

Ida, and the *Pingala*, (see Motoyama, H., *Theories of the Chakras*, Wheaton, Il. (1981) Theosophical Pub. House*)*. The *Sushumna* is deemed to be metaphysical column that runs vertically; it is said to be the channel for linking the Chakras and their various dimensions of consciousness. The *Ida* and *Pingala Nadis* crisscross, intersecting at the major Chakras. It is theorised that the *Sushumna* corresponds to the central canal of the spinal cord, and the *Ida* and *Pingala* to the sympathetic nerve stems located on either side of the spinal cord. *Prana* is distributed to the peripheral areas of the body through an elaborate matrix of thousands of minor *nadi* channels. Thus, "this system of *nadi* channels is analogous to the spinal nerves, which comprise the peripheral nervous system and serve a similar function. Just as the peripheral spinal nerves conduct the life energy of the nervous system to glands, organs, and tissues, the *nadis* distribute *prana* to all of the body, converting into different forms of vital energy appropriate for various organs, glands, and tissues." Motoyama, H., *Theories of the Chakras*, Wheaton, Il. (1981) Theosophical Pub. House, p.26

[4] Jung 1932, 1975 cited in Sannella, 1987, Sannella, L. (1987). *The Kundalini Experience*. Lower Lake, Calif.: Integral Pub.Sannella, 1987.

[5] <http://www.kundaliniresearch.org/links.html>.

[6] Diagnostic and Statistical Manual of Mental Disorders, 4th Edition. The DSM categorises mental health disorders and is a manual published by the American Psychiatric Association

[7] Sovatsky, (2010), *On Being Moved: Kundalini and the Complete Maturation of the Spiritual Body*, Man in India, 90 (1-2), pp. 339-352

[8] Sovatsky, S, (2010), p. 343-355

[9] Sovatsky, S, (2010), pp. 339-352

[10] Graphic art for this figure produced by Jodie Beckley from original art by Melanie Bedford, copyright held by Childosophy.

[11] See full story in Pert, C., *Molecules of Emotion*, (1997) New York,

NY., Scribner. To note here also in ascending order, the Chakras are located at the base of the spine (1st or Root Chakra), (2nd or Sacral Chakra), above the naval (3rd or solar plexus Chakra), the centre of the chest (4th or Heart Chakra), middle of the neck (5th or Throat Chakra), just above the brow area (6th or Third-eye Chakra), and top of the head (7th or Crown Chakra) p. 245

[12] Pert, C. (1997). *Molecules of Emotion.* New York, NY: Scribner. Pert also was the pharmacologist most famous for discovering the opiate receptor. See also Pert, C. and Marriott, N. (2006). *Everything you need to know to feel go(o)d.* Carlsbad, Calif.: Hay House.

[13] Pert, (1997), p. 20.

[14] *Candacepert.com, 2013*

[15] Pert C, & Marriot, N, (2006).. *Everything You Need to Know to Feel Go(o)d* p.211, Carlsbad, Calif., Hay House.

[16] Glassey, D. (2010). 'The Vitalistic Healing Model | Mind, Body, Spirit'. [online] Retrieved from: http://icpa4kids.org/Wellness-Articles/the-vitalistic-healing-model.html [Accessed: 01 Sep 2012].

[17] For me to make the link or to see a similarity for physics to match the theory I had put forth, may have taken additional years of research and I would also have had to have a deep understanding of physics. My line of research regarding quantum physics had given me a good understanding of the subject, but to take this further leap to explore solid-state physics would not have emerged without this contribution.

[18] See also Ashcroft, N. and Mermin, N. (1976). *Solid-State Physics.* New York: Holt, Rinehart and Winston, and Kittel, C. and Kittel, B. (1986). *Introduction to Solid-State Physics.* Wiley New York.

[19] Ashcroft, N. and Mermin, N. (1976). *Solid-State Physics.* New York: Holt, Rinehart and Winston

[20] This perspective is referred to as the "Normative-Descriptive Approach", since it applies norms of development to describe the

growth process.
http://www.gesellinstitute.org/pdf/AgesAndStagesHandout.pdf

PART II

CHILDREN NEED TO BE SAFE AND SECURE

[1] Nursery Rhyme - Mother Goose's Melody (London, c. 1765) with my amendment

[2] The Chakra themes are chosen from the work of Judith, A., *Eastern Body, Western Mind*, (1996, 2004) Berkeley, Calif., Celestial Arts. There are a variety of other sources that I have used and referred to over the years that announce the same energy themes of the Chakras, however, Judith's appear the most identifiable and almost universal as far as Western interpretations are concerned.

[3] For each of these seven sections of the *Foundational Needs Model* the associated themes from Judith, A., *Eastern Body, Western Mind* (2004) Berkeley, Calif., Celestial Arts

[4] For each of these seven sections of the *Foundational Needs Model* the associated Anatomy and body system correlations are from Myss, C., *Anatomy of the Spirit*, (1996) and *Why People Don't Heal and How They Can*, (2004) New York, Gramercy Books

[5] Bowlby and Ainsworth (1953) Bowlby, J. and Ainsworth, M. (2013) *The Origins of Attachment Theory, Attachment Theory: Social, Developmental, and Clinical Perspectives*, p. 45.

[6] T.R. Insel, *Oxytocin* – 'A Neuropeptide for Affiliation: Evidence from Behavioral, Receptor Autoradiographic, and Comparative Studies', Psychoneuroendocrinology 17, no. 1 (1992): 3- 35

[7] See Dawe et al (2007) *Cell Migration from Baby to Mother* in Journal of Cell Adhesion and Migration (2007 Jan-Mar) 1(1): 19–27 206 See

also Buyon JP., *The Effects of Pregnancy on Autoimmune Diseases*, Journal of Leukocyte Biology (1998 Mar) 63(3):281-7

[8] For a great article on Microchimerism, see a study done by the Clinical Research Division, Fred Hutchinson, Cancer Research Center, Seattle, Washington, USA. Chan, W. F., Gurnot, C., Montine, T. J., Sonnen, J. A., Guthrie, K. A., & Nelson, J. L. *Male Microchimerism in the Human Female Brain* (2006) PLoS One, 7(9), e45592

[9] The word *Zouyuzei* (in Chinese) translates to "sitting out the month." (Jaappa' (in Hindi). During the first 30 days after birth, both mother and child follow a strict set of rules that support the care of both mother and baby. Confinement is an ancient tradition dating back 2000 years, but it is still widely practiced throughout Asia today. See Wilms, S., *The Female Body in Medieval China: A Translation and Interpretation of the "Women's Recipes" in Sun Simiao's Beiji qianjinyaofang*, (2002) University of Arizona<http://arizona.openrepository.com/arizona/handle/10150/280225>

[10] *The Committee on Integrating the Science of Early Childhood Development* (2000) identified how essential the attachment bond is to a child's development.

[11] Bowlby, J., *A Secure Base*, (1988) New York, Basic Books

[12] Carlson, M. and Earls, F., *Psychological and Neuroendocrinological Sequelae of Early Social Deprivation in Institutionalized Children in Romania*, Annals of the New York Academy of Sciences, (1997) 807 (1), pp. 419-428, p.416 -- HPA (hypothalamic-pituitary-adrenal) axis is a central part of the neuroendocrine system and the physiology of stress and regulates the energy storage and expenditure.

[13] The *Effects of Early Social-Emotional and Relationship Experience on the Development of Young Orphanage Children*, by The St. Petersburg, USA Orphanage Research Team, in *Monographs of the Society for Research in Child Development*, Volume 73, Issue 3, pages 1– 15, December 2008,

Ainsworth, Bell and Stayton (1974)

[14] Taige et al, *Antenatal Maternal Stress and Long-term Effects on Child Neurodevelopment: How and Why?* Journal of Child Psychology and Psychiatry, (2007, Mar-Apr) 48(3-4):245-61

[15] Shonkoff JP, Boyce W, McEwen BS., *Neuroscience, Molecular Biology, and the Childhood Roots of Health Disparities: Building a New Framework for Health Promotion and Disease Prevention*, JAMA (2009) 301(21): 2252-2259

[16] Yeo, R. A., Gangestad, S. W., & Thoma, R. J., *Developmental Instability and Individual Variation in Brain Development Implications for the Origin of Neurodevelopmental Disorders* (2007) Current Directions in Psychological Science, 16(5), 245-249, Chicago

[17] See for more detailed analysis *Complex Trauma in Children and Adolescents*, White Paper from the National Child Traumatic Stress Network Complex Trauma Task Force (2003)

[18] Gary Dees, *You, But Better: How to Overcome Stress and Anxiety and Fulfill Your Potential*, (2015) Booktango

[19] Freud, S. *Analysis of a Phobia of a Five Year Old Boy*, ithe Pelican Freud Library (1977) Vol 8, Case Histories 1, pages 169-306

[20] Freud, S. and Strachey, J., *Three Essays on the Theory of Sexuality* (1962) p. 141-149, New York, Basic Books.

In *Three Essays on Sexuality*, Freud outlined these stages as oral, anal, phallic, latent, and genital. The satisfaction of a sexual desire is attributed to each stage. Whether this desire is realised or not, plays a role in adult personality. These functions form a symbolic meaning for the child in the adjustments and adaptations the individual makes in coping with the anxieties and stresses of life. Many have challenged Freud's dominance of the idea of sexual gratification as the innate drive and critiqued his thinking in general. *cf* Dufresne, *Against Freud: Critics Talk Back,* (2007) Stanford, Stanford University Press.

21 Without going into too much detail about Freudian theory, the reason for this conclusion by Freud was because this interpretation fit his introduction of a particular myth of *Oedipus Rex*. As Freud has been important to our understanding of children in the past, I should explain that the Oedipal drama is a myth that speaks to the desire of the son to be in a sexual union with his mother so he kills the father to do so. Freud tells us that the Oedipus complex is an active part of every human psyche; that every child desires to be the love object of their parent in this way (boys to their mothers and girls to their fathers), and wants the other parent out of the way

22 See Jonathon Lear, *Freud* (2005) Psychology Press, chapter 2: 55-87 Lear says one is disrupted by anxiety every time one tries to formulate a thought but one never gets around to having that thought, and as displayed in the case of Elisabeth Von R., this can turn into a physical manifestation which is tied to the mental aspect. Freud, with his renowned medical background, made the connection between body and mind when he spoke of conversion disorders and the effect of repressed memory on the physical body of some of his patients.

23 Dunlop and Fabian (2007) *Outcomes of good practice in transition processes for children entering primary school,* working papers early childhood development, 42 (report)

24 Children in foster care had increased vulnerability to autoimmune disorders (see Bruce, Fisher, Pears, & Levine (2009) cited in *Understanding the Effects of Maltreatment on Brain Development,* https://www.childwelfare.gov/pubPDFs/brain_development.pdf

25 A wonderful book that looks at the impact of sexual boundary violations; by exploring an extreme human experience, childhood sexual abuse, the book allows an insight into a hidden, silenced, and destructive aspect of human relations. Anna Luise Kirkengen, *Inscribed Bodies: Health Impact of Childhood Sexual Abuse,* (2001) Kluwer Academic Publishers.

[26] Kendall-Tackett, K., Williams, L. and Finkelhor, D., Impact of Sexual Abuse on Children: A *Review and Synthesis of Recent Empirical Studies*, Psychological bulletin (1993) 113 (1), p. 164

[27] Impett, E., Daubenmier, J. and Hirschman, A., *Minding the Body: Yoga, Embodiment, and Well-Being*, (2006) Sexuality Research & Social Policy, 3 (4), pp. 39-48. Childosophy www.childosophy.com has developed programs that incorporate the concepts of the book in a child friendly way that links the child's behaviours to the unmet need as well as Yoga practices incorporating the theme of the Needs. Such approaches support children to gain a deeper understanding of why they do what they do and how they may begin to meet their own needs.

[28] Benyamini, Idler, Leventhal, & Leventhal, 2000; Cohen, Alper, Doyle, Treanor, & Turner, cited in Ryan et al, *Vitalizing Effects of Being Outdoors and in Nature* (2010) Journal of Environmental Psychology, 30 (2010) 159–168 see also Ryan et al (2010) *Vitalizing Effects of Being Outdoors and in Nature* Journal of Environmental Psychology (2010) 30 159–168.

[29] *Perceived Eating Norms and Vegetable Consumption in Children*, Maxine Sharps, Eric Robinson, Int J Behav Nutr Phys Act. (2015) 12: 135, Published online, 2015, October 14

[30] Steptoe, A., Pollard, T. M., & Wardle, J. (1995). Development of a measure of the motives underlying the selection of food: the food choice questionnaire. *Appetite*, 25(3), 267-284

CHILDREN NEED TO FEEL

[31] Robert Frost. "A Servant to Servants." Robert Frost (1874–1963). North of Boston. 1915.

[32] http://www.panda.org.au/practical-information/about-postnatal-depression/33-postnatal-depression-and-childbirth-trauma

33 Candace Pert, (1997), *Molecules of Emotion*. New York, NY: Scribner. p. 20.

34 Aurobindo, Sri, (1992*) The Synthesis of Yoga*, Pondicherry, Sri Aurobindo Ashram Trust, pp. 799–800, See also Carlin Flora, *Gut Almighty* (2007) Psychology Today, Vol 40, Issue 3, 68-75

35 *Aron, E, The Highly Sensitive Person: How to Thrive When the World Overwhelms You, (2003)* Kensington. In the book, the author shares her extensive research identifying HSP as a specific trait. Although the term is usually used to describe humans, the characteristic was found to be present in nearly all higher animals and inherited by 15% to 20% of the population.

36 Bedwetting is considered persistent after the age of three when bladder control is more established. Bedwetting can usually be traced to a repressed fear of a male authority figure, or the emotional expression that is not possible in this regard. See Louise Hay, *Heal your Body*, (1998) Carlsbad, Hay House; Lise Bourbeau, *Your Body's Telling you: Love Yourself* (2001) Canada, Les Editions and Annette, Noontil, *The Body is the Barometer of the Soul* (2002) McPhersons, Australia -- Bedwetting has been a topic of interest for many decades and offers much insight into both the psychological and biological interaction resulting in the child from fear-based experiences. See Gerard, M., *Enuresis: A Study in Etiology* (1939) American Journal of Orthopsychiatry, 9 (1), pp. 48-58, and Pierce, C et al. *Enuresis and Dreaming: Experimental Studies* (1961) Archives of General Psychiatry, 4 (2), p. 166.

37 HeartMath ® Institute has been researching the connection between body and mind, specifically the heart and the brain for decades. *Science of the Heart: Exploring the Role of the Heart in Human Performance: An Overview of Research Conducted by the HeartMath Institute* has a chapter on intuition research. This is an ebook: https://www.heartmath.org/research/science-of-the-heart/ *accessed April, 2016*

38 Seligman, M. (2011). *Flourish*. North Sydney, N.S.W.: Random

House Australia. Goleman, D. (1995). *Emotional intelligence.* New York: Bantam Books. p. 84

[39] Professor Martin E.P. Seligman, in announcing the recipients of the Templeton Positive Neuroscience Awards cited on www.authentichappiness.sas.upenn.edu/newsletter.aspx?id=1545

[40] Repetti, R., Taylor, S. and Seeman, T., *Risky Families: Family Social Environments and the Mental and Physical Health of Offspring,* Psychological Bulletin, 128 (2), p. 330

[41] Lahey, B., Conger, R., Atkeson, B. and Treiber, F., *Parenting Behavior and Emotional Status of Physically Abusive Mothers,* Journal of Consulting and Clinical Psychology, 52 (6), p. 1062.

[42] Chambers, C., Reid, G., Craig, K., Mcgrath, P., and Finley, G., *Agreement Between Child and Parent Reports of* Pain (1998) The Clinical Journal of Pain, 14 (4), pp. 336—342

[43] Lander et al, Social Work Public Health (2013) 28(0): 194–205, *The Impact of Substance Use Disorders on Families and Children: From Theory to Practice* and Carnes. P., *Sexual Addiction and Compulsion: Recognition, Treatment, & Recovery* (2000) Ph.D. CNS Spectrums, 5(10): 63-72, International Institute of Trauma and Addiction Professionals, https://www.iitap.com.

[44] Gibb, B. and Abela, J., *Emotional Abuse, Verbal Victimization, and the Development of Children's Negative Inferential Styles and Depressive Symptoms* (2008) Cognitive Therapy and Research, 32 (2), pp. 161-176

[45] Cognitive behavioural therapy (CBT) is said to help people learn more realistic explanatory styles, that is, to change the negative or pessimistic attributions to life and self into more positive ones. CBT holds at its base an assumption that a person's disposition or outlook on life is related directly to his or her patterns of thought. Pessimistic or negative thinking has an affect on one's sense of self, behaviour, and physical state. Silverman WK, Pina AA, Viswesvaran C., *Evidence-based Psychosocial Treatments for Phobic and Anxiety Disorders in Children and Adolescents,* Journal of Clinical Child and Adolescent

Psychology, (2008 Jan,) 37(1): 105- 130

[46] Elias C, Berk, L (2002) Self-regulation in young children: Is there a role for sociodramatic play? Early Childhood Research Quarterly Vol 17, Issue 2, Summer 2002, Pages 216–238

[47] Accessed http://www.sensory-processingdisorder.com/sensory-integration-activities.html

[48] Lester, S., and Russell, W., *Play for a Change: Play, Policy and Practice: A Review of Contemporary Perspectives* (2008) London, National Children's Bureau, p. 9

[49] Oaklander, V., *The Therapeutic Process With Children and Adolescents*, (1997) Gestalt Review, 1(4), 292-317

[50] Whitebread, D. (2012) The Importance of Play, A report on the value of children's play with a series of policy recommendations p. 26 of the report. Cambridge University.

[51] Freud, *Formulations on the Two Principles of Mental Functioning* (1958) in J. Strachey (Ed. and Trans.) *The Standard Edition of the Complete Psychological Works of Sigmund Freud* (Vol. 12, pp. 213-227), London, Hogarth Press (Original work published 1911)

[52] Liss, M., et al, *Empowering or Oppressing? Development and Exploration of the Enjoyment of Sexualization Scale*, Personality and Social Psychology Bulletin, January, 2011, vol. 37, no. 1 55-68

[53] https://www.psychology.org.au/publications/tip_sheets/girls_positive_image/

CHILDREN NEED TO ACT

[1] John O'Donohue, *Anam Cara: A Book of Celtic Wisdom (1998)*

[2] Hillman, J., *The Soul's Code: In Search of Character and Calling (1997)* New York, Random House

[3] Ritzer, G., *Sociological Theory*, (1996) New York, McGraw-Hill Companies

[4] O'Connor, T. and Scott, S., *Parenting and Outcomes for Children* (2007) report, p, 15

[5] United Nations Committee on the Rights of the Child, 2001, General Comment No. 1, par 11

[6] Reaves, J., *Survey Gives Children Something to Cry About* (2000) Times, New York, 5 October and ABC News, *Calls for Ban on Parents Smacking Children*, (2013) Retrieved from: http://www.abc.net.au/news/2013-07-26/calls-for-ban-on-parents-smacking-

[7] Dickens, C. (n.d.), *Hard times*, Champaign, Ill., Project Gutenberg.

[8] Foucault, *Discipline and Punish* (1997) Vintage, p.26-27

[9] Cekaite, A., *Shepherding the Child: Embodied Directive Sequences in Parent-Child Interactions, An Interdisciplinary Journal of Language* (2010) Discourse & Communication Studies, 30 (1), pp. 1-25

[10] Perry, B., *Applying Principles of Neurodevelopment to Clinical Work with Maltreated and Traumatized Children: The Neurosequential Model of Therapeutics* (2006) Guilford Press

[11] Barber, B. and Harmon, E., *Violating the Self: Parental Psychological Control of Children and Adolescents* (2002) American Psychological Association

[12] Benard, B, *Fostering Resilience in Children* (1995) ERIC Digest, www.eric.ed.gov

[13] Bybee, J., *Guilt and Children* (1998) San Diego, Academic Press

[14] Benard, B, *Fostering Resilience in Children* (1995) ERIC Digest, www.eric.ed.gov and Eccles, J., Midgley, C., Wigfield, A., Buchanan, C., Reuman, D., Flanagan, C. and Mac Iver, D. *Development During Adolescence: The Impact of Stage* Environment Fit on Young

Adolescents' Experiences in Schools and in Families (1993) American psychologist, 48 (2), p. 90

15 "Holding" as a metaphor for the ways in which children get stuck and have difficulty processing their emotions. Often, a child holds when the parent or caregiver does not allow the child's opinions, feelings, ideas, or suggestions to be validated. *Cf,* Oaklander, V., *Hidden Treasure* (2006) London, Karnac

16 Hillman, J., *The Soul's Code: In Search of Character and Calling (1997)* New York, Random House

17 Daw, N and Shohamy, D., 'The Cognitive Neuroscience of Motivation and Learning' Social Cognition, Vol. 26, No. 5, 2008, pp. 593–620

18 Cole, C. and Coyne, J., 'Situational Specificity of Laboratory induced Learned Helplessness in Humans' (1977) Journal of Abnormal Psychology, 86 (6), p. 615–623

19 Journal of Personality and Social Psychology, 2011, Vol. 101, No. 2, 354–36

20 Nietzsche, F, Kaufmann, W. and Hollingdale, R. *(1968). The will to power. p. 481.* New York: Vintage Books.

21 Personal communication, January 2008. For other details on Krishnamurti's philosophies see Krishnamurti, J. (1991). *The collected works of J. Krishnamurti.* Dubuque, Iowa: Kendall/Hunt.

22 The metaphysical cause of illness and disease may be examined thorough the work of Louise Hay, *Heal your Body (1998)* Carlsbad, Hay House; Lise Bourbeau *Your Body's Telling You: Love Yourself* (2001) Canada, Les Editions; Annette, Noontil, *The Body is the Barometer of the Soul* (2002) McPhersons, Australia

23 Egger, H., Costello, E., Erkanli, A. and Angold, A. (1999). 'Somatic complaints and psychopathology in children and

adolescents: stomach aches, musculoskeletal pains, and headaches'. *Journal of the American Academy of Child & Adolescent Psychiatry*, 38 (7), pp. 852--860.

[24] Dinan, T, G. et al., *Collective Unconscious: How Gut Microbes Shape Human Behavior* (2015) Journal of Psychiatric Research, Volume 63, 1 – 9

CHILDREN NEED TO LOVE

[26]The Beatles, July, 1967

[26] Gilligan, Carol, *Moral Orientation and Moral Development* (2008) The Feminist Philosophy Reader, by Alison Bailey and Chris J. Cuomo, Boston, McGraw-Hill, N. pg. 469

[27] Lawrence Kohlberg's stages of moral development constitute an adaptation of a psychological theory originally conceived by the Swiss psychologist. Kohlberg followed the development of moral judgment far beyond the ages studied earlier by Piaget. See also Piaget, Jean, *The Moral Judgment of the Child (1932)* London, Kegan Paul, Trench, Trubner and Co see also Piaget, Jean, *The Moral Judgment of the Child* (1932) London, Kegan Paul, Trench, Trubner and Co

[28] Noddings, N., *Caring, A Feminine Approach to Ethics & Moral Education* (1984) Berkeley, University of California Press, p. 11

[29] Coles, R., *The Moral Life of Children* (1986-a) Boston, Atlantic Monthly -Press; Coles, R., (1986-b), *The Political Life of Children*, Boston, Atlantic Monthly Press

[30] Noddings, N. *The Challenge to Care in Schools* (1992). New York, Teachers College Press

[31] de Botton, A., *The News; A User's Manual* (2014) Pantheon, p.180

[32] de Botton, 2014, p. 180

[33] Dalai Lama, 2016,

<http://www.dalailama.com/messages/compassion>

[34] Dalai Lama, 2016

[35] Caspi, A., Moffitt, T., Morgan, J., Rutter, M., Taylor, A., Arseneault, L., Tully, L., Jacobs, C., Kim-Cohen, J., and Polo-Tomas, M., *Maternal Expressed Emotion Predicts Children's Antisocial Behavior Problems: Using Monozygotic-twin Differences to Identify Environmental Effects on Behavioral Development* (2004) Developmental psychology, 40 (2), p. 149

[36] Steinfeldt, J., Vaughan, E., Lafollette, J. and Steinfeldt, M., *Bullying Among Adolescent Football Players: Role of Masculinity and Moral Atmosphere* (2012) Psychology of Men & Masculinity, 13 (4), p. 340

[37] Szalavitz, M. and Perry, B., *Born for Love* (2010) New York, William Morrow

[38] Adolphs, cited in Iacoboni, M., *Imitation, Empathy, and Mirror Neurons* (2009) Annual Review of Psychology, 60 pp. 653-670 p.667

[39] Iacoboni, M. *Imitation, Empathy, and Mirror Neurons* (2009) Annual review of psychology, 60, pp. 653-670, p.667

[40] Ryff, C. and Singer, B. *Interpersonal Flourishing: A Positive Health Agenda for the N Millennium* (2000) Personality and Social Psychology Review, 4 (1), pp. 30-44

[41] Labay, L. and Walco, G. (2004). 'Brief report: empathy and psychological adjustment in siblings of children with cancer'. *Journal of paediatric psychology*, 29 (4), pp. 309--314.

[42] Lieberman, A., *The Emotional Life of the Toddler* (2007) New York, Free Press

[43] Agnew, Z., Bhakoo, K. and Puri, B., *The Human Mirror System: A Motor Resonance Theory of Mind-Reading* (2007) Brain Research Reviews, 54 (2), pp. 286-293

[44] Agnew, Bhakoo, & Puri, 2007, p. 286

[45] Williams, J., Whiten, A., Suddendorf, T., and Perrett, D., *Imitation, Mirror N and Autism* (2001) Neuroscience & Biobehavioral Reviews, 25 (4), pp. 28—295

[46] Agnew, Bhakoo, & Puri, 2007

[47] Agnew, Bhakoo, & Puri, 2007

[48] The theory of morphic resonance is dependent upon the morphic field theory, which posits that all living organisms have a prototypical energetic field that support growth and evolution. Morphic field theory may sound very similar or at least familiar as another interpretation of the motivating, energetic force, or the *push*. Sheldrake, R., *A New Science of Life* (1981) Los Angeles, J.P. Tarcher; Sheldrake, R., *The Presence of the Past* (1988) New York, Times Books

[49] *Science of the Heart: Exploring the Role of the Heart in Human Performance*, < https://www.heartmath.org/resources/downloads/science-of-the-heart/ >

[50] HeartMath ® Institute has been researching the connection between body and mind, specifically the heart and the brain for decades. *Science of the Heart: Exploring the Role of the Heart in Human Performance An Overview of Research Conducted by the HeartMath Institute* contains a chapter on intuition research. A link to download the book is: https://www.heartmath.org/research/science-of-the-heart/ (accessed April 2016)

[51] Armour, J. A., *Neurocardiology: Anatomical and Functional Principles*, Boulder Creek, CA., HeartMath Research Center, Institute of HeartMath, Publication, (03-011)

[52] Armour, J. A. (2003)

[53] www.littleways.com/about

[54] Froh, J. J., Bono, G., Fan, J., Emmons, R. A., Henderson, K., Harris, C., Wood, A. M., 'Nice Thinking! An Educational Intervention that Teaches Children to Think Gratefully' *(*2014) School Psychology Review, *43*(2), 132

[55] Emmons, R A. and McCullough, M.E., 'Counting Blessings versus Burdens: An Experimental Investigation of Gratitude and Subjective Well-Being in Daily Life' (2003) Journal of Personality and Social Psychology, *Vol. 84(2), Feb., 377-389*

[56] Emmons, R A. and McCullough, M.E. (2003)

CHILDREN NEED TO SPEAK

[57] Jean Berko Gleeson interview with Krista Tippet (2016) *On Being* https://onbeing.org/programs/jean-berko-gleason-unfolding-language-unfolding-life/

[58] <http://www.abc.net.au/radionational/programs/newdimensions/esp2c-autistic-children2c-remote-viewing2c-telepathy2c-and-/6365562 >See also Diana Powell (2008) *The ESP Enigma: The Scientific Case for Psychic Phenomena*, Walker Books

[59] Padgett, David A., and Ronald Glaser. "How stress influences the immune response." Trends in immunology 24.8 (2003): 444-448.

[60] Faith Jegede 2012 in a TED talk - This grab is from their website

TED is a nonprofit devoted to spreading ideas, usually in the form of short, powerful talks (18 minutes or less). TED began in 1984 as a conference where Technology, Entertainment and Design converged, and today covers almost all topics — from science to business to global issues — in more than 100 languages. Meanwhile, independently run TEDx events help share ideas in communities around the world. The link to Faith Jegede's talk:

https://www.ted.com/talks/faith_jegede_what_i_ve_learned_from_my_autistic_brothers/transcript?language=en

[61] See *The Empty Fortress* (1967), *A Good Enough Parent*, (1987) for accounts on cases. Bruno Bettelheim derived his thinking from the qualitative investigation of clinical cases that the cold or refrigerator mother as he termed caused emotional problems for the child and later that Autism was a disorder of parenting.

[62] *Immunization Safety Review: Thimerosal-Containing Vaccines and Neurodevelopmental Disorders.* (2001) Institute of Medicine (US) Immunization Safety Review Committee; Stratton K, Gable A, McCormick MC, editors. Washington DC

[63] Bourbeau, L. (2001) *Your body's telling you: Love Yourself,* Canada; Les Editions.

[64] Elman, J. (1993). 'Learning and development in neural networks: The importance of starting small'. *Cognition*, 48 (1), pp. 71--99.

[65] Krebs, C., *A Revolutionary Way of Thinking* (1998) Melbourne, Hill of Content, p. 174

[66] Split-brain research has upheld that language processing is principally a process that occurs in the left side of the brain. For instance, when words appear only in the left visual field, the right brain must transfer that information to the left-brain, in order to interpret it. The study at the University of California, Santa Barbara (UCSB), "Dynamic network structures of inter hemispheric coordination", Karl W. Doron, Danielle S. Bassett, and Michael S. Gazzaniga (2012) shows that people will respond with less accuracy when the right brain has only been shown information. There appears a highly complex interaction between both brain spheres. The brain works as whole, not as fragmented parts. The findings are

the result of using sensitive neuroscientific equipment and analysis techniques from network science. The researchers contend this work demonstrates that recently developed techniques are giving access to previously unapproachable understandings into the role of inter hemispheric coordination in cognition.

[67] E. Mayer, 'Gut Feelings: The Emerging Biology of Gut–Brain Communication' (2011) Nature Reviews Neuroscience, 12, 453-466 (August)

[68] Anthony J. DeCasper and William P. Fifer, 'Of Human Bonding: Newborns Prefer their Mothers' Voices' (1980) Science, New Series, Vol. 208, No. 4448 (Jun. 6) pp. 1174-1176, American Association for the Advancement of Science

[69] Seltzer, L. J., Prososki, A. R., Ziegler, T. E., & Pollak, S. D., *Instant Messages vs. Speech: Hormones and Why We Still Need to Hear Each Other* '(2012) Evolution and Human Behavior, *33*(1), 42-45

[70] Chandler, D., *Semiotics* (2002) London, Routledge, p.11

[71] Andrew Stables, *Living and Learning as Semiotic Engagement* (2005) p. 103, Lewiston, Edwin Mellon Press

[72] Dilts, Bandler & DeLozier, 1980 p. 2, cited in Tosey, P., & Mathison, J. 'Neuro Linguistic Programming as an Innovation in Education and Teaching' (2010) Innovations in Education and Teaching International (2010) *47*(3), 317-326

[73] Wittgenstein, L., *Rules and Meanings,* (1973) Harmondsworth, Penguin, Chicago

[74] Pinker, S., *The Language Instinct* (1994) New York, W. Morrow and Co.

[75] Pinker, 1994, p. 130

[76] Hudson, R. A., *Sociolinguistics* (1996) Cambridge University Press

[77] When I worked as an integration aide, the children I worked with were on the autism spectrum. The instructions that came from psychologists in way of relational approaches for teachers seemed counter intuitive to what I felt the child needed. Given the focus 20 years ago was still mostly about trying to convert the child and have them adapt to "fit in". There seemed a general sentiment that the autistic child was on an established developmental pathway and adults needed to redirect them; the blank slate thinking. Autistic children are still today largely measured and compared against other children and the adults they are projected to become.

[78] M. Bayat *Evidence of Resilience in Families of Children with Autism* (2007) Journal of Intellectual Disability Research, Vol 51 Issue 9, 702–714, September

[79] Andrew Solomon, *Far From the Tree; Parents, Children, and the Search for Identity* (2014)

[80] ABC, AIFS, *Life at 5* (2013) - About the Series - ABC TV *Life at Five* Transcript from the show, http://www.abc.net.au/tv/life/about_the_series/life_at_5.htm Based upon the research of the AIFS, Ann Sanson is the Acting Director of the Australian Institute of Family Studies and Project Director of the Growing Up in Australia study. Robert Johnstone is the Growing Up in Australia study Data Manager at the Australian Institute of Family Studies. The LSAC Research Consortium consists of the Consortium Advi.

[81] ABC: AIFS, *Life at Five* (2013)

[82] *Life at 5* (2013) About the Series - ABC TV *Life at Five*, Transcript from the show, http://www.abc.net.au/tv/life/about_the_series/life_at_5.htm Based upon the research of the AIFS. Ann Sanson is the Acting Director of the Australian Institute of Family Studies and Project Director of the Growing Up in Australia study. Robert Johnstone is the Growing Up in Australia study Data Manager at the Australian

Institute of Family Studies. The LSAC Research Consortium consists of the Consortium Advi.

[83] Caroline Myss, *Defy Gravity: Healing Beyond the Bounds of Reason* (2009) Hay House

[84] Bussey. K. (1999) 'Children's Categorization and Evaluation of Different Types of Lies and Truths'. Child Development, 70 (6): 1338-1347. November/December, 1999

[85] Pennebaker and Susman, 1988, cited in Finkenauer, C and Rime, B. (1998), 'Socially shared emotional experiences vs emotional experiences kept secret: Differential statistics and consequences,' Journal of Social and Clinical Psychology, 17: 295-318.

[86] Finkenauer and Rime, 1998, p. 125.

[87] Smart, C., *Children's Personal Lives* (2011) in, May, V. eds. *Sociology of Personal Life* (2011) New York, Palgrave Macmillan, pp. 98-107

[88] Mitra, D., 'The Significance of Students: Can Increasing Student Voice in Schools Lead to Gains in Youth Development?' (2004) The Teachers College Record, 106 (4), pp. 651-688

[89] Mitra, 2004

CHILDREN NEED TO SEE

[90] The Disney Corporation attributes this quote to Walt Disney. But apparently Disney archivist Dave Smith says it was actually created by a Disney employee for the Epcot ride Horizons in the 1980s.

[91] Evan Kidd, a researcher at Australian National University, and colleagues found that adults who had imaginary friends as children scored higher on creativity tests than those who did not.

[92] https://faculty.washington.edu/chudler/syne.html

⁹³ Winnicott in Jacobson, E., *The Self and the Object World: Vicissitudes of their Infantile Cathexes and their Influence on Ideational and Affective Development* (1954) Psychoanalytic Study of the Child, 9:75-127. p. 160

⁹⁴ Lacan, J. and Miller, J., *The Seminar of Jacques Lacan* (1988) New York, Norton, Lacan, J., Fink, H. and Fink, B. *Ecrits* (2006) New York, W.W. Norton & Co.

⁹⁵ Brooks-Gunn, J., & Lewis, M., *Mirror-Image Stimulation and Self Recognition in Infancy* (1975)

⁹⁶ For cognitive psychologists, the mirror is also used in a common research testing self-awareness in infants. This is known as the Rouge test, and in effect works by applying a dot on an infant's face before putting them in front of a mirror. If the infant is drawn to the dot by touching it, it is said that they realise their own existence and have achieved self-awareness. See Amsterdam, B. *Mirror Self-image Reactions before Age Two* (1972, Developmental Psychology 5, (4): 297–305) Again, the paradigm I am supporting does not discount the child's self-awareness it argues strongly that the child's self awareness is unified and knows the difference in perception of experiences and the felt sense, not just the cognitive ability (thought process and interpretations) of the things it sees and touches, and seeks to keep maintain unity – to keep feelings and thoughts in harmony.

⁹⁷ Louise Hay, *Mirror Work: 21 Days to Heal Your Life* (2016) Hay House Publishing, Carlsbad, CA

⁹⁸ Winnicott, D. W., *Transitional Objects and Transitional Phenomena* (1953) The International Journal of Psycho-Analysis, *34*, 89

⁹⁹ Winnicott, 1971, p. 98-99.

¹⁰⁰ Rofrano (2006) See Therese, M., 2013, for a full discussion on this. In part, Frances Rofrano (2006) states that by viewing Winnicott (1971) through the lens of Martin Buber's Philosophy

("encounter" and "'dialogue"') 'It could be said that spirit does not reside in the immanent or the transcendent but manifests itself through the narrative of self of the child created in the transitional space between I and Thou.'

[101] Smith, L. and Gasser, M., 'The Development of Embodied Cognition: Six lessons from Babies' (2005) Artificial Life, 11 (1-2), pp. 13-29

[102] Smith & Gasser, (2005) p.13.

[103] Smith & Gasser, (2005)

[104] Smith & Gasser, (2005) p.21

[105] Simms, E., *The Child in the World: Embodiment, Time and Language in Early Childhood* (2008) Great reference for child embodiment.

[106] http://www.artofliving.org/in-en/archive/1329

[107] Good, T., *21st Century Education* (2008) Los Angeles, SAGE Publications, p. 267

[108] Groen, M., *The Whig Party and the Rise of Common Schools 1837-1854: Party and Policy Re-examined* (2008) American Educational History Journal, 35 (2), pp. 251-260

[109] Burbules, N. and Berk, R., Critical Thinking and Critical Pedagogy: Relations, Differences, and Limits; Critical Theories in Education: Changing Terrains of Knowledge and Politics (1999) in T. Popkewitz and L. Fendler (eds), *Critical Theories in Education: Changing Terrains of Knowledge and Politics* (pp. 45–65)

[110] Burbules & Berk, 1999

[111] Moore, R. and Moore, D. *Better Late than Early* (1975) New York, Reader's Digest Press

[112] Montessori, M., *The Absorbent Mind* (1967) New York, Holt, Rinehart and Winston, p. 240

[113] Montessori cited in Miller, R., *What are Schools For?* Brandon, VT., Holistic Education Press

[114] Montessori, 1967, p. 69

[115] Montessori, M. and Costelloe, M., *The Secret of Childhood* (1974) New York: Ballantine Books, p. 38

[116] Montessori, (1967),

[117] Montessori, (1967) p. 41

[118] Miller, J (2012) *Education for Sustainability Holistic Education: Learning for an Interconnected World*, Source [www.eolss.net] Accessed 22/08/2012

[119] Miller, J (2012)

[120] Vaughn, B., Coppola, G., Verissimo, M., Monteiro, L., Santos, A., Posada, G., Carbonell, O., Plata, S., Waters, H., Bost, K. and others, 'The Quality of Maternal Secure-Base Scripts Predicts Children's Secure-Base Behavior at Home in Three Sociocultural Groups' (2007) International Journal of Behavioral Development, 31 (1), pp. 65-76

[121] Cohen, L. B., & Salapatek, P. (Eds., *Infant Perception: From Sensation to Cognition: Basic Visual Processes*' (2013) Vol. 1, Academic Press

[122] Bergen, D., *The Role of Pretend Play in Children's Cognitive Development* (2002) Early Childhood Research & Practice, *4*(1)

[123] Smilansky, S., & Shefatya, L., *Facilitating Play: A Medium for Promoting Cognitive, Socio-Emotional and Academic Development in Young Children* (1990) Psychosocial & Educational.

[124] The effect of meditation on the brain has been widely

documented by Jon Kabat-Zinn.

[125] Howard Gardner, 1993, 15 Gardner, H., *Frames of Mind* (1983) New York, Basic Books, Walters & Gardner, 1986

[126] Walter, J. and Gardner, H., *The Theory of Multiple Intelligences: Some Issues and Answers* (1986) in Sternberg, R. and Wagner, R. eds. *Practical Intelligence* New York, NY., Cambridge University Press., p. pp. 163-182

[127] The eight distinct intelligences as proposed by Gardner are musical - rhythmic, visual - spatial, verbal - linguistic, logical - mathematical, bodily - kinesthetic, interpersonal, intrapersonal, and naturalistic. See Slavin, R., *Educational Psychology* (2009) 9th ed. Boston, Pearson, Pp. 117

[128] Thomas Armstrong has drawn parallels with Gardner's *MI* and Rudolph Steiner's philosophies in that they both have an educational approach to the understanding of the child's needs and potentials. Armstrong, T., *Multiple Intelligences in the Classroom* (1994) Alexandria, Va., Association for Supervision and Curriculum Development

[129] Prouty, S., *Waldorf Education and the Neurodevelopment of Intelligence: An Integrative Review*, (1994) Antioch New England Graduate School, ProQuest

[130] Gesell, A., *Maturation and the Patterning of Behaviour* (1933) in Murchinson, C. eds., *A Handbook of Child Psychology* (1934) 2nd ed., Worchester, Clark University

[131] Judith, A, (1996, 2004) *Eastern Body, Western Mind*, Berkeley, Calif., Celestial Arts. p. 338-387

[132] Wernovsky, Gila,b; Shillingford, Amanda Ja,b; Gaynor, J. William, (2005) *Central Nervous System Outcomes in Children with Complex Congenital Heart Disease*, Current Opinion in Cardiology, Volume 20, March, Issue 2, pp 94-99, Pediatrics

[133] Blair, Lawrence *Rhythms of Vision: The Changing Patterns of Belief* (1975) London

[134] Owens, J., Maxim, R., Nobile, C., Mcguinn, M. and Msall, M. *Parental and Self-report of Sleep in Children with Attention-Deficit/Hyperactivity Disorder* Archives of Pediatrics & Adolescent Medicine, 154 (6), p. 549

[135] Owens et al., 2000, p. 549

[136] Valli, K., Revonsuo, A., Palkas,O., Ismail, K., Ali, K. and Punamaki, R., *The Threat Simulation Theory of the Evolutionary Function of Dreaming: Evidence from Dreams of Traumatized Children* (2005) Consciousness and Cognition, 14 (1), pp. 188-218

[137] Nielsen, T., Powell, R. and Kuiken, D., *Nightmare Frequency is Related to a Propensity for Mirror Behaviors*, Consciousness and Cognition, 22 (4), pp. 1181-1188

[138] Lieberman, A. *The Emotional Life of the Toddler* (2007) New York, Free Press

[139] Agnew, Z., Bhakoo, K. and Puri, B., *The Human Mirror System, a Motor Resonance Theory of Mind-Reading* (2007) *Brain Research Reviews*, 54 (2), pp. 286-293

[140] Agnew, Bhakoo, & Puri, 2007, p. 286

CHILDREN NEED TO KNOW

[141] "Twinkle, Twinkle, Little Star" is a popular English lullaby. The lyrics are from an early 19th-century English poem by Jane Taylo

[142] Antinuclear antibody or ANA testing is an indicator of autoimmune conditions specifically targeting skin isues.

[143] Consciousness, Bioenergy and Healing: Self-Healing and Energy Medicine for the 21st Century. See page 106 – 107 for Victor Adamenko's (1972) studies.

[144] Shenefelt, P. D., & Shenefelt, D. A. (2014). Spiritual and religious aspects of skin and skin disorders. *Psychology Research and Behavior Management*, 7, 201–212.

[145] Denby K, Duffy N, Tausk F. 'Psychoneuroimmunology in Dermatology.' In: Norman RA, Shenefelt PD, Rupani RN, editors. *Integrative Dermatology*. New York, NY, USA: Oxford University Press; 2014.

[146] *Akuaba* are wooden ritual fertility dolls from Ghana and nearby areas. My doll was a of the *Ashanti* people. See https://en.wikipedia.org/wiki/Akuaba.

[147] Shenefelt, P. D., & Shenefelt, D. A. (2014). 'Spiritual and religious aspects of skin and skin disorders'. Psychology Research and Behavior Management, 7, 201–212.

[148] *The Philosophy of Childhood* gives a definition of what the philosophy of childhood is. Matthews was also an advocate for the child as an active agent in their own philosophical questioning of life and self, and wrote extensively from this position. cf., *Philosophy & the* Matthews G.B., *Young Child* (1980) See also Matthews, 1994, *The Philosophy of Childhood*, Harvard University Press

[149] *How the Human Body is Connected to the Life Cycles of the Earth, the Planets, and the Stars,* Oxford University Press, 1 edition (March 1, 2015) Karel Schrijver, Senior Fellow, Lockheed Martin Advanced Technology Center, California, Iris Schrijver, Professor of Pathology and Pediatrics, Stanford University School of Medicine Pathology Department

[150] *How 40,000 Tons of Cosmic Dust Falling to Earth Affects You and Me* Our bodies are made of remnants of stars and massive explosions in

the galaxies, authors say. By Simon Worrall published January 28 2015. <http://news.nationalgeographic.com/2015/01/150128-big-bang-universe-supernova-astrophysics-health-space-ngbooktalk/>

[151] The Cartesian body-mind dualism has discounted any interconnections between mind and body. Researchers have also learned that most traditional systems of Chinese medicine appreciate and incorporate into their practice the complex and powerful relationship between the mind and the body. The body's organ systems hold memory, and the unconscious mind, in turn influences the body's responses. This is similar to many Asian philosophies, such as Ayurveda and Tibetan medicine, which see human beings as part of an interconnected, universal energy field. See Hicks, Angela, *Chinese Medicine* (1996) London, Thorsons,

[152] Freud, *Phobia of a Five Year Old Boy* (1909) Huish p28

[153] Haire, M., *Phobia, Paradox, and Persuasion in the Case of Little Hans* (2005) Hons Thesis, Deakin University, (Haire, nee Therese)

[154] De Souza, 2009; Hay & Nye, 2006; Coles, 1990; Hyde, Ota and Yust, 2013, cited in Therese, M. (2013) *A Philosophy of Childhood: The Foundational Needs and Wellbeing*, Deakin University.

[155] De Souza, M., *Spirituality and Wellbeing* (2009) International Journal of Children's Spirituality, 14 (3), pp. 181-184

[156] Hay and Nye *The Spirit of the Child* (2006) London, Fount, p. 22-24, refers to Alistair Hardy's 1965 work on religious experience having a biological basis. They break the concept of relational consciousness into four elements: 1) awareness of self 2) awareness of others 3) awareness of the environment and 4) (for some people) awareness of a transcendent other (Hay and Nye, 2006 p. 109). This definition is closely linked to an emerging sense of identity in young children, which is often centred on their own needs. It involves children recognising both their independence and interdependence,

reflecting the importance attached to many religious traditions of being less obsessed with oneself or with material possessions.

[157] Ken Wilber gives 5 definitions of spirituality in the chapter, and these definitions are for the most part vertical; that is, hierarchical, staged, or linear. Definition 3, sees spirituality as a separate line of development all together, and Wilber maintains that infancy and childhood definitely have spirituality, but only the lowest stages of spirituality. Definition 4 maintains that infants and children are directly in touch with spiritual realities (devotional, objective, or mystical) or at least they can be. This is, however, according to Wilber, person centered. It is useful to remember that Hay and Nye's relational consciousness is counter to Wilber's understanding, in that they see the child as having a specific relational consciousness that sees them relating to the self, others, nature, and God. Wilber's Definition 5, spirituality is a peak experience, and peak experiences, according to Wilber, offer the most credible definition of childhood spirituality. He says this is genuine spirituality in the sense of Wordsworth, "Not in entire forgetfulness...but trailing clouds of glory we come," namely the deeper psychic (or soul) dimension that some suggest is present from prenatal through early years, but then fades as frontal (egoic) development gets underway. For full discussion refer to, Therese, M., *The Integral Child* (2010) Man in India, 90 (1-2), p.p. 319-338

[158] Ferrer, J. (2002). *Revisioning transpersonal theory*. Albany: State University of New York Press - Leonard & Murphy, 1995; Murphy, 1992; Rothberg, 1996, 1999; Welwood, 2000; Wilber, 2000, 2001; cited in Ferrer, 2002, p. 1

[159] This staged (vertical) spirituality is also resonant to James Fowler's (1981) work in *Stages of Faith* in which Fowler proposes a staged development of faith (or spiritual development) across the lifespan.[159] The spiritual staged model of Wilber's is also related to the theories of Jean Piaget (1953) and Erik Erikson (1968) regarding

aspects of psychological development in children and adults also from a lifespan perspective.

[160] Hyde, A (2013), 'The Yoga of Critical Discourse', *Journal of Transformative Education*, 2013 11:114

[161] Ferrer, J. (2003). 'Integral transformative practice: A participatory perspective'. *Journal of Transpersonal Psychology*, 35 (1), pp. 21--42. Ferrer, J (2013a). 'Embodied Spirituality: Now and Then', [online] Integralworld.net Retrieved from: http://www.integralworld.net/ferrer2.html [Accessed: 17 July 2012]. Ferrer. J (2013b). 'Integral Transformative Practice: A Participatory Perspective,' [online] Integralworld.net Retrieved from: http://www.integralworld.net/ferrer.html [Accessed: 3 May 2012].

[162] Hyde, Brendan, Cathy Ota, and Karen-Marie Yust. "Spirituality and physicality." (2012): 1-3.

[163] Emmons, R., *The Psychology of Ultimate Concerns* (1999) New York, Guilford Press

[164] Maslow, (1943): A Theory of Human Motivation'. *Psychological review*, 50 (4), p. 370

[165] Shariff, A. and Norenzayan, A. (2007). 'God Is Watching You Priming God Concepts Increases Prosocial Behavior in an Anonymous Economic Game'. *Psychological Science*, 18 (9), pp. 803--809.

[166] Shariff & Norenzavan, 2007

[167] De Roos, Miedema & Iedema, 2001

[168] Hay & Nye, 1999 *The Spirit of the Child* (2006) London

169 Hill and Pargament, 2008, see Pargament, K. I. (2011). *Spiritually integrated psychotherapy: Understanding and addressing the sacred.* Guilford Press.

170 Also in a similar manner to Kübler-Ross, E. (1983), Bluebond-Langer opened discussion about the child's view on death and dying demonstrating the depth and knowing of children. See also Kübler-Ross, E., *On Children and Death* (1983) New York, Macmillan (Bluebond-Langner, 1996)

171 Bluebond-Langner, M. (1989). Worlds of dying children and their well siblings. *Death Studies, 13*(1), 1-16.*viii*

172 John O'Donohue, *Anam Cara: A Book of Celtic Wisdom (1998)*

PART III

CHAPTER FIVE

1 Albert Einstein from the memoirs of William Miller, an editor, quoted in Life magazine, May 2, 1955; Expanded, p. 281

2 Bishop, S. R. et al., *Mindfulness: A Proposed Operational Definition,* Clinical Psychology; Science and Practice, Volume 11, Issue September (2004) Pages 230–241 <http://onlinelibrary.wiley.com/doi/10.1093/clipsy.bph077/full>

3 A good reference is *Mindfulness: What Is It? Where Does It Come From?* Ronald D. Siegel, et al., from Didonna, F. (Ed.) *Clinical Handbook of Mindfulness* (2008) New York, Springer Mindful approaches have been researched for their efficacy in the parent-child relationships with great promise in a reduction in stress, enhanced parenting satisfaction, decreased child aggression, and increased child prosocial behaviors. Jeanette A.Sawyer Cohen and Randy J. Semple, *Mindful Parenting: A Call for Research* (2009) Journal of Child and Family Studies, Volume 19, Issue 2, April (2010) pp 145-151 Singh

et al., (2009) *Mindful Parenting Decreases Aggression and Increases Social Behavior in Children with Developmental Disabilities* Journal of Behavior Modification, November, 2007, Vol. 31 no. 6 749-771

[4] Matthews, G., *Philosophy and the Young Child* (1980) Cambridge, Mass., Harvard University Press, p.2

[5] Hart, T., *The Secret Spiritual World of Children,* (2003) California, New World Library, p.54

CONCLUSION

[6] *The Face of the Deep: The Religious Ideas of C.G. Jung* (1967) Charles Bartruff Hanna

www.ingramcontent.com/pod-product-compliance
Lightning Source LLC
Chambersburg PA
CBHW021113300426
44113CB00006B/136